STAR
WARS ®

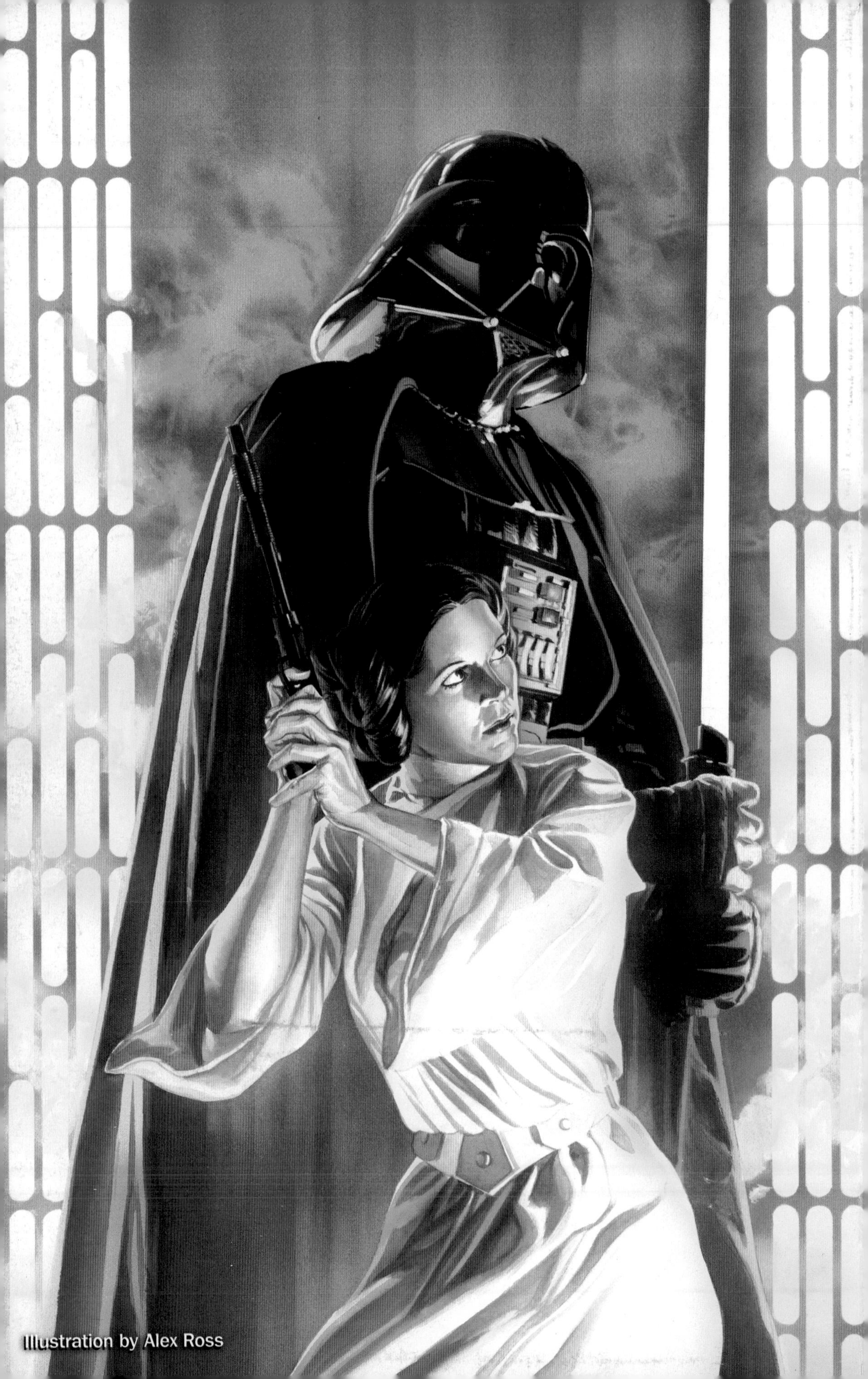

Illustration by Alex Ross

THE REBELLION

FROM THE BATTLE OF YAVIN TO FIVE YEARS AFTER

Open resistance begins to spread across the galaxy in protest of the Empire's tyranny. Rebel groups unite, and the Galactic Civil War begins. This era starts with the Rebel victory that secured the Death Star plans, and ends a year after the death of the Emperor high over the forest moon of Endor. This is the era in which the events in *A New Hope*, *The Empire Strikes Back*, and *Return of the Jedi* take place.

The events in this story take place shortly after the events in *Star Wars: Episode IV—A New Hope*.

VOLUME ONE | IN THE SHADOW OF YAVIN

Script	Art	Colors	Lettering
BRIAN WOOD	**CARLOS D'ANDA**	**GABE ELTAEB**	**MICHAEL HEISLER**

THE ASSASSINATION OF DARTH VADER

Script	Art	Colors	Lettering
BRIAN WOOD	**RYAN ODAGAWA**	**GABE ELTAEB**	**MICHAEL HEISLER**

Front Cover Art
ALEX ROSS

President and Publisher
MIKE RICHARDSON

Collection Designer
JIMMY PRESLER

Editor
RANDY STRADLEY

Assistant Editor
FREDDYE LINS

STAR WARS® VOLUME 1: IN THE SHADOW OF YAVIN
Star Wars © 2013 Lucasfilm Ltd. & ™. All rights reserved. Used under authorization. Text and
illustrations for Star Wars are © 2013 Lucasfilm Ltd. Dark Horse Books® and the Dark Horse
logo are registered trademarks of Dark Horse Comics, Inc. All rights reserved. No portion of this
publication may be reproduced or transmitted, in any form or by any means, without the express
written permission of Dark Horse Comics, Inc. Names, characters, places, and incidents featured
in this publication either are the product of the author's imagination or are used fictitiously. Any
resemblance to actual persons (living or dead), events, institutions, or locales, without satiric intent,
is coincidental.

This volume collects issues #1–#6 of the Dark Horse comic-book series Star Wars, as well as "Star
Wars: The Assassination of Darth Vader," first published in Free Comic Book Day 2013.

Published by Dark Horse Books, a division of Dark Horse Comics, Inc.
10956 SE Main Street, Milwaukie, OR 97222

DarkHorse.com StarWars.com

International Licensing: (503) 905-2377
To find a comics shop in your area, call the Comic Shop Locator Service toll-free at 1-888-266-4226

Library of Congress Cataloging-in-Publication Data

Wood, Brian, 1972-
Star Wars. Volume one, In the shadow of Yavin / script, Brian Wood ; art, Carlos D'Anda ; colors, Gabe
Eltaeb ; lettering, Michael Heisler.
    pages cm
Summary: "Princess Leia forms a stealth squadron of her best pilots--including Luke Skywalker--to
expose a spy and find the Rebel Alliance a safe home"-- Provided by publisher.
ISBN 978-1-61655-170-4
[1. Graphic novels.] I. D'Anda, Carlos, illustrator. II. Title. III. Title: In the shadow of Yavin.
PZ7.7.W65St 2013
741.5'973--dc23
                                  2013015114

First edition: September 2013
ISBN 978-1-61655-170-4

10 9 8 7 6 5 4 3 2 1
Printed in China

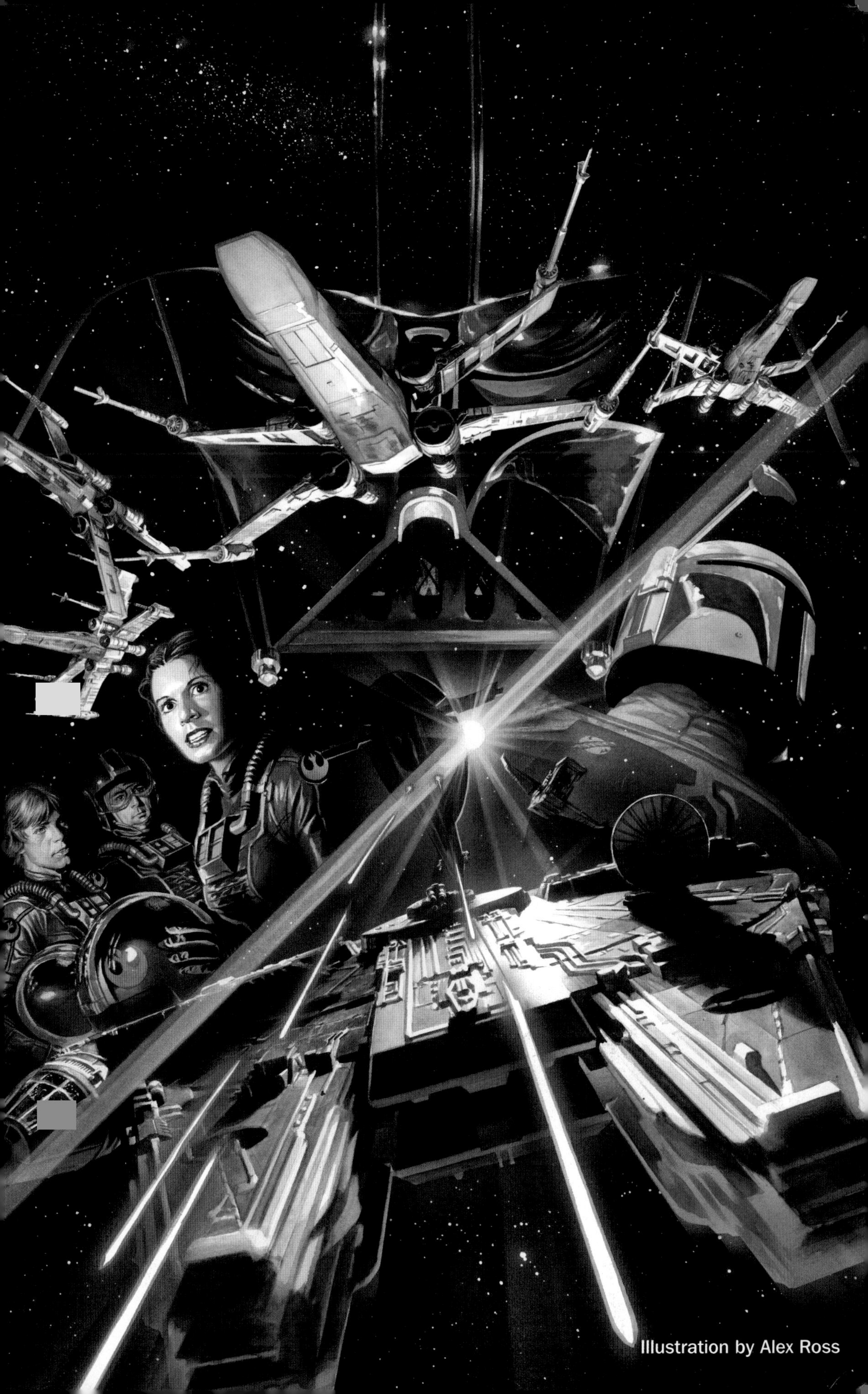

Illustration by Alex Ross

IN THE SHADOW OF YAVIN

The Rebel Alliance destroyed the Galactic Empire's fearsome space station, the Death Star, but the losses they suffered in the midst of that victory were substantial.

Rebel leader Princess Leia Organa witnessed the destruction of her homeworld; farm-boy-turned-hero Luke Skywalker lost the only family he knew, as well as a boyhood friend; and smuggler Han Solo made a decision to fight the Empire that will have consequences he can't even begin to anticipate.

Now, in the quest for a new base from which to continue the war against the Empire, Leia, Luke, and ace pilot Wedge Antilles have journeyed to the edge of the Outer Rim.

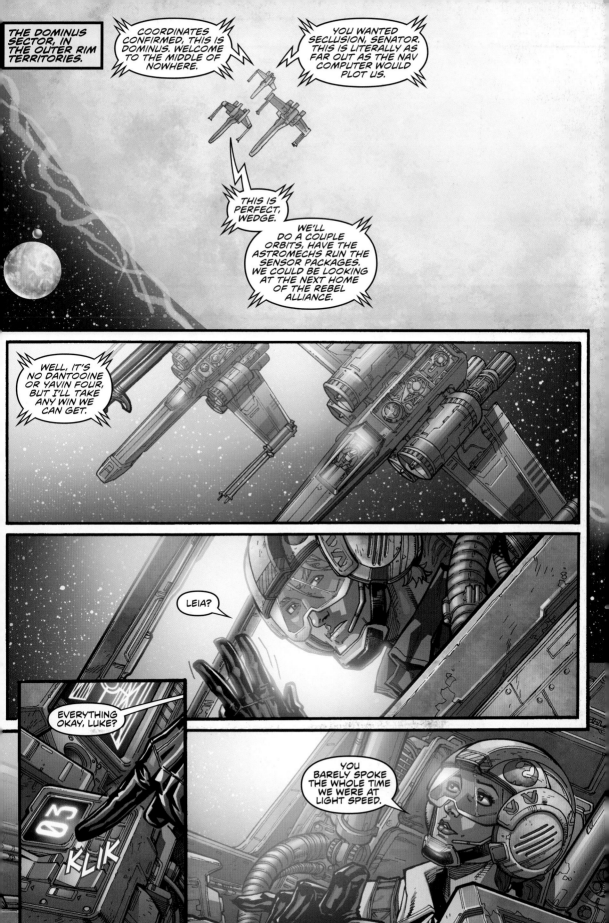

THE DOMINUS SECTOR, IN THE OUTER RIM TERRITORIES.

COORDINATES CONFIRMED, THIS IS DOMINUS. WELCOME TO THE MIDDLE OF NOWHERE.

YOU WANTED SECLUSION, SENATOR. THIS IS LITERALLY AS FAR OUT AS THE NAV COMPUTER WOULD PLOT US.

THIS IS PERFECT, WEDGE.

WE'LL DO A COUPLE ORBITS, HAVE THE ASTROMECHS RUN THE SENSOR PACKAGES. WE COULD BE LOOKING AT THE NEXT HOME OF THE REBEL ALLIANCE.

WELL, IT'S NO DANTOOINE OR YAVIN FOUR, BUT I'LL TAKE ANY WIN WE CAN GET.

LEIA?

EVERYTHING OKAY, LUKE?

KLIK

YOU BARELY SPOKE THE WHOLE TIME WE WERE AT LIGHT SPEED.

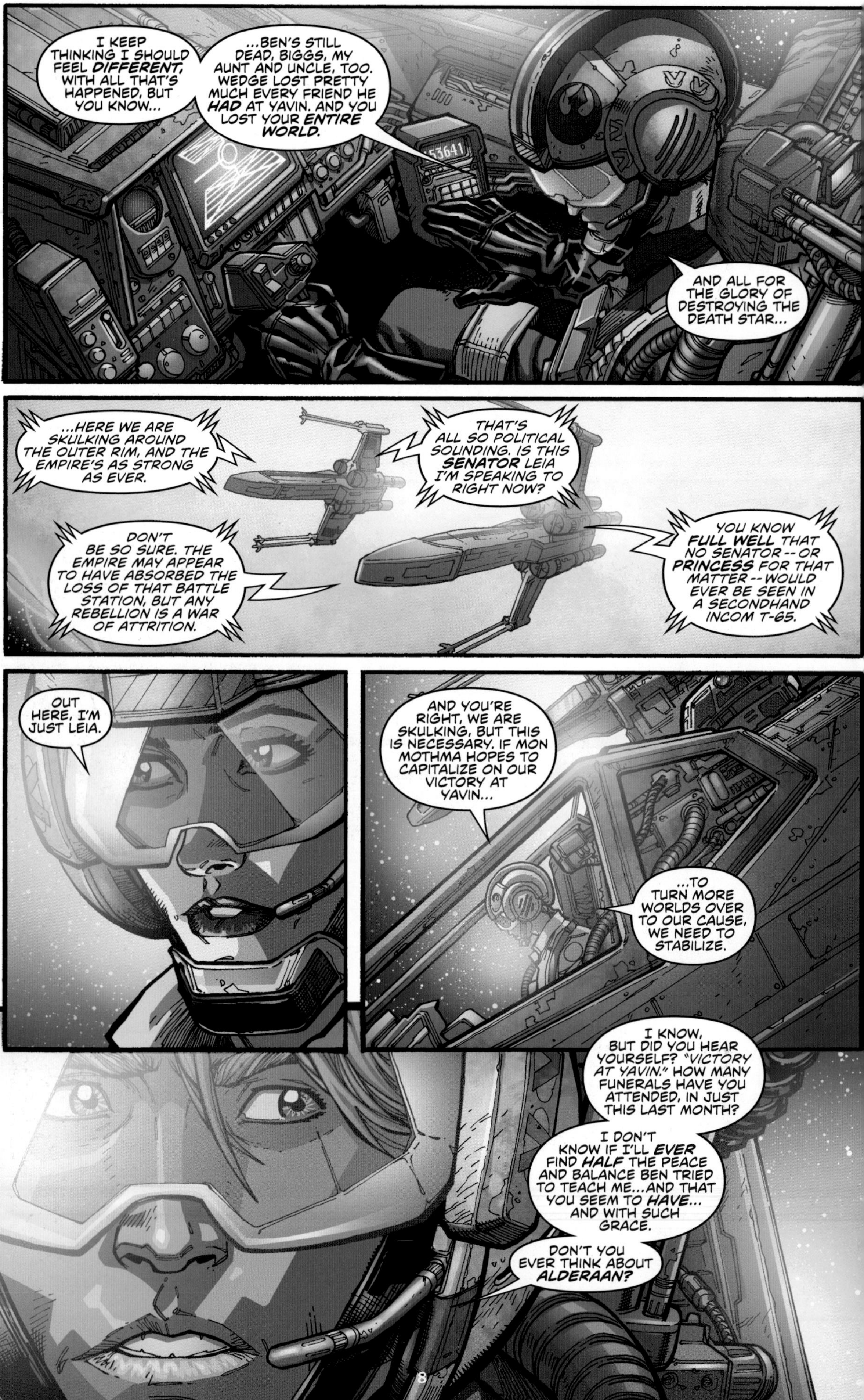
I KEEP THINKING I SHOULD FEEL DIFFERENT, WITH ALL THAT'S HAPPENED, BUT YOU KNOW...
...BEN'S STILL DEAD, BIGGS, MY AUNT AND UNCLE, TOO. WEDGE LOST PRETTY MUCH EVERY FRIEND HE HAD AT YAVIN. AND YOU LOST YOUR ENTIRE WORLD.
53641
AND ALL FOR THE GLORY OF DESTROYING THE DEATH STAR...
...HERE WE ARE SKULKING AROUND THE OUTER RIM, AND THE EMPIRE'S AS STRONG AS EVER.
THAT'S ALL SO POLITICAL SOUNDING. IS THIS SENATOR LEIA I'M SPEAKING TO RIGHT NOW?
DON'T BE SO SURE. THE EMPIRE MAY APPEAR TO HAVE ABSORBED THE LOSS OF THAT BATTLE STATION, BUT ANY REBELLION IS A WAR OF ATTRITION.
YOU KNOW FULL WELL THAT NO SENATOR -- OR PRINCESS FOR THAT MATTER -- WOULD EVER BE SEEN IN A SECONDHAND INCOM T-65.
OUT HERE, I'M JUST LEIA.
AND YOU'RE RIGHT, WE ARE SKULKING, BUT THIS IS NECESSARY. IF MON MOTHMA HOPES TO CAPITALIZE ON OUR VICTORY AT YAVIN...
...TO TURN MORE WORLDS OVER TO OUR CAUSE, WE NEED TO STABILIZE.
I KNOW, BUT DID YOU HEAR YOURSELF? "VICTORY AT YAVIN." HOW MANY FUNERALS HAVE YOU ATTENDED, IN JUST THIS LAST MONTH?
I DON'T KNOW IF I'LL EVER FIND HALF THE PEACE AND BALANCE BEN TRIED TO TEACH ME...AND THAT YOU SEEM TO HAVE... AND WITH SUCH GRACE.
DON'T YOU EVER THINK ABOUT ALDERAAN?

NOT ENOUGH.

I LOOK FORWARD TO THESE LONG TRIPS. IT GIVES ME TIME TO *THINK*, SOMETHING I HAVE PRECIOUS LITTLE OF AS AN OFFICER OF THE ALLIANCE.

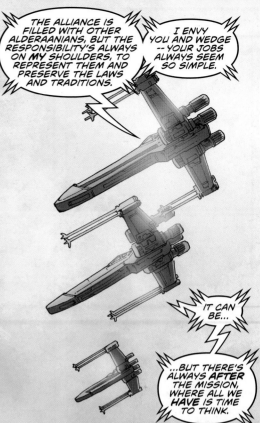

THE ALLIANCE IS FILLED WITH OTHER ALDERAANIANS, BUT THE RESPONSIBILITY'S ALWAYS ON *MY* SHOULDERS, TO REPRESENT THEM AND PRESERVE THE LAWS AND TRADITIONS.

I ENVY YOU AND WEDGE -- YOUR JOBS ALWAYS SEEM SO SIMPLE.

IT CAN BE...

...BUT THERE'S ALWAYS *AFTER* THE MISSION, WHERE ALL WE *HAVE* IS TIME TO THINK.

IS THIS WHY YOU'VE BEEN FLYING THESE MISSIONS WITH US?

THAT'S HOW I SOLD IT TO MON MOTHMA. LUKE, LISTEN...

WE'VE *ALL* LOST MORE THAN A LIFETIME'S WORTH OF LOVED ONES, ALL IN A FEW SHORT MONTHS.

IF GENERAL KENOBI WAS TEACHING YOU HOW TO FIND A BALANCE, A WAY TO USE THE FORCE TO TURN THAT PAIN INTO SOMETHING POSITIVE...

...YOU SHOULD STICK WITH IT. WE NEED YOU.

THANKS, I THINK I WILL. FOR BEN, *AND* FOR MY FATHER.

KRRSSSHHKK... SORRY TO BREAK IN, KIDS, BUT WE GOT TROUBLE. SWITCH TO THE TACTICAL CHANNEL, AND CALL SIGNS FROM HERE ON OUT.

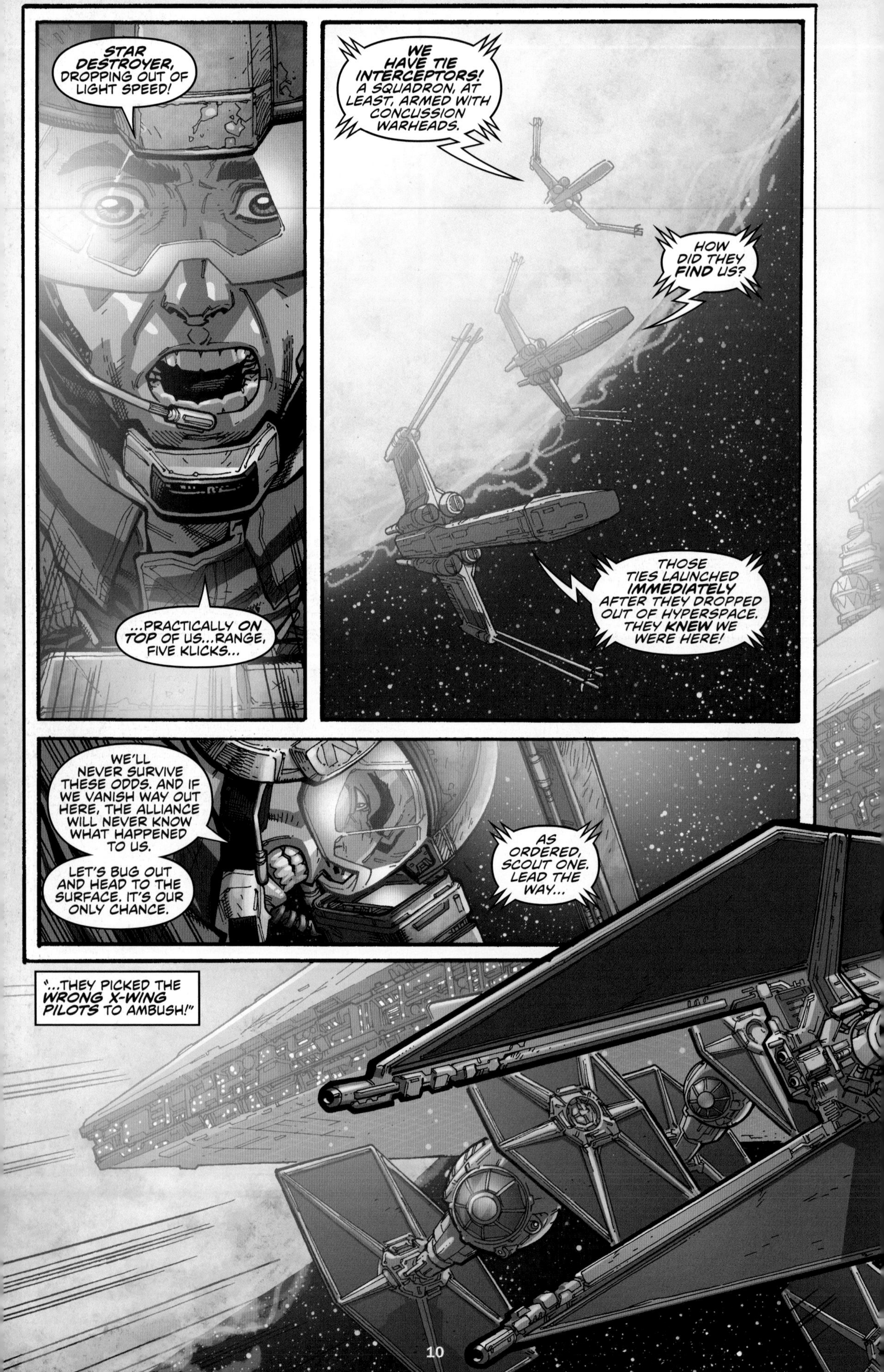
STAR DESTROYER, DROPPING OUT OF LIGHT SPEED!
...PRACTICALLY ON TOP OF US...RANGE, FIVE KLICKS...
WE HAVE TIE INTERCEPTORS! A SQUADRON, AT LEAST, ARMED WITH CONCUSSION WARHEADS.
HOW DID THEY FIND US?
THOSE TIES LAUNCHED IMMEDIATELY AFTER THEY DROPPED OUT OF HYPERSPACE. THEY KNEW WE WERE HERE!
WE'LL NEVER SURVIVE THESE ODDS. AND IF WE VANISH WAY OUT HERE, THE ALLIANCE WILL NEVER KNOW WHAT HAPPENED TO US.
LET'S BUG OUT AND HEAD TO THE SURFACE. IT'S OUR ONLY CHANCE.
AS ORDERED, SCOUT ONE. LEAD THE WAY...
"...THEY PICKED THE WRONG X-WING PILOTS TO AMBUSH!"

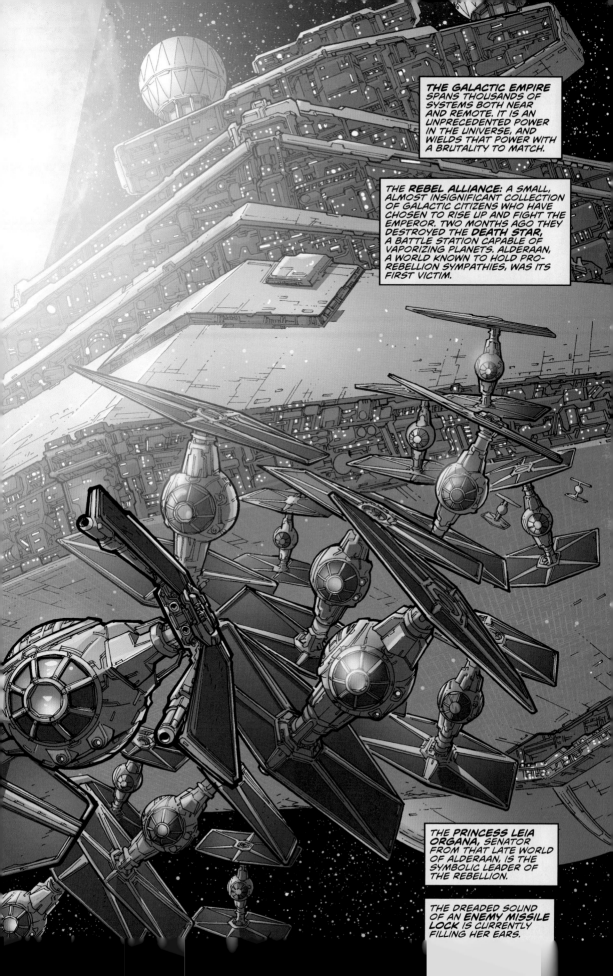

THE GALACTIC EMPIRE SPANS THOUSANDS OF SYSTEMS BOTH NEAR AND REMOTE. IT IS AN UNPRECEDENTED POWER IN THE UNIVERSE, AND WIELDS THAT POWER WITH A BRUTALITY TO MATCH.

THE **REBEL ALLIANCE:** A SMALL, ALMOST INSIGNIFICANT COLLECTION OF GALACTIC CITIZENS WHO HAVE CHOSEN TO RISE UP AND FIGHT THE EMPEROR. TWO MONTHS AGO THEY DESTROYED THE **DEATH STAR,** A BATTLE STATION CAPABLE OF VAPORIZING PLANETS. ALDERAAN, A WORLD KNOWN TO HOLD PRO-REBELLION SYMPATHIES, WAS ITS FIRST VICTIM.

THE **PRINCESS LEIA ORGANA,** SENATOR FROM THAT LATE WORLD OF ALDERAAN, IS THE SYMBOLIC LEADER OF THE REBELLION.

THE DREADED SOUND OF AN **ENEMY MISSILE LOCK** IS CURRENTLY FILLING HER EARS.

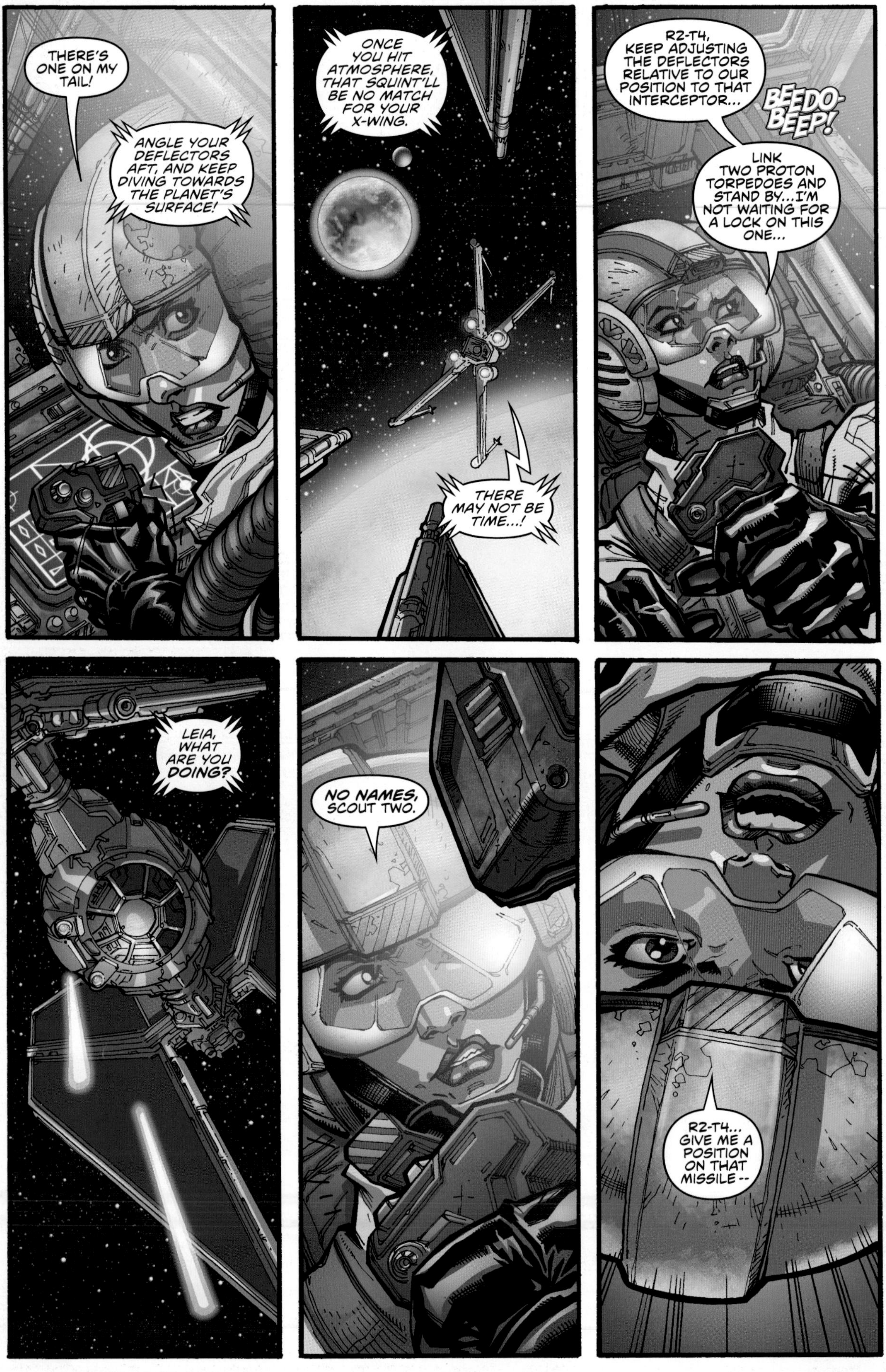
THERE'S ONE ON MY TAIL!
ANGLE YOUR DEFLECTORS AFT, AND KEEP DIVING TOWARDS THE PLANET'S SURFACE!
ONCE YOU HIT ATMOSPHERE, THAT SQUINT'LL BE NO MATCH FOR YOUR X-WING.
THERE MAY NOT BE TIME...!
R2-T4, KEEP ADJUSTING THE DEFLECTORS RELATIVE TO OUR POSITION TO THAT INTERCEPTOR...
BEEDO-BEEP!
LINK TWO PROTON TORPEDOES AND STAND BY...I'M NOT WAITING FOR A LOCK ON THIS ONE...
LEIA, WHAT ARE YOU DOING?
NO NAMES, SCOUT TWO.
R2-T4... GIVE ME A POSITION ON THAT MISSILE--

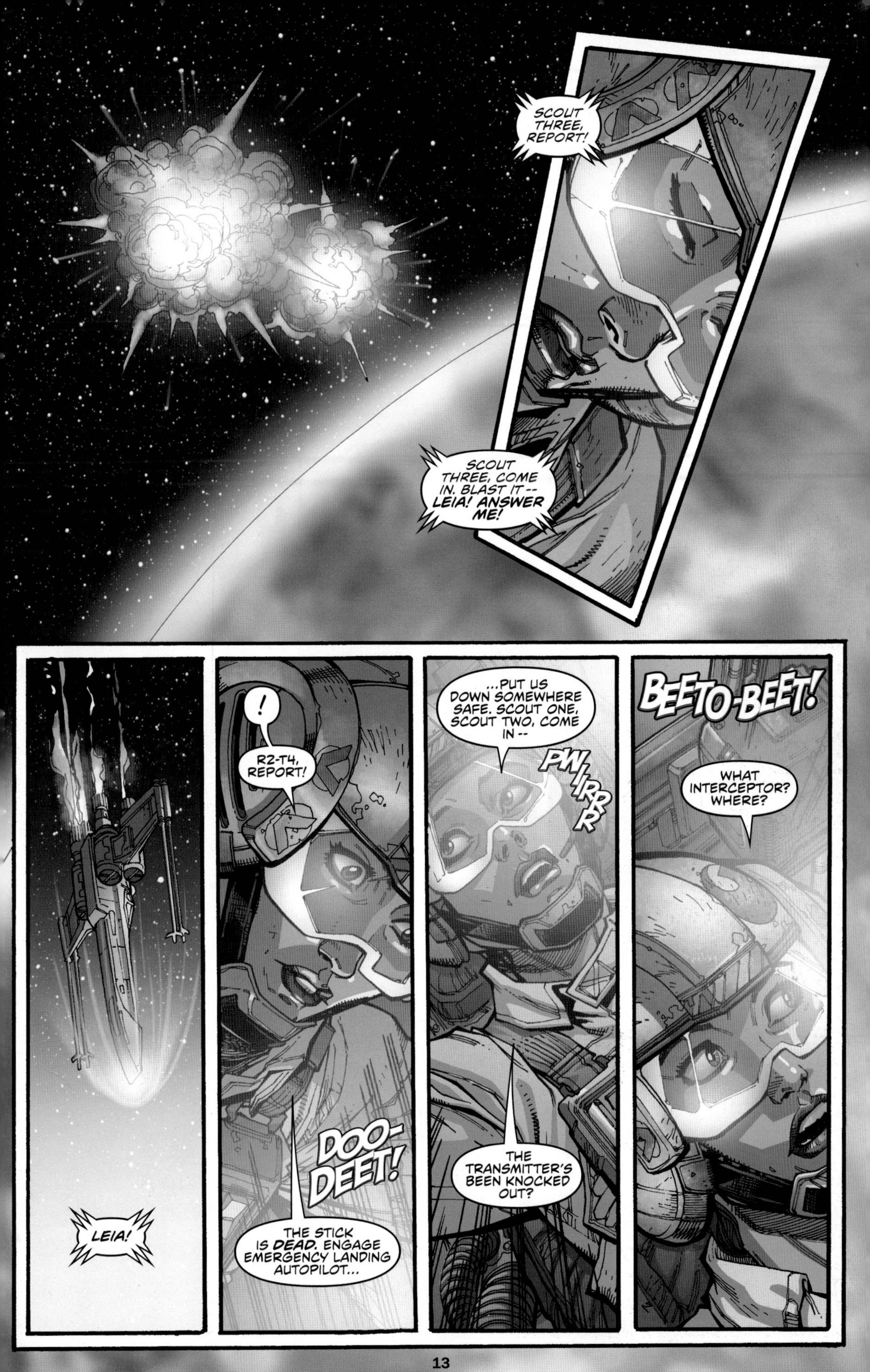
SCOUT THREE, REPORT!
SCOUT THREE, COME IN. BLAST IT -- LEIA! ANSWER ME!
LEIA!
!
R2-T4, REPORT!
DOO-DEET!
THE STICK IS DEAD. ENGAGE EMERGENCY LANDING AUTOPILOT...
...PUT US DOWN SOMEWHERE SAFE. SCOUT ONE, SCOUT TWO, COME IN --
PWIRRR
THE TRANSMITTER'S BEEN KNOCKED OUT?
BEETO-BEET!
WHAT INTERCEPTOR? WHERE?

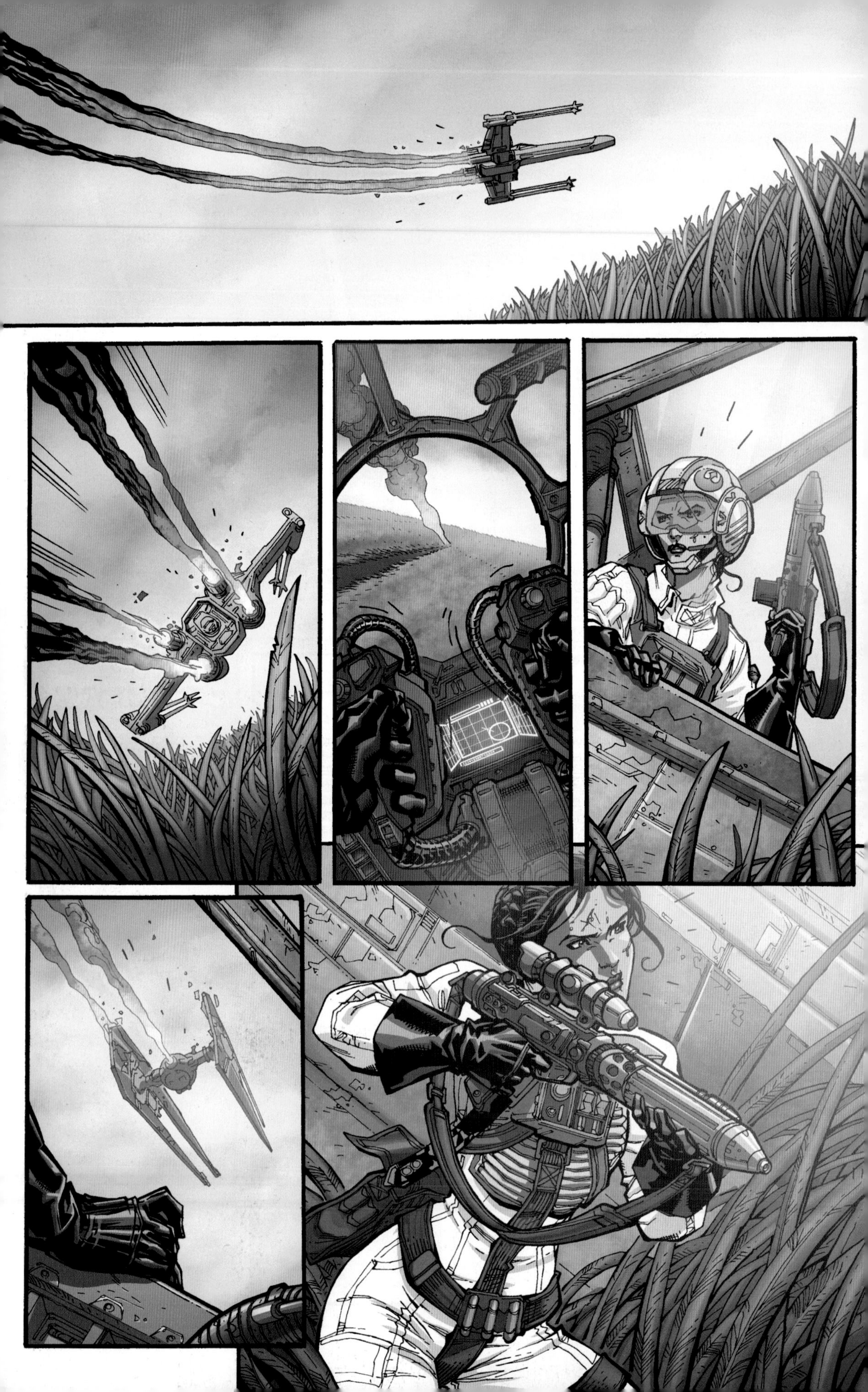

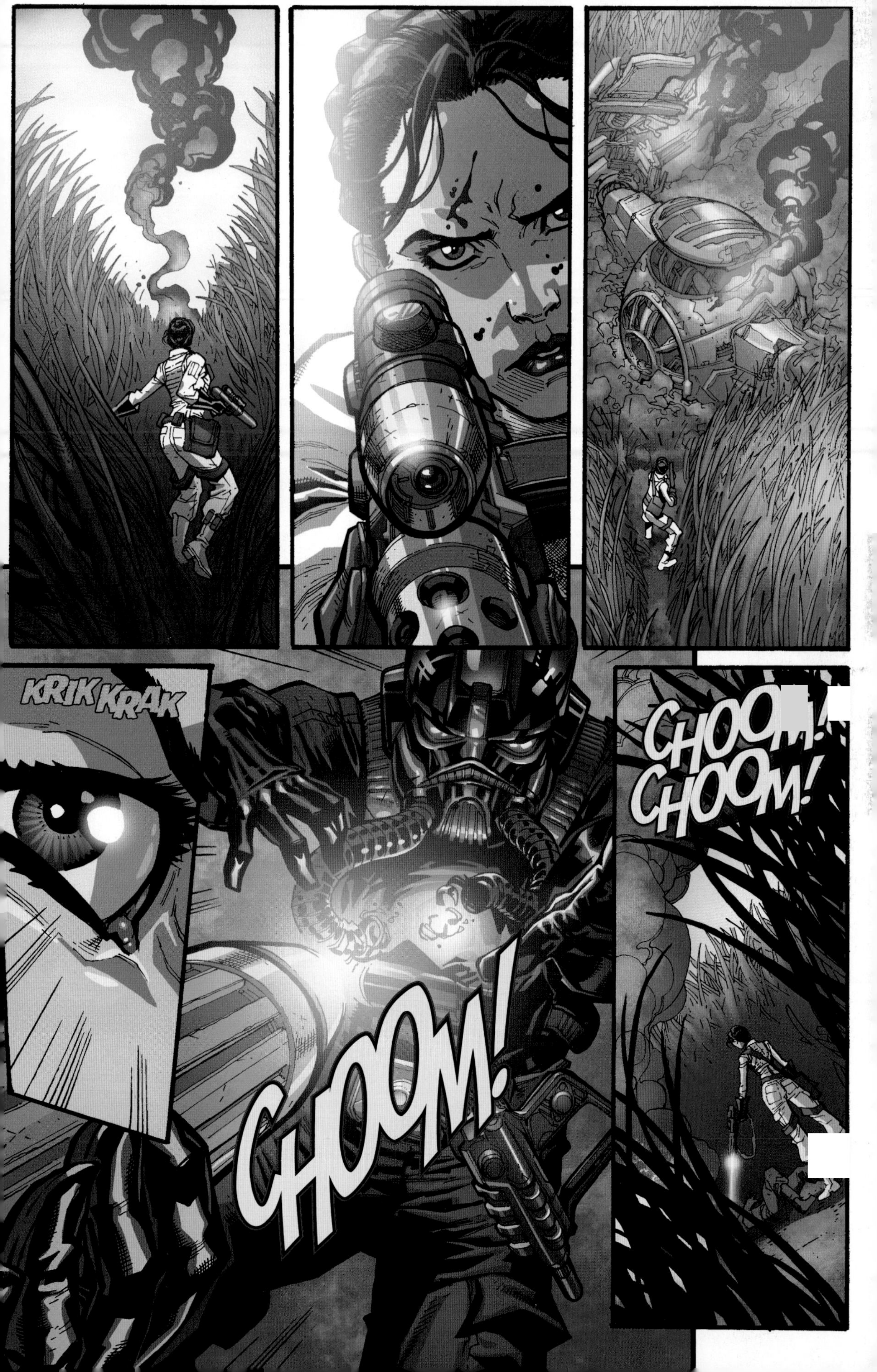
KRIK KRAK
CHOOM!
CHOOM!
CHOOM!

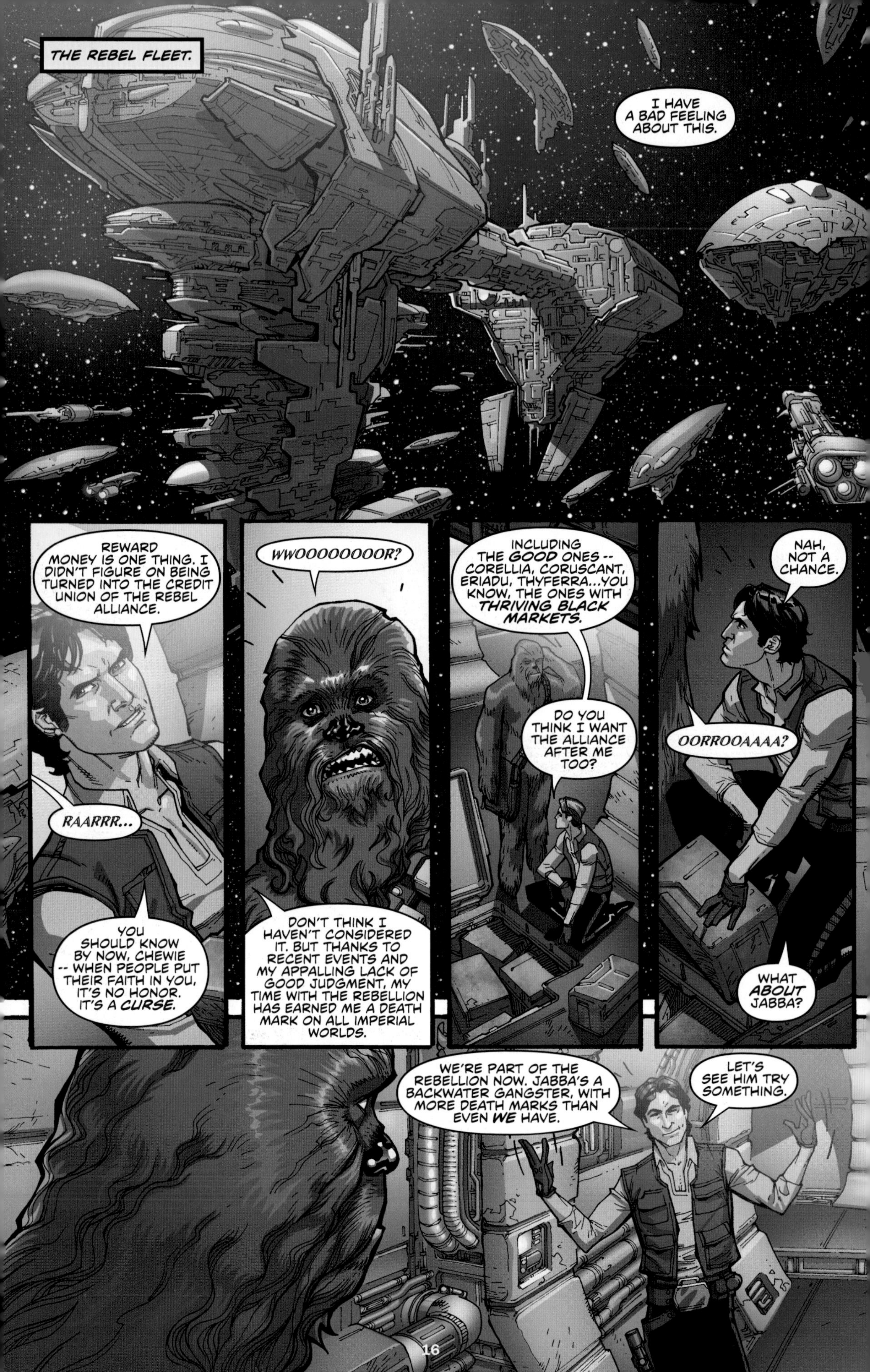
THE REBEL FLEET.
I HAVE A BAD FEELING ABOUT THIS.
REWARD MONEY IS ONE THING. I DIDN'T FIGURE ON BEING TURNED INTO THE CREDIT UNION OF THE REBEL ALLIANCE.
RAARRR...
YOU SHOULD KNOW BY NOW, CHEWIE -- WHEN PEOPLE PUT THEIR FAITH IN YOU, IT'S NO HONOR. IT'S A CURSE.
WWOOOOOOOOR?
DON'T THINK I HAVEN'T CONSIDERED IT. BUT THANKS TO RECENT EVENTS AND MY APPALLING LACK OF GOOD JUDGMENT, MY TIME WITH THE REBELLION HAS EARNED ME A DEATH MARK ON ALL IMPERIAL WORLDS.
INCLUDING THE GOOD ONES -- CORELLIA, CORUSCANT, ERIADU, THYFERRA...YOU KNOW, THE ONES WITH THRIVING BLACK MARKETS.
DO YOU THINK I WANT THE ALLIANCE AFTER ME TOO?
NAH, NOT A CHANCE.
OORROOAAAA?
WHAT ABOUT JABBA?
WE'RE PART OF THE REBELLION NOW. JABBA'S A BACKWATER GANGSTER, WITH MORE DEATH MARKS THAN EVEN WE HAVE.
LET'S SEE HIM TRY SOMETHING.

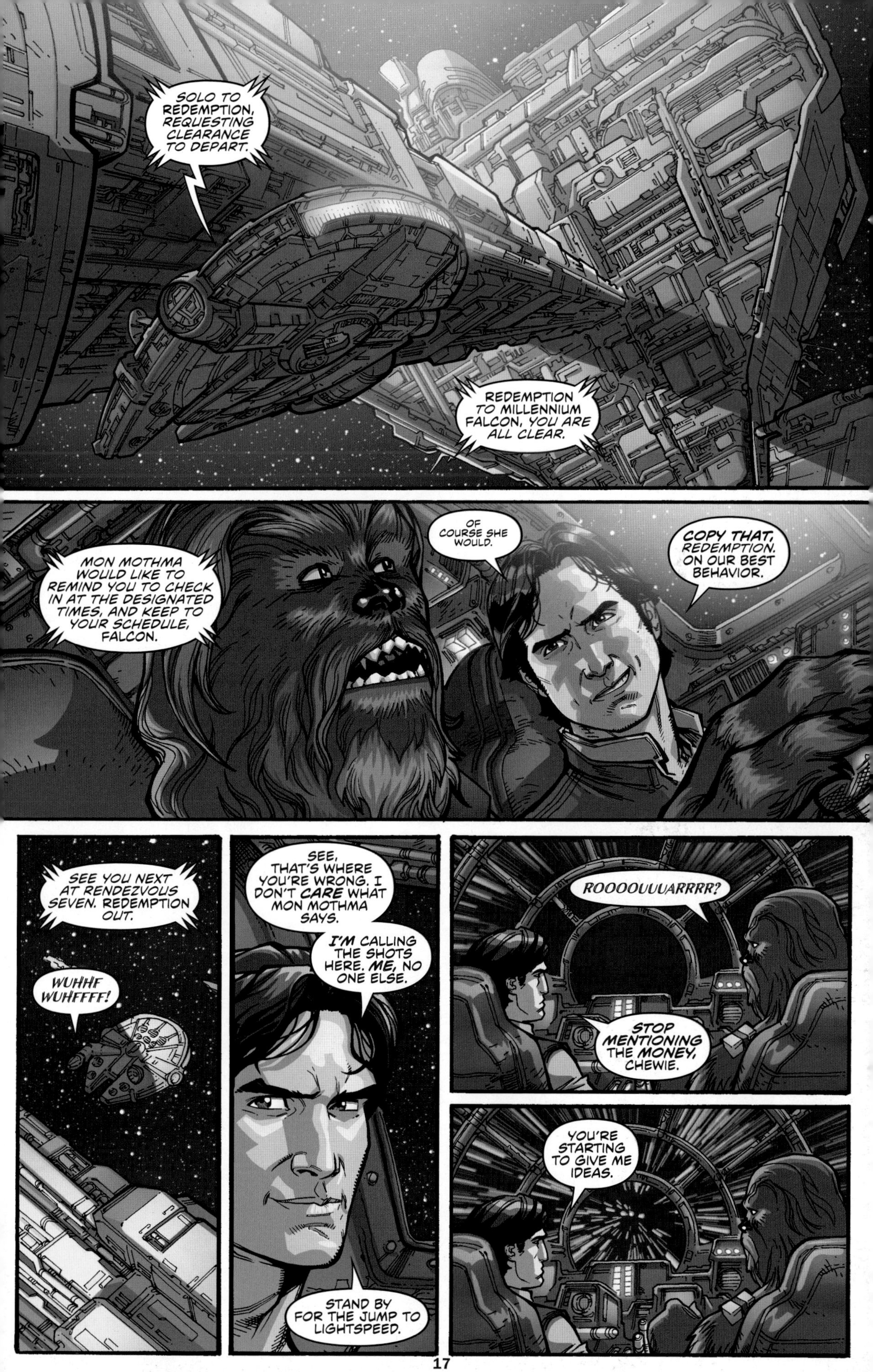
SOLO TO REDEMPTION, REQUESTING CLEARANCE TO DEPART.
REDEMPTION TO MILLENNIUM FALCON, YOU ARE ALL CLEAR.
MON MOTHMA WOULD LIKE TO REMIND YOU TO CHECK IN AT THE DESIGNATED TIMES, AND KEEP TO YOUR SCHEDULE, FALCON.
OF COURSE SHE WOULD.
COPY THAT, REDEMPTION. ON OUR BEST BEHAVIOR.
SEE YOU NEXT AT RENDEZVOUS SEVEN. REDEMPTION OUT.
WUHHF WUHFFFF!
SEE, THAT'S WHERE YOU'RE WRONG. I DON'T CARE WHAT MON MOTHMA SAYS.
I'M CALLING THE SHOTS HERE. ME, NO ONE ELSE.
STAND BY FOR THE JUMP TO LIGHTSPEED.
ROOOOUUUARRRR?
STOP MENTIONING THE MONEY, CHEWIE.
YOU'RE STARTING TO GIVE ME IDEAS.

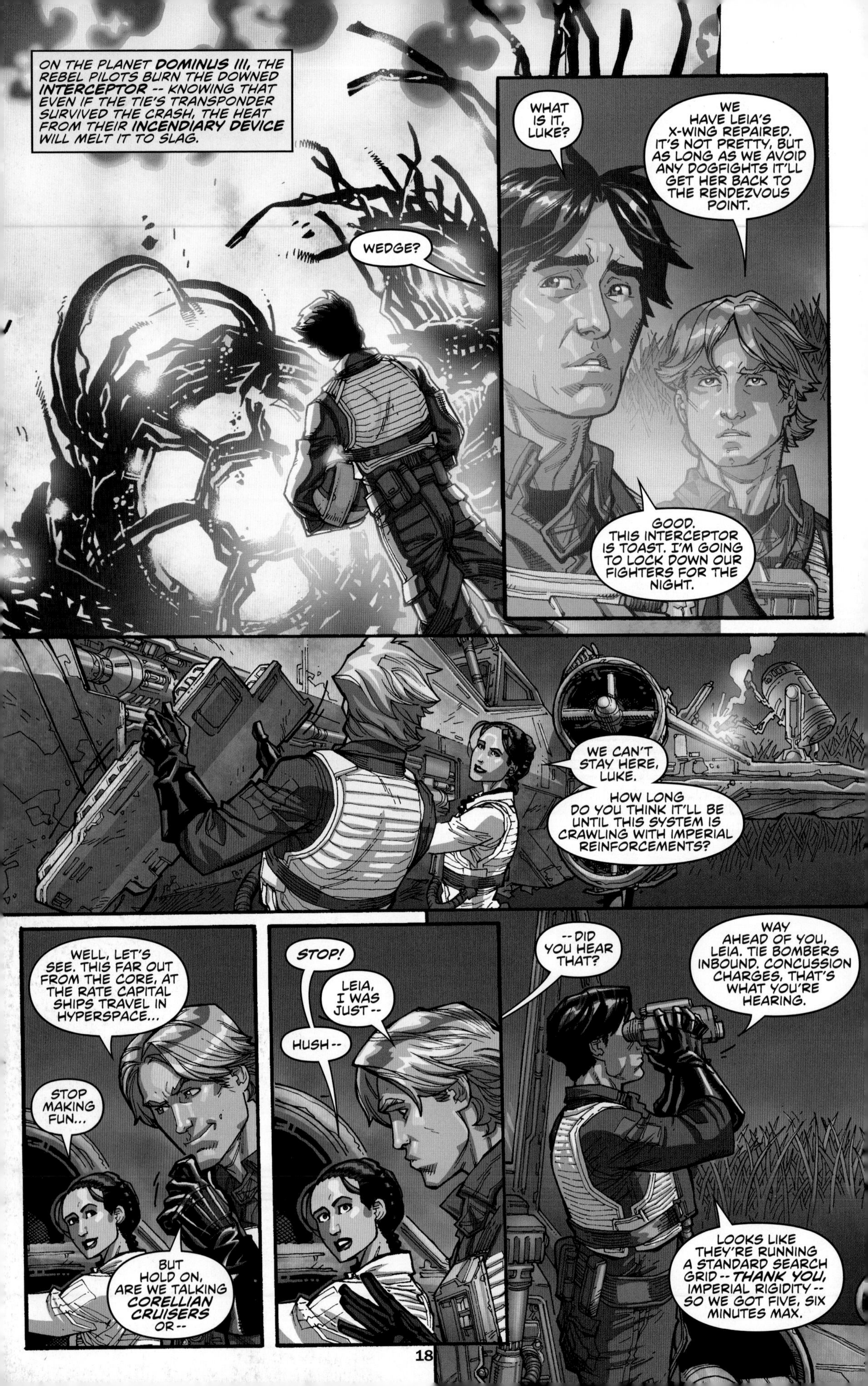
ON THE PLANET DOMINUS III, THE REBEL PILOTS BURN THE DOWNED INTERCEPTOR -- KNOWING THAT EVEN IF THE TIE'S TRANSPONDER SURVIVED THE CRASH, THE HEAT FROM THEIR INCENDIARY DEVICE WILL MELT IT TO SLAG.
WEDGE?
WHAT IS IT, LUKE?
WE HAVE LEIA'S X-WING REPAIRED. IT'S NOT PRETTY, BUT AS LONG AS WE AVOID ANY DOGFIGHTS IT'LL GET HER BACK TO THE RENDEZVOUS POINT.
GOOD. THIS INTERCEPTOR IS TOAST. I'M GOING TO LOCK DOWN OUR FIGHTERS FOR THE NIGHT.
WE CAN'T STAY HERE, LUKE.
HOW LONG DO YOU THINK IT'LL BE UNTIL THIS SYSTEM IS CRAWLING WITH IMPERIAL REINFORCEMENTS?
WELL, LET'S SEE. THIS FAR OUT FROM THE CORE, AT THE RATE CAPITAL SHIPS TRAVEL IN HYPERSPACE...
STOP MAKING FUN...
BUT HOLD ON, ARE WE TALKING CORELLIAN CRUISERS OR --
STOP!
LEIA, I WAS JUST --
HUSH --
-- DID YOU HEAR THAT?
WAY AHEAD OF YOU, LEIA. TIE BOMBERS INBOUND. CONCUSSION CHARGES, THAT'S WHAT YOU'RE HEARING.
LOOKS LIKE THEY'RE RUNNING A STANDARD SEARCH GRID -- THANK YOU, IMPERIAL RIGIDITY -- SO WE GOT FIVE, SIX MINUTES MAX.

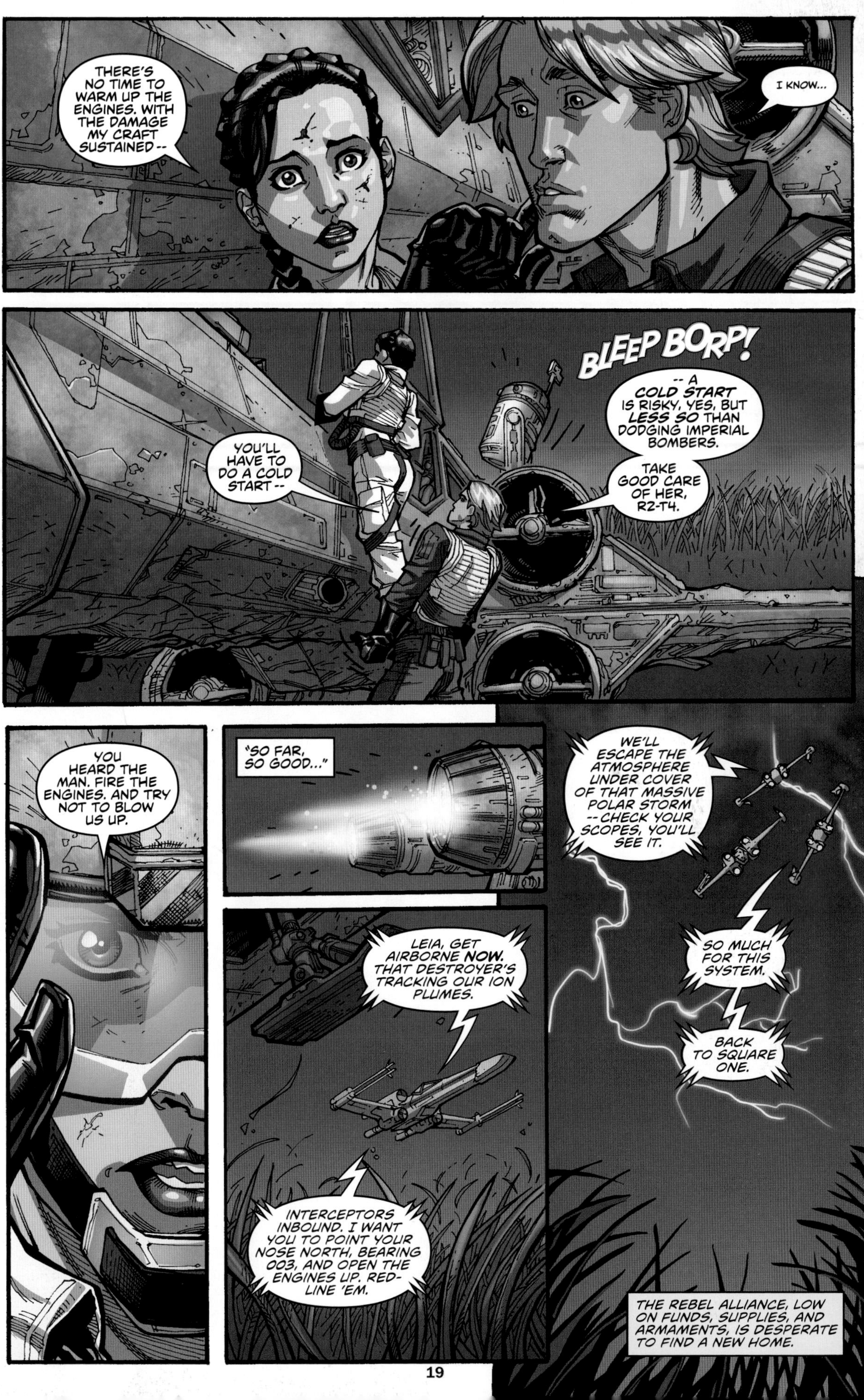
THERE'S NO TIME TO WARM UP THE ENGINES. WITH THE DAMAGE MY CRAFT SUSTAINED --
I KNOW...
BLEEP BORP!
YOU'LL HAVE TO DO A COLD START --
-- A COLD START IS RISKY, YES, BUT LESS SO THAN DODGING IMPERIAL BOMBERS.
TAKE GOOD CARE OF HER, R2-T4.
YOU HEARD THE MAN. FIRE THE ENGINES. AND TRY NOT TO BLOW US UP.
"SO FAR, SO GOOD..."
LEIA, GET AIRBORNE NOW. THAT DESTROYER'S TRACKING OUR ION PLUMES.
INTERCEPTORS INBOUND. I WANT YOU TO POINT YOUR NOSE NORTH, BEARING 003, AND OPEN THE ENGINES UP. RED-LINE 'EM.
WE'LL ESCAPE THE ATMOSPHERE UNDER COVER OF THAT MASSIVE POLAR STORM -- CHECK YOUR SCOPES, YOU'LL SEE IT.
SO MUCH FOR THIS SYSTEM.
BACK TO SQUARE ONE.
THE REBEL ALLIANCE, LOW ON FUNDS, SUPPLIES, AND ARMAMENTS, IS DESPERATE TO FIND A NEW HOME.

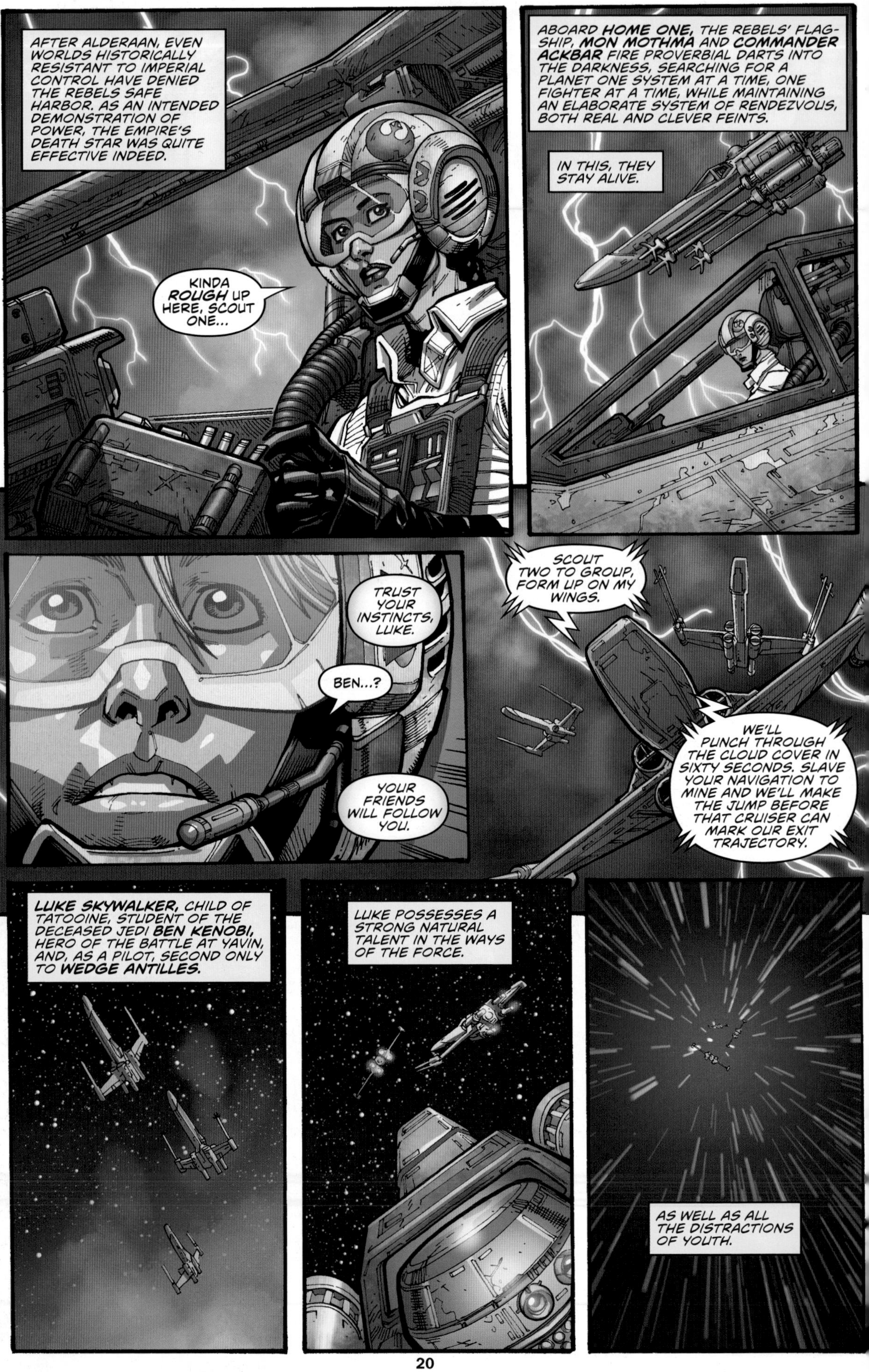
AFTER ALDERAAN, EVEN WORLDS HISTORICALLY RESISTANT TO IMPERIAL CONTROL HAVE DENIED THE REBELS SAFE HARBOR. AS AN INTENDED DEMONSTRATION OF POWER, THE EMPIRE'S DEATH STAR WAS QUITE EFFECTIVE INDEED.
KINDA ROUGH UP HERE, SCOUT ONE...
ABOARD HOME ONE, THE REBELS' FLAGSHIP, MON MOTHMA AND COMMANDER ACKBAR FIRE PROVERBIAL DARTS INTO THE DARKNESS, SEARCHING FOR A PLANET ONE SYSTEM AT A TIME, ONE FIGHTER AT A TIME, WHILE MAINTAINING AN ELABORATE SYSTEM OF RENDEZVOUS, BOTH REAL AND CLEVER FEINTS.
IN THIS, THEY STAY ALIVE.
TRUST YOUR INSTINCTS, LUKE.
BEN...?
YOUR FRIENDS WILL FOLLOW YOU.
SCOUT TWO TO GROUP, FORM UP ON MY WINGS.
WE'LL PUNCH THROUGH THE CLOUD COVER IN SIXTY SECONDS. SLAVE YOUR NAVIGATION TO MINE AND WE'LL MAKE THE JUMP BEFORE THAT CRUISER CAN MARK OUR EXIT TRAJECTORY.
LUKE SKYWALKER, CHILD OF TATOOINE, STUDENT OF THE DECEASED JEDI BEN KENOBI, HERO OF THE BATTLE AT YAVIN, AND, AS A PILOT, SECOND ONLY TO WEDGE ANTILLES.
LUKE POSSESSES A STRONG NATURAL TALENT IN THE WAYS OF THE FORCE.
AS WELL AS ALL THE DISTRACTIONS OF YOUTH.

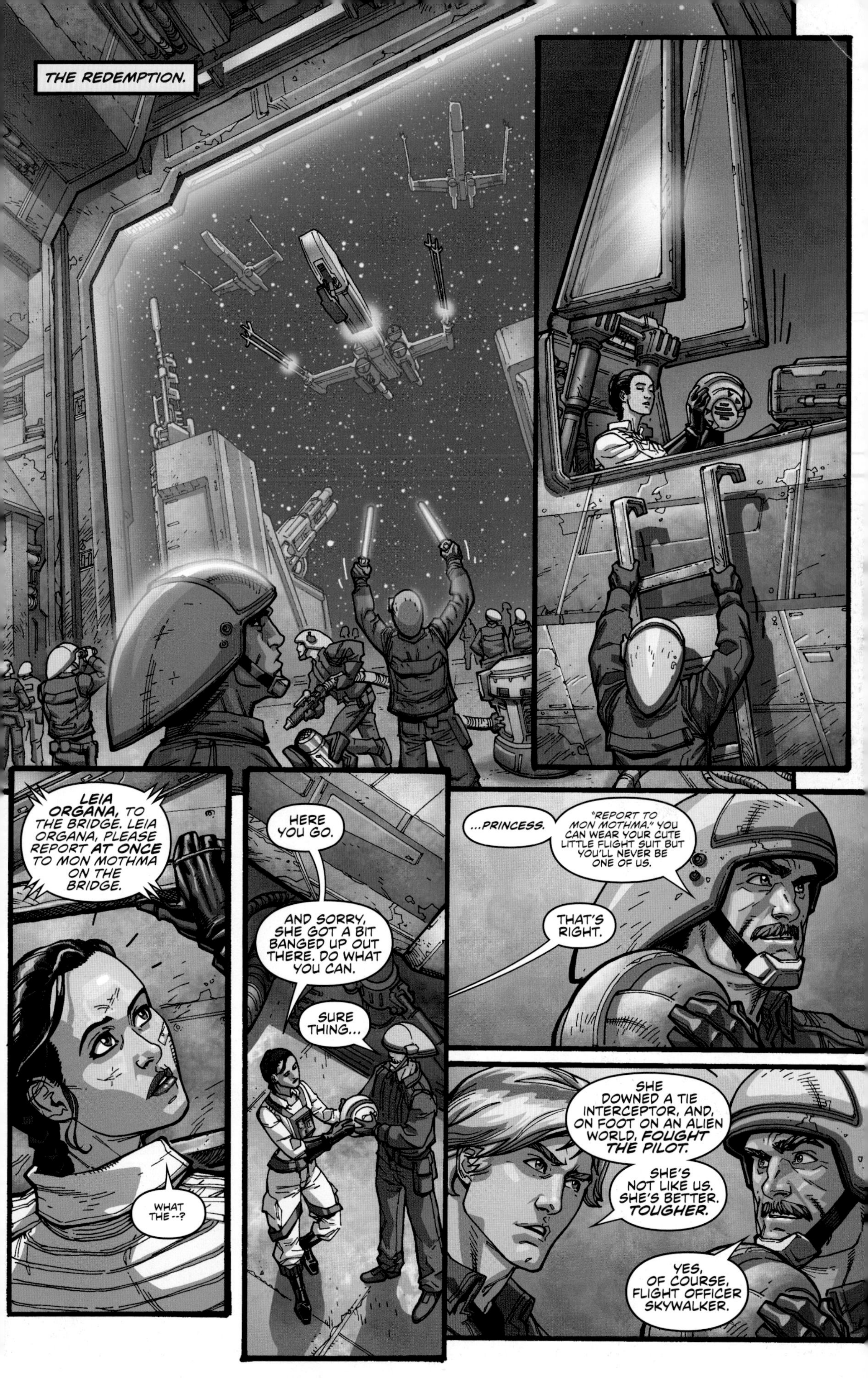
THE REDEMPTION.
LEIA ORGANA, TO THE BRIDGE. LEIA ORGANA, PLEASE REPORT AT ONCE TO MON MOTHMA ON THE BRIDGE.
WHAT THE--?
HERE YOU GO.
AND SORRY, SHE GOT A BIT BANGED UP OUT THERE. DO WHAT YOU CAN.
SURE THING...
...PRINCESS.
"REPORT TO MON MOTHMA." YOU CAN WEAR YOUR CUTE LITTLE FLIGHT SUIT BUT YOU'LL NEVER BE ONE OF US.
THAT'S RIGHT.
SHE DOWNED A TIE INTERCEPTOR, AND, ON FOOT ON AN ALIEN WORLD, FOUGHT THE PILOT.
SHE'S NOT LIKE US. SHE'S BETTER. TOUGHER.
YES, OF COURSE, FLIGHT OFFICER SKYWALKER.

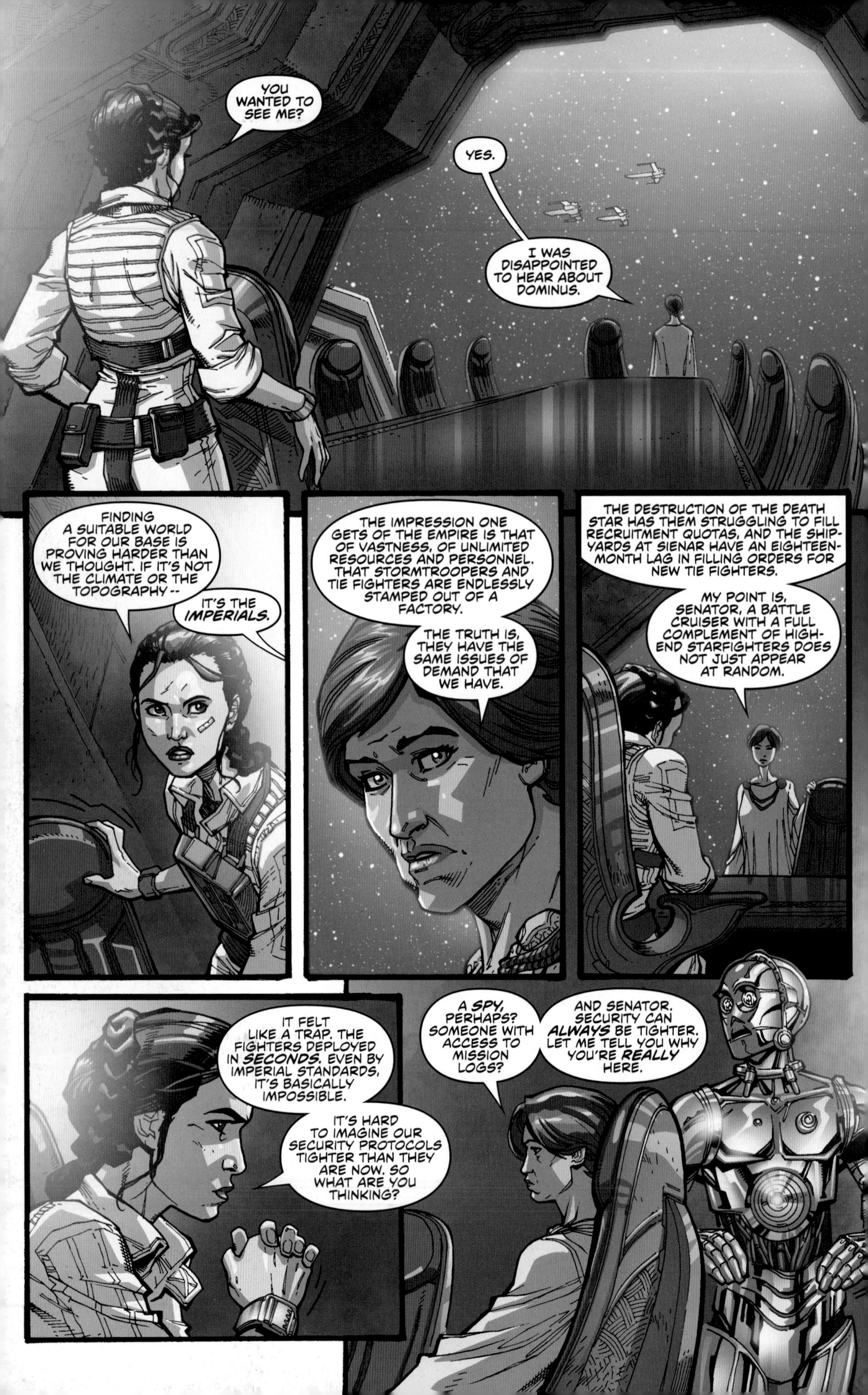
YOU WANTED TO SEE ME?
YES.
I WAS DISAPPOINTED TO HEAR ABOUT DOMINUS.
FINDING A SUITABLE WORLD FOR OUR BASE IS PROVING HARDER THAN WE THOUGHT. IF IT'S NOT THE CLIMATE OR THE TOPOGRAPHY --
IT'S THE *IMPERIALS.*
THE IMPRESSION ONE GETS OF THE EMPIRE IS THAT OF VASTNESS, OF UNLIMITED RESOURCES AND PERSONNEL. THAT STORMTROOPERS AND TIE FIGHTERS ARE ENDLESSLY STAMPED OUT OF A FACTORY.
THE TRUTH IS, THEY HAVE THE SAME ISSUES OF DEMAND THAT WE HAVE.
THE DESTRUCTION OF THE DEATH STAR HAS THEM STRUGGLING TO FILL RECRUITMENT QUOTAS, AND THE SHIPYARDS AT SIENAR HAVE AN EIGHTEEN-MONTH LAG IN FILLING ORDERS FOR NEW TIE FIGHTERS.
MY POINT IS, SENATOR, A BATTLE CRUISER WITH A FULL COMPLEMENT OF HIGH-END STARFIGHTERS DOES NOT JUST APPEAR AT RANDOM.
IT FELT LIKE A TRAP. THE FIGHTERS DEPLOYED IN *SECONDS.* EVEN BY IMPERIAL STANDARDS, IT'S BASICALLY IMPOSSIBLE.
IT'S HARD TO IMAGINE OUR SECURITY PROTOCOLS TIGHTER THAN THEY ARE NOW. SO WHAT ARE YOU THINKING?
A *SPY,* PERHAPS? SOMEONE WITH ACCESS TO MISSION LOGS?
AND SENATOR. SECURITY CAN *ALWAYS* BE TIGHTER. LET ME TELL YOU WHY YOU'RE *REALLY* HERE.

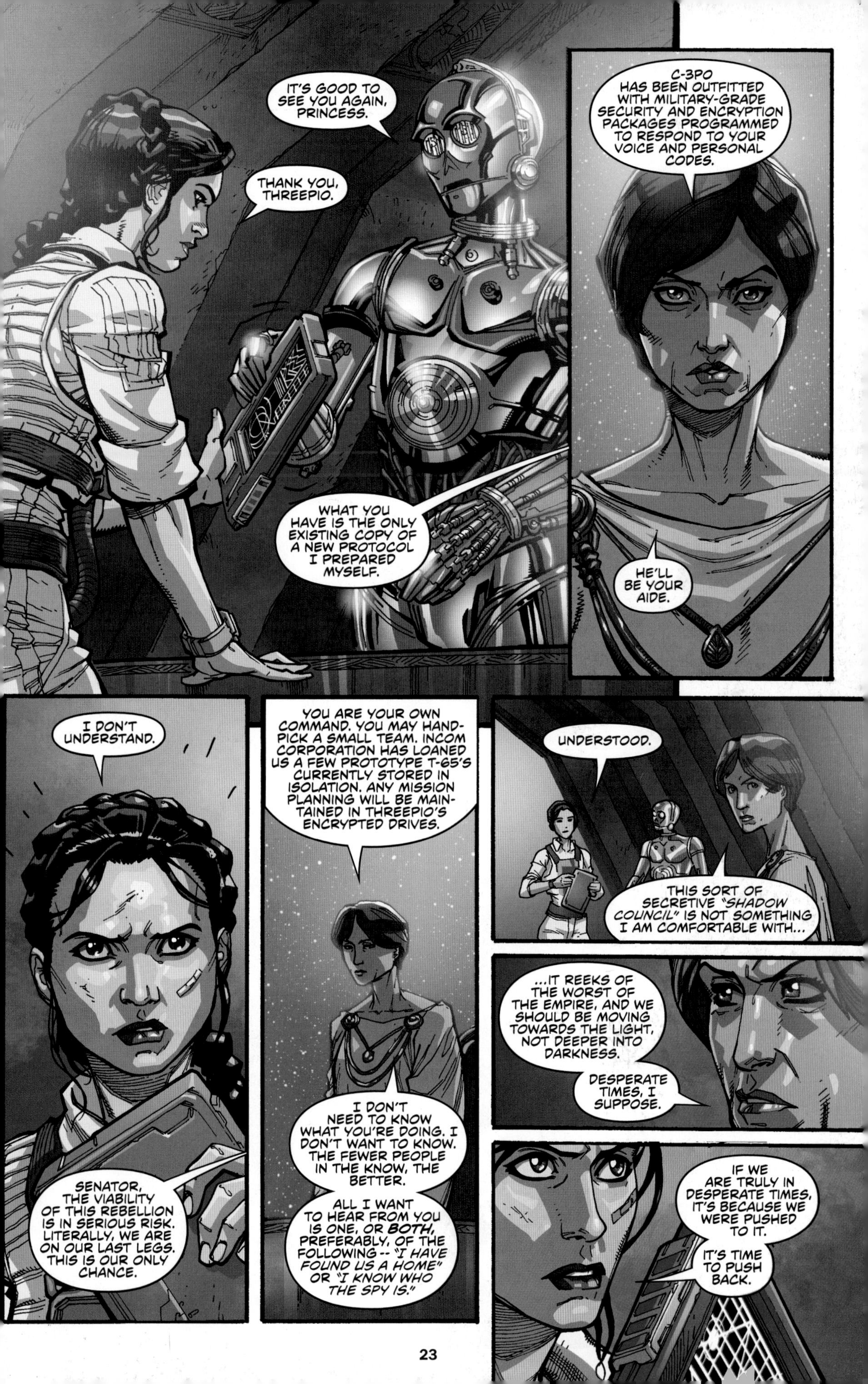
IT'S GOOD TO SEE YOU AGAIN, PRINCESS.
THANK YOU, THREEPIO.
WHAT YOU HAVE IS THE ONLY EXISTING COPY OF A NEW PROTOCOL I PREPARED MYSELF.
C-3PO HAS BEEN OUTFITTED WITH MILITARY-GRADE SECURITY AND ENCRYPTION PACKAGES PROGRAMMED TO RESPOND TO YOUR VOICE AND PERSONAL CODES.
HE'LL BE YOUR AIDE.
I DON'T UNDERSTAND.
SENATOR, THE VIABILITY OF THIS REBELLION IS IN SERIOUS RISK. LITERALLY, WE ARE ON OUR LAST LEGS. THIS IS OUR ONLY CHANCE.
YOU ARE YOUR OWN COMMAND. YOU MAY HAND-PICK A SMALL TEAM. INCOM CORPORATION HAS LOANED US A FEW PROTOTYPE T-65'S CURRENTLY STORED IN ISOLATION. ANY MISSION PLANNING WILL BE MAINTAINED IN THREEPIO'S ENCRYPTED DRIVES.
I DON'T NEED TO KNOW WHAT YOU'RE DOING. I DON'T WANT TO KNOW. THE FEWER PEOPLE IN THE KNOW, THE BETTER.
ALL I WANT TO HEAR FROM YOU IS ONE, OR *BOTH*, PREFERABLY, OF THE FOLLOWING -- *"I HAVE FOUND US A HOME"* OR *"I KNOW WHO THE SPY IS."*
UNDERSTOOD.
THIS SORT OF SECRETIVE *"SHADOW COUNCIL"* IS NOT SOMETHING I AM COMFORTABLE WITH...
...IT REEKS OF THE WORST OF THE EMPIRE, AND WE SHOULD BE MOVING TOWARDS THE LIGHT, NOT DEEPER INTO DARKNESS.
DESPERATE TIMES, I SUPPOSE.
IF WE ARE TRULY IN DESPERATE TIMES, IT'S BECAUSE WE WERE PUSHED TO IT.
IT'S TIME TO PUSH BACK.

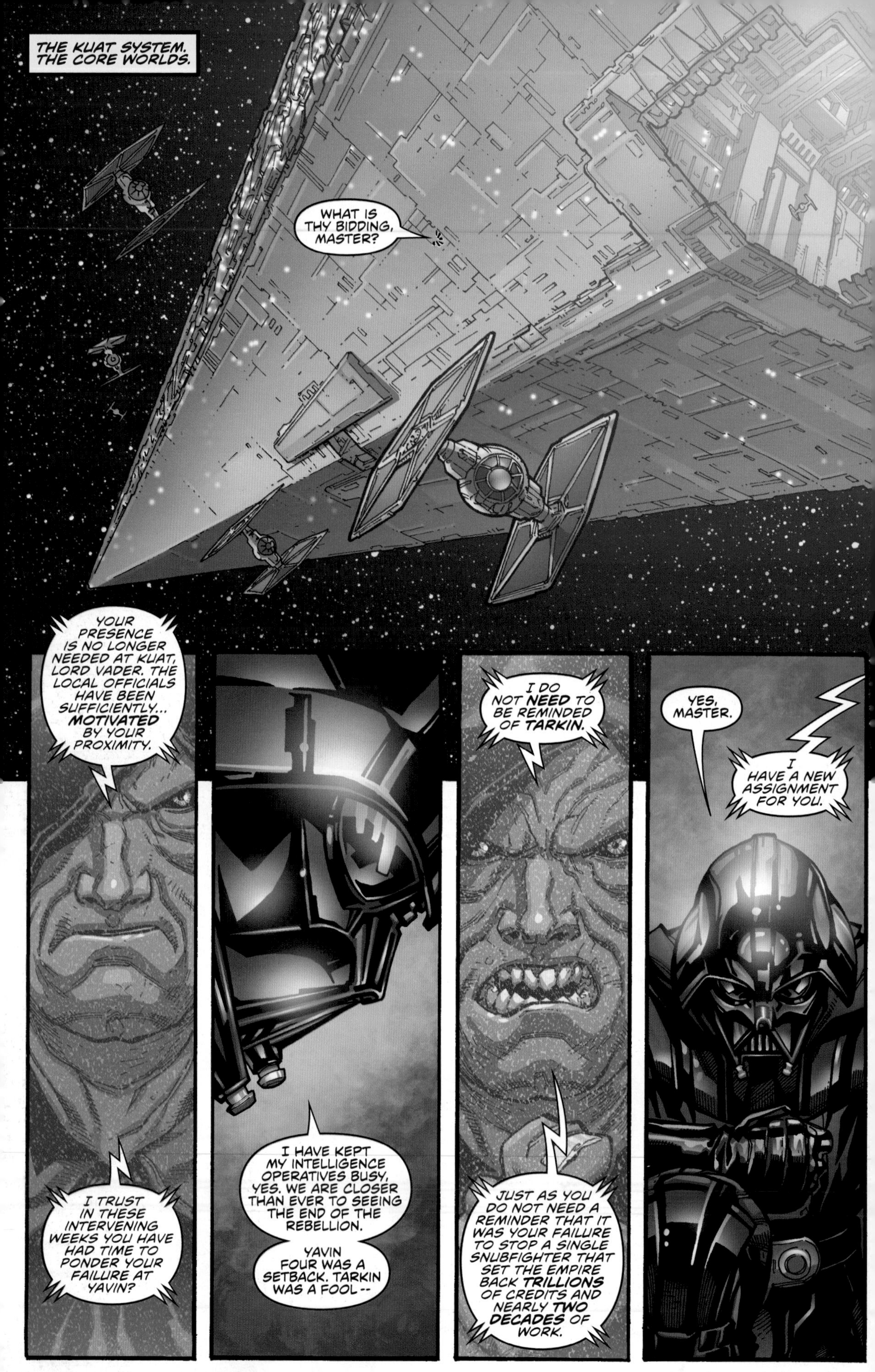
THE KUAT SYSTEM. THE CORE WORLDS.
WHAT IS THY BIDDING, MASTER?
YOUR PRESENCE IS NO LONGER NEEDED AT KUAT, LORD VADER. THE LOCAL OFFICIALS HAVE BEEN SUFFICIENTLY... MOTIVATED BY YOUR PROXIMITY.
I TRUST IN THESE INTERVENING WEEKS YOU HAVE HAD TIME TO PONDER YOUR FAILURE AT YAVIN?
I HAVE KEPT MY INTELLIGENCE OPERATIVES BUSY, YES. WE ARE CLOSER THAN EVER TO SEEING THE END OF THE REBELLION.
YAVIN FOUR WAS A SETBACK. TARKIN WAS A FOOL --
I DO NOT NEED TO BE REMINDED OF TARKIN.
JUST AS YOU DO NOT NEED A REMINDER THAT IT WAS YOUR FAILURE TO STOP A SINGLE SNUBFIGHTER THAT SET THE EMPIRE BACK TRILLIONS OF CREDITS AND NEARLY TWO DECADES OF WORK.
YES, MASTER.
I HAVE A NEW ASSIGNMENT FOR YOU.

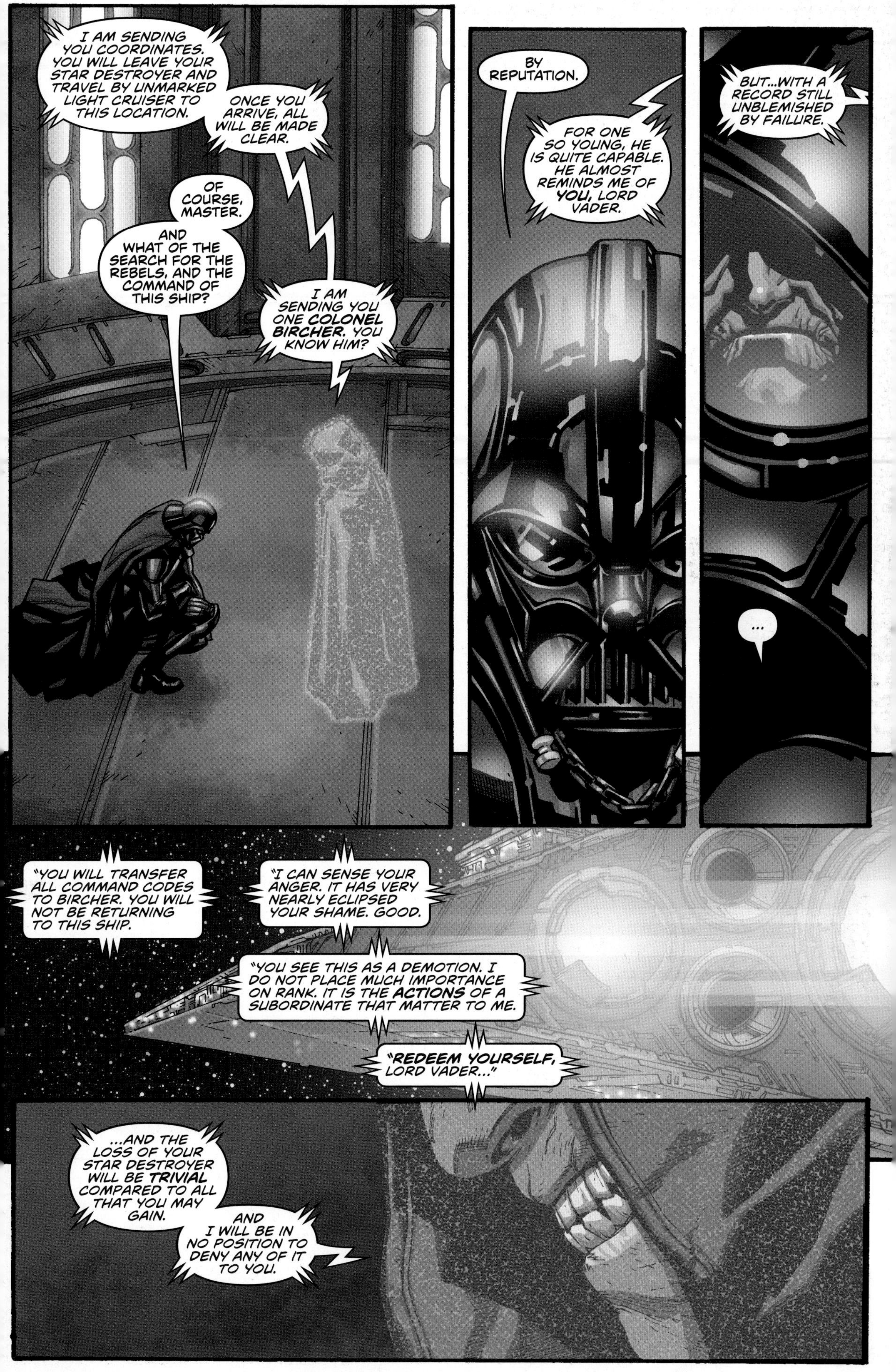
I AM SENDING YOU COORDINATES. YOU WILL LEAVE YOUR STAR DESTROYER AND TRAVEL BY UNMARKED LIGHT CRUISER TO THIS LOCATION.
ONCE YOU ARRIVE, ALL WILL BE MADE CLEAR.
OF COURSE, MASTER.
AND WHAT OF THE SEARCH FOR THE REBELS, AND THE COMMAND OF THIS SHIP?
I AM SENDING YOU ONE COLONEL BIRCHER. YOU KNOW HIM?
BY REPUTATION.
FOR ONE SO YOUNG, HE IS QUITE CAPABLE. HE ALMOST REMINDS ME OF YOU, LORD VADER.
BUT...WITH A RECORD STILL UNBLEMISHED BY FAILURE.
...
"YOU WILL TRANSFER ALL COMMAND CODES TO BIRCHER. YOU WILL NOT BE RETURNING TO THIS SHIP.
"I CAN SENSE YOUR ANGER. IT HAS VERY NEARLY ECLIPSED YOUR SHAME. GOOD.
"YOU SEE THIS AS A DEMOTION. I DO NOT PLACE MUCH IMPORTANCE ON RANK. IT IS THE ACTIONS OF A SUBORDINATE THAT MATTER TO ME.
"REDEEM YOURSELF, LORD VADER..."
...AND THE LOSS OF YOUR STAR DESTROYER WILL BE TRIVIAL COMPARED TO ALL THAT YOU MAY GAIN.
AND I WILL BE IN NO POSITION TO DENY ANY OF IT TO YOU.

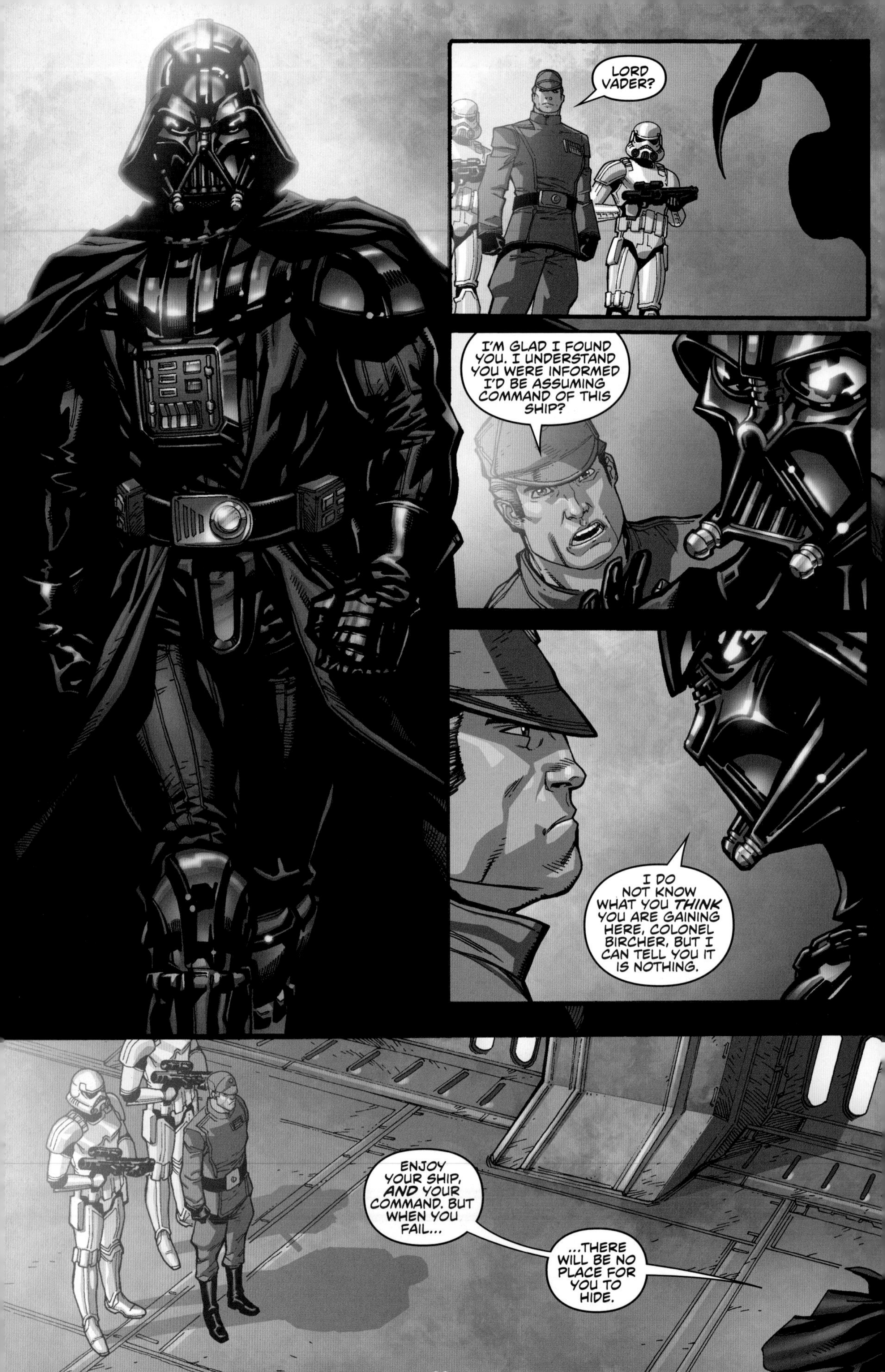
LORD VADER?
I'M GLAD I FOUND YOU. I UNDERSTAND YOU WERE INFORMED I'D BE ASSUMING COMMAND OF THIS SHIP?
I DO NOT KNOW WHAT YOU *THINK* YOU ARE GAINING HERE, COLONEL BIRCHER, BUT I CAN TELL YOU IT IS NOTHING.
ENJOY YOUR SHIP, ***AND*** YOUR COMMAND. BUT WHEN YOU FAIL...
...THERE WILL BE NO PLACE FOR YOU TO HIDE.

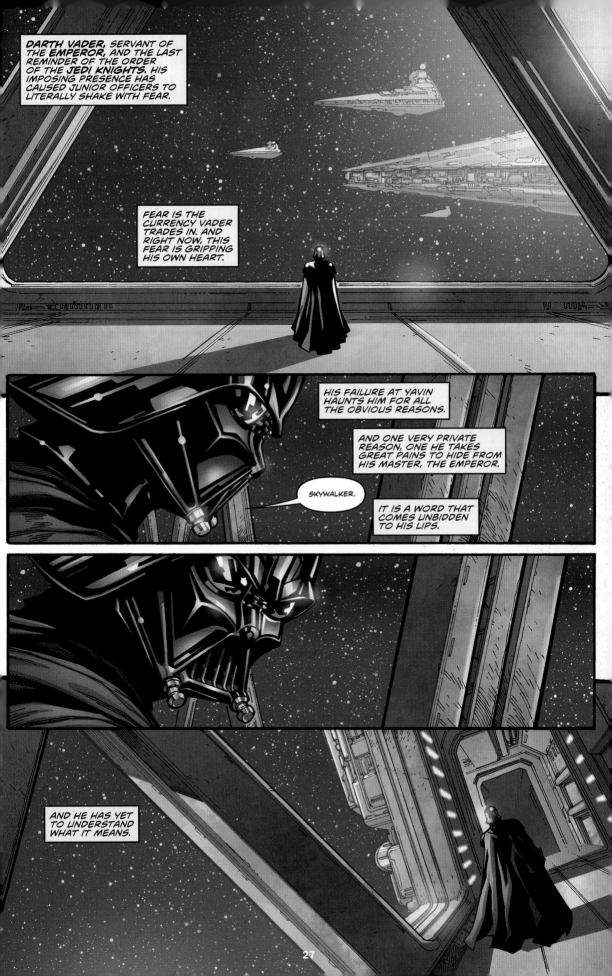

DARTH VADER, SERVANT OF THE EMPEROR, AND THE LAST REMINDER OF THE ORDER OF THE JEDI KNIGHTS. HIS IMPOSING PRESENCE HAS CAUSED JUNIOR OFFICERS TO LITERALLY SHAKE WITH FEAR.

FEAR IS THE CURRENCY VADER TRADES IN. AND RIGHT NOW, THIS FEAR IS GRIPPING HIS OWN HEART.

HIS FAILURE AT YAVIN HAUNTS HIM FOR ALL THE OBVIOUS REASONS.

AND ONE VERY PRIVATE REASON, ONE HE TAKES GREAT PAINS TO HIDE FROM HIS MASTER, THE EMPEROR.

SKYWALKER.

IT IS A WORD THAT COMES UNBIDDEN TO HIS LIPS.

AND HE HAS YET TO UNDERSTAND WHAT IT MEANS.

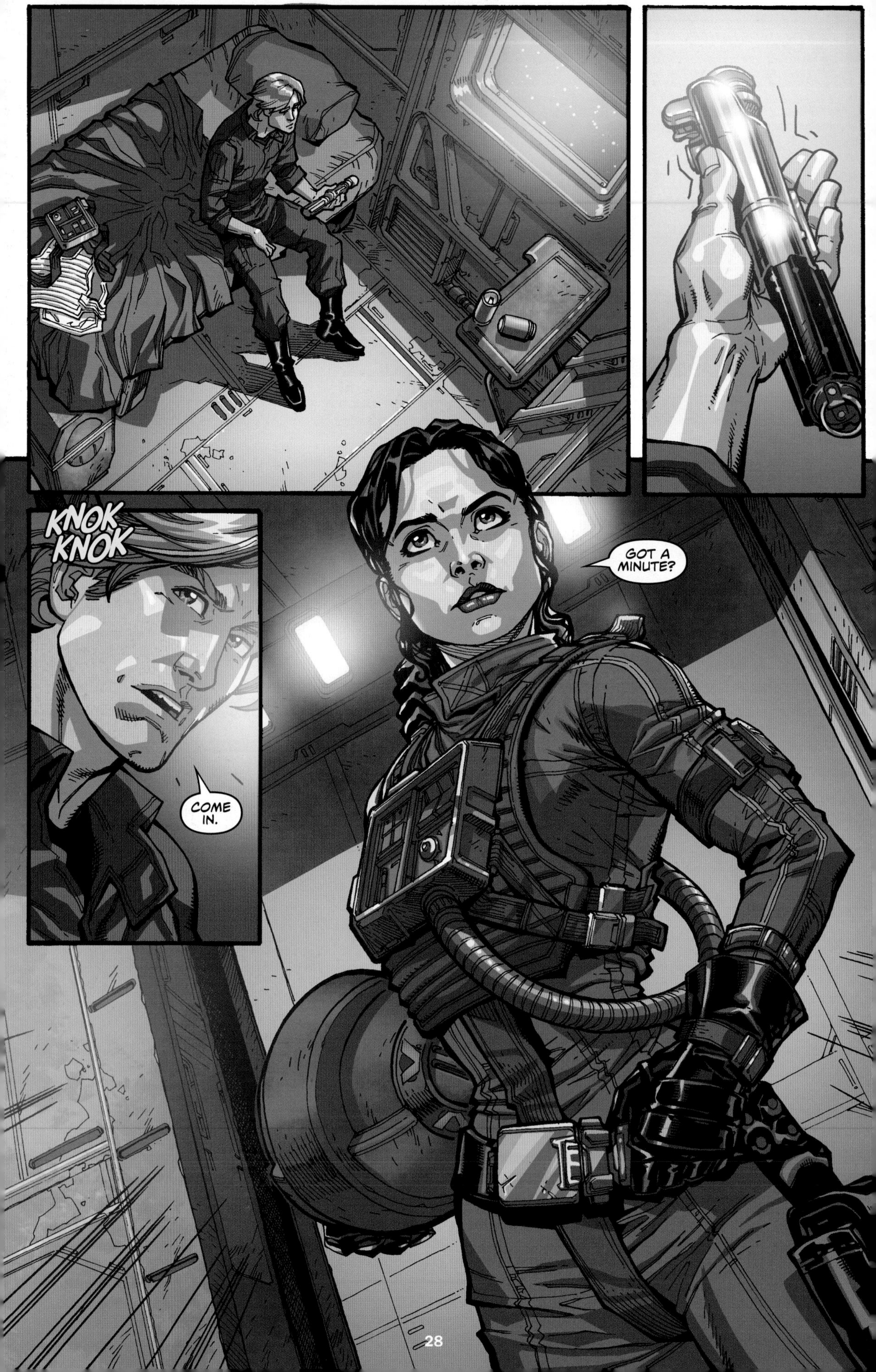
KNOK
KNOK
COME IN.
GOT A MINUTE?

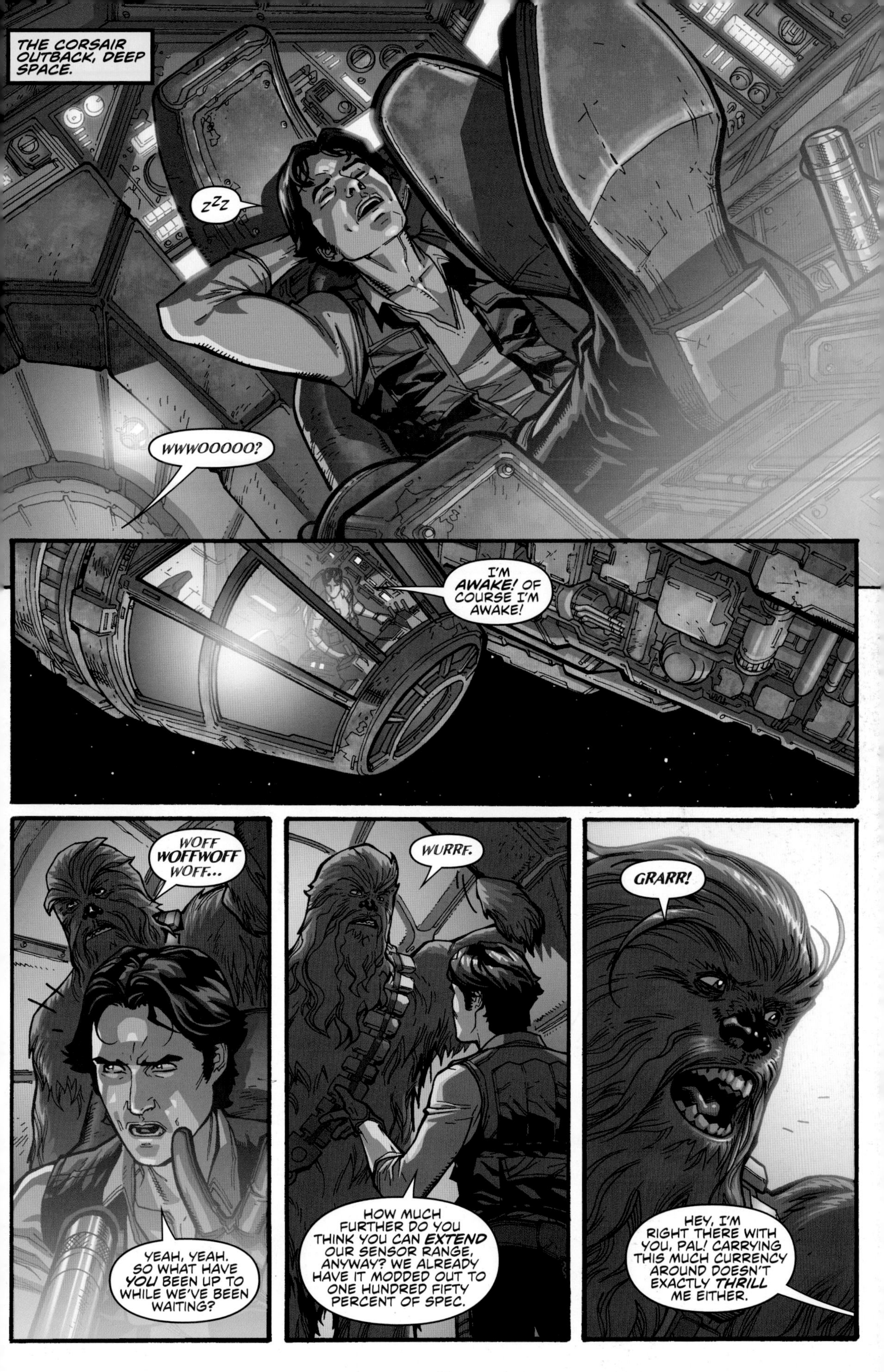
THE CORSAIR OUTBACK, DEEP SPACE.
ZZZ
WWWOOOOO?
I'M AWAKE! OF COURSE I'M AWAKE!
WOFF WOFFWOFF WOFF...
YEAH, YEAH. SO WHAT HAVE YOU BEEN UP TO WHILE WE'VE BEEN WAITING?
WURRF.
HOW MUCH FURTHER DO YOU THINK YOU CAN EXTEND OUR SENSOR RANGE, ANYWAY? WE ALREADY HAVE IT MODDED OUT TO ONE HUNDRED FIFTY PERCENT OF SPEC.
GRARR!
HEY, I'M RIGHT THERE WITH YOU, PAL! CARRYING THIS MUCH CURRENCY AROUND DOESN'T EXACTLY THRILL ME EITHER.

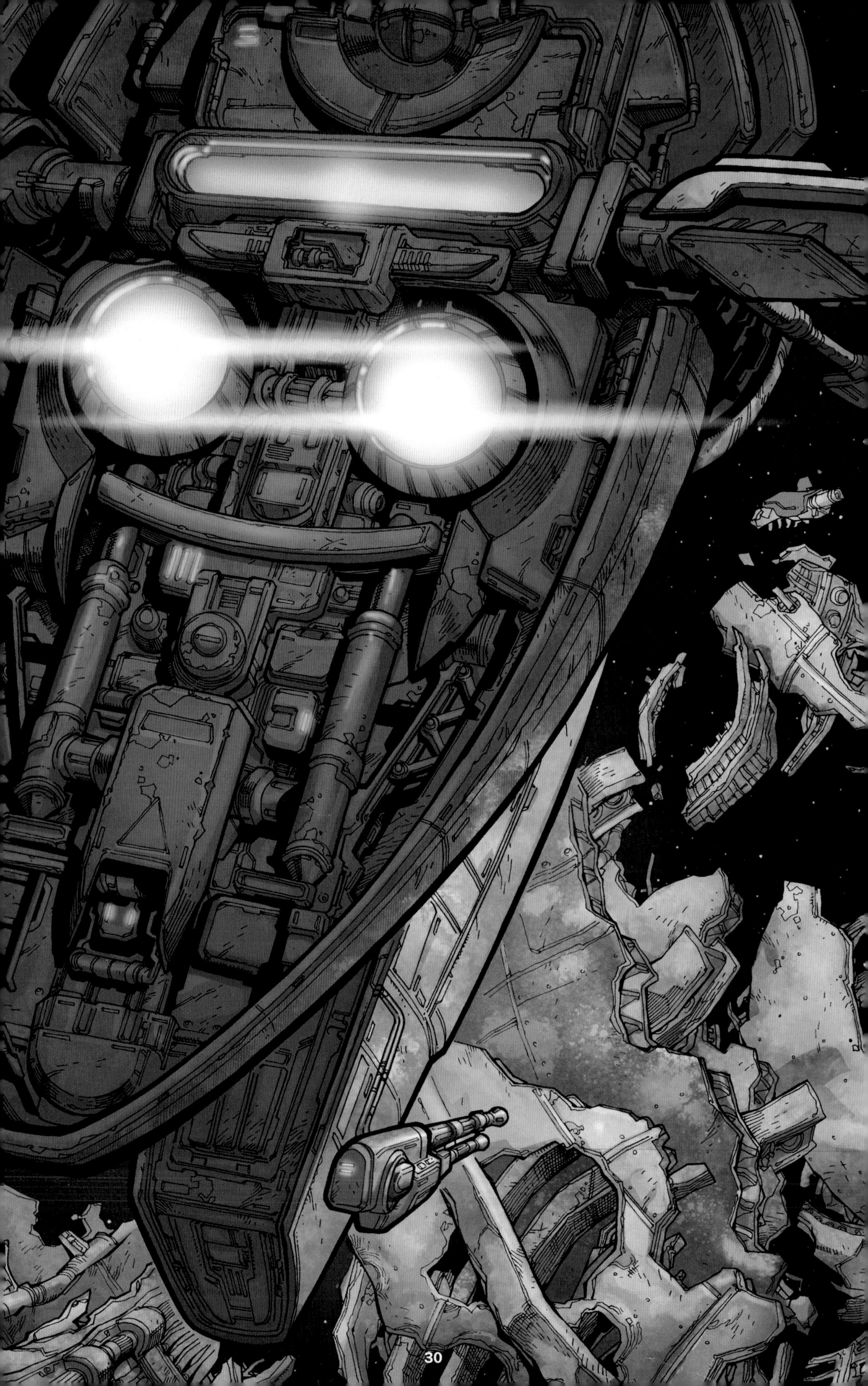

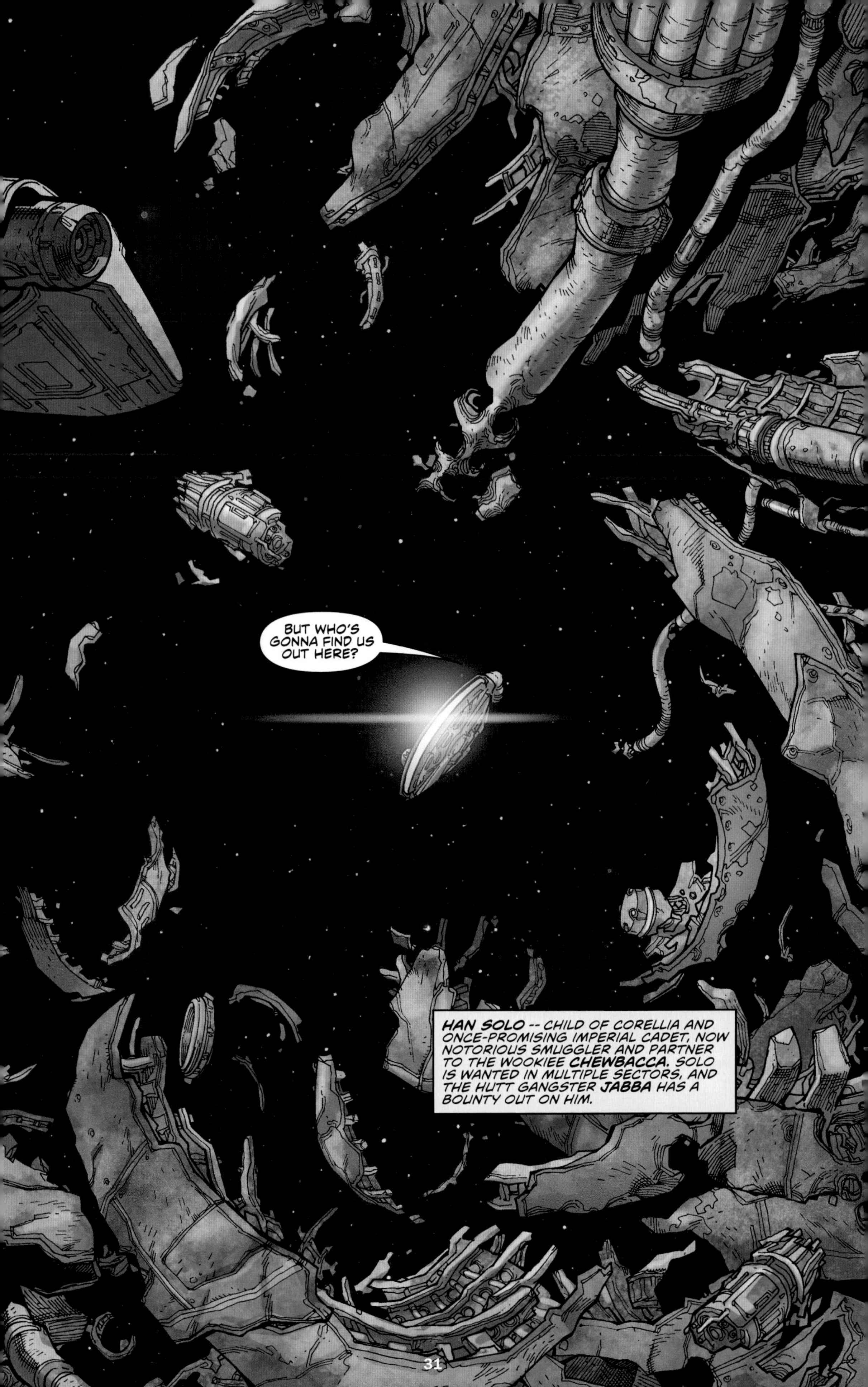
BUT WHO'S GONNA FIND US OUT HERE?
HAN SOLO -- CHILD OF CORELLIA AND ONCE-PROMISING IMPERIAL CADET, NOW NOTORIOUS SMUGGLER AND PARTNER TO THE WOOKIEE CHEWBACCA. SOLO IS WANTED IN MULTIPLE SECTORS, AND THE HUTT GANGSTER JABBA HAS A BOUNTY OUT ON HIM.

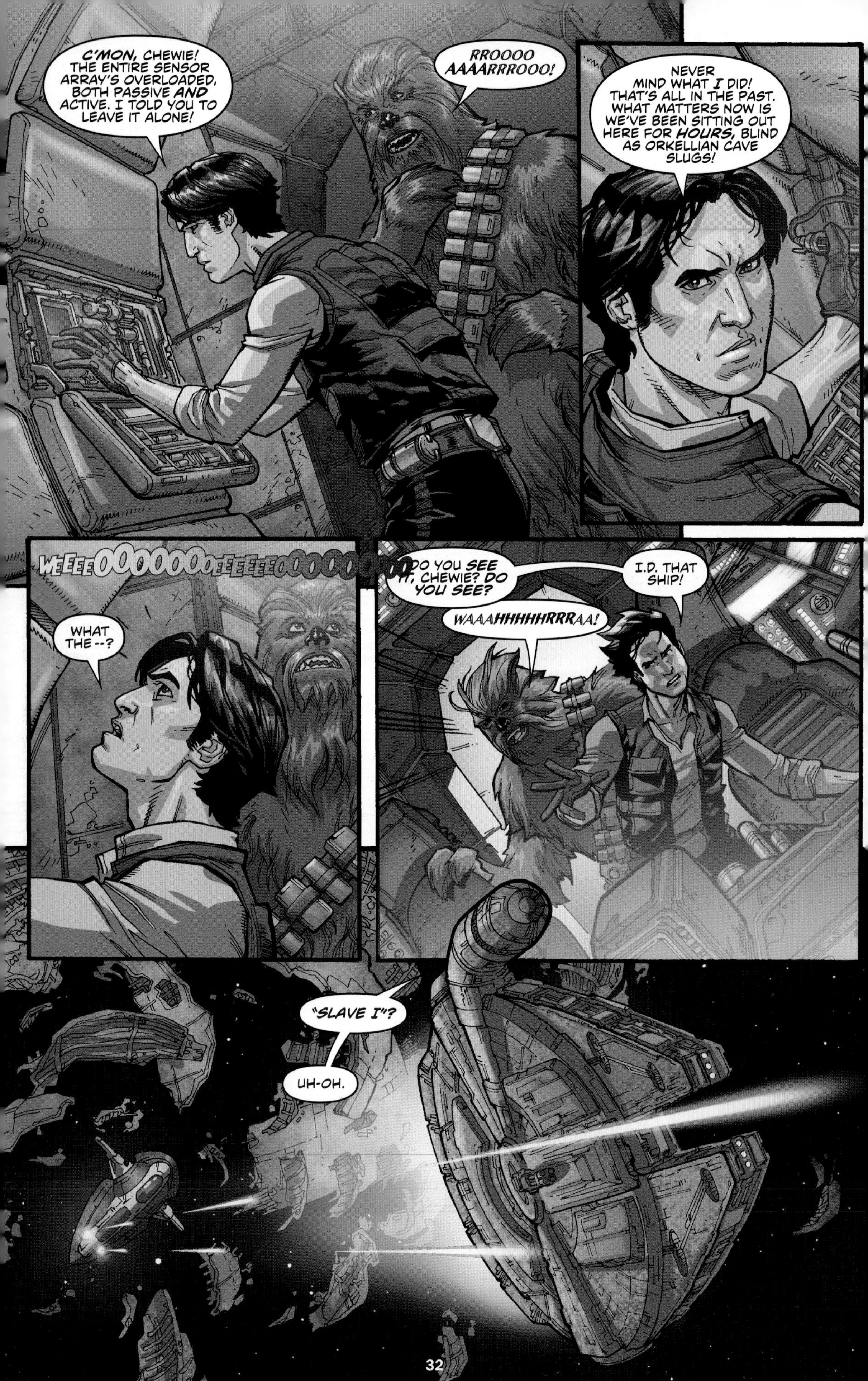
C'MON, CHEWIE! THE ENTIRE SENSOR ARRAY'S OVERLOADED, BOTH PASSIVE AND ACTIVE. I TOLD YOU TO LEAVE IT ALONE!
RROOOO AAAARRROOO!
NEVER MIND WHAT I DID! THAT'S ALL IN THE PAST. WHAT MATTERS NOW IS WE'VE BEEN SITTING OUT HERE FOR HOURS, BLIND AS ORKELLIAN CAVE SLUGS!
WEEEEOOOOOOOEEEEEEOOOOOOOOO
WHAT THE--?
DO YOU SEE IT, CHEWIE? DO YOU SEE?
I.D. THAT SHIP!
WAAAHHHHHRRRAA!
"SLAVE I"?
UH-OH.

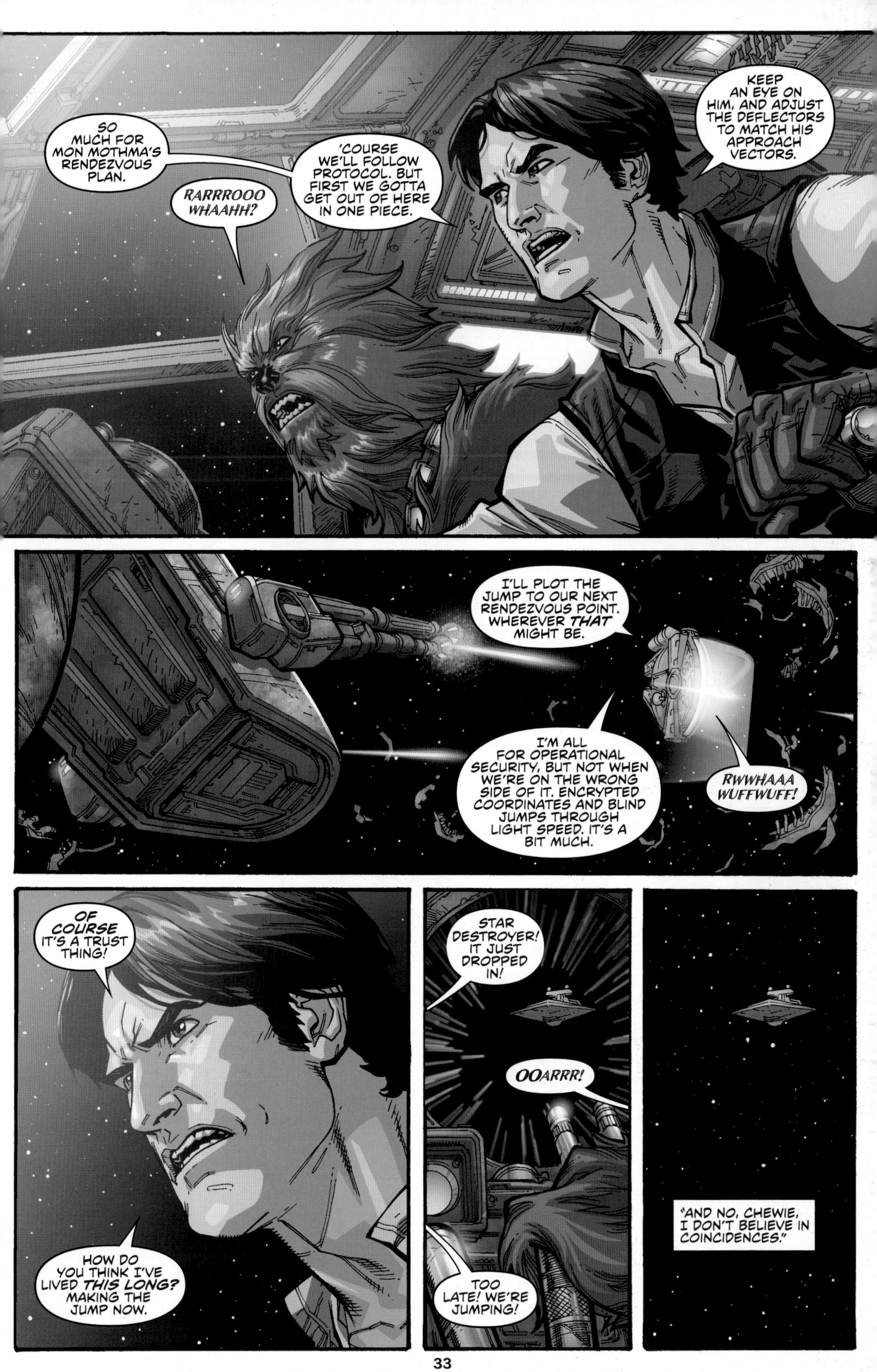
SO MUCH FOR MON MOTHMA'S RENDEZVOUS PLAN.
RARRROOO WHAAHH?
'COURSE WE'LL FOLLOW PROTOCOL. BUT FIRST WE GOTTA GET OUT OF HERE IN ONE PIECE.
KEEP AN EYE ON HIM, AND ADJUST THE DEFLECTORS TO MATCH HIS APPROACH VECTORS.
I'LL PLOT THE JUMP TO OUR NEXT RENDEZVOUS POINT. WHEREVER THAT MIGHT BE.
RWWHAAA WUFFWUFF!
I'M ALL FOR OPERATIONAL SECURITY, BUT NOT WHEN WE'RE ON THE WRONG SIDE OF IT. ENCRYPTED COORDINATES AND BLIND JUMPS THROUGH LIGHT SPEED. IT'S A BIT MUCH.
OF COURSE IT'S A TRUST THING!
HOW DO YOU THINK I'VE LIVED THIS LONG? MAKING THE JUMP NOW.
STAR DESTROYER! IT JUST DROPPED IN!
OOARRR!
TOO LATE! WE'RE JUMPING!
"AND NO, CHEWIE, I DON'T BELIEVE IN COINCIDENCES."

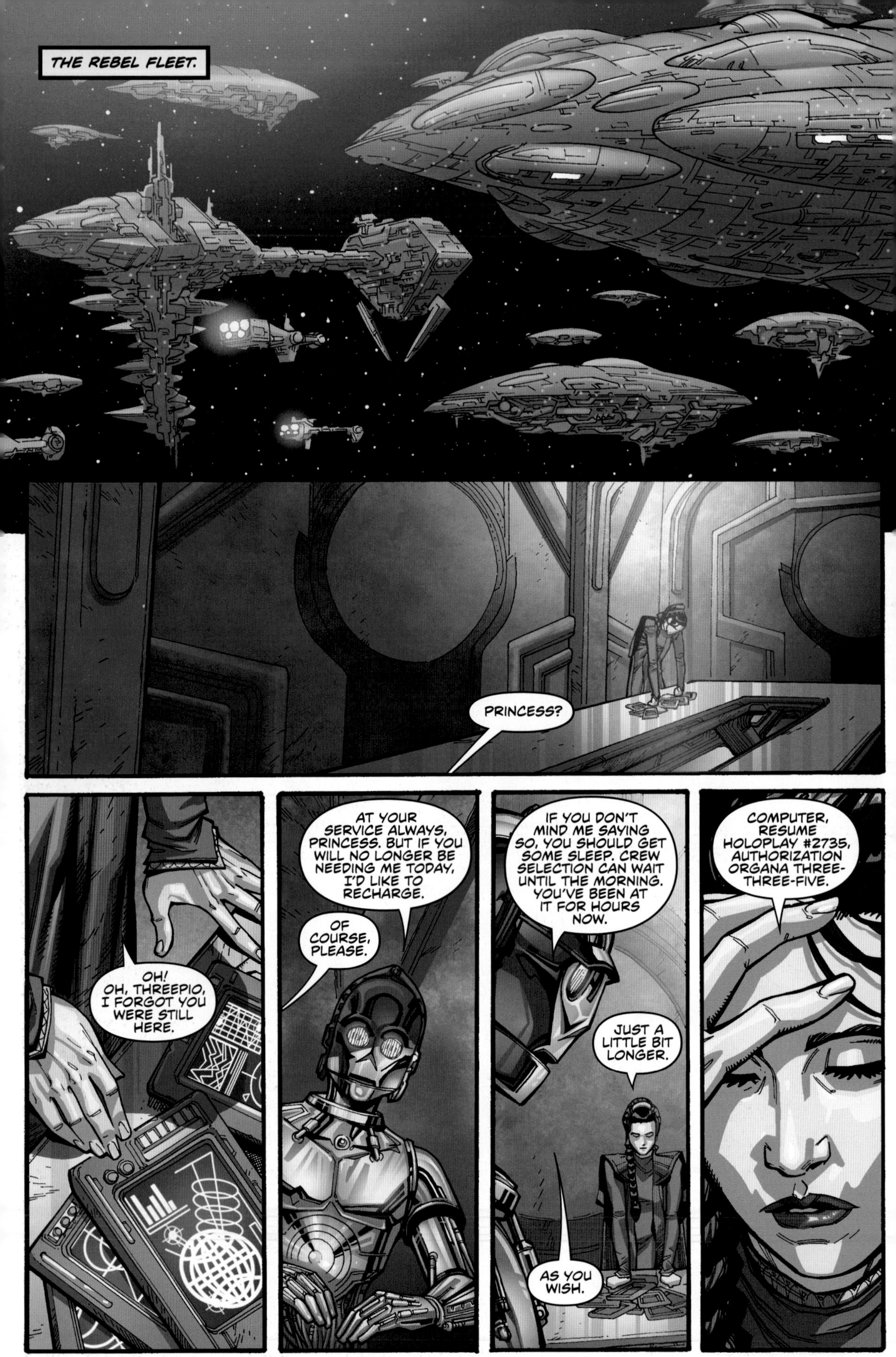
THE REBEL FLEET.
PRINCESS?
OH! OH, THREEPIO, I FORGOT YOU WERE STILL HERE.
AT YOUR SERVICE ALWAYS, PRINCESS. BUT IF YOU WILL NO LONGER BE NEEDING ME TODAY, I'D LIKE TO RECHARGE.
OF COURSE, PLEASE.
IF YOU DON'T MIND ME SAYING SO, YOU SHOULD GET SOME SLEEP. CREW SELECTION CAN WAIT UNTIL THE MORNING. YOU'VE BEEN AT IT FOR HOURS NOW.
JUST A LITTLE BIT LONGER.
AS YOU WISH.
COMPUTER, RESUME HOLOPLAY #2735, AUTHORIZATION ORGANA THREE-THREE-FIVE.

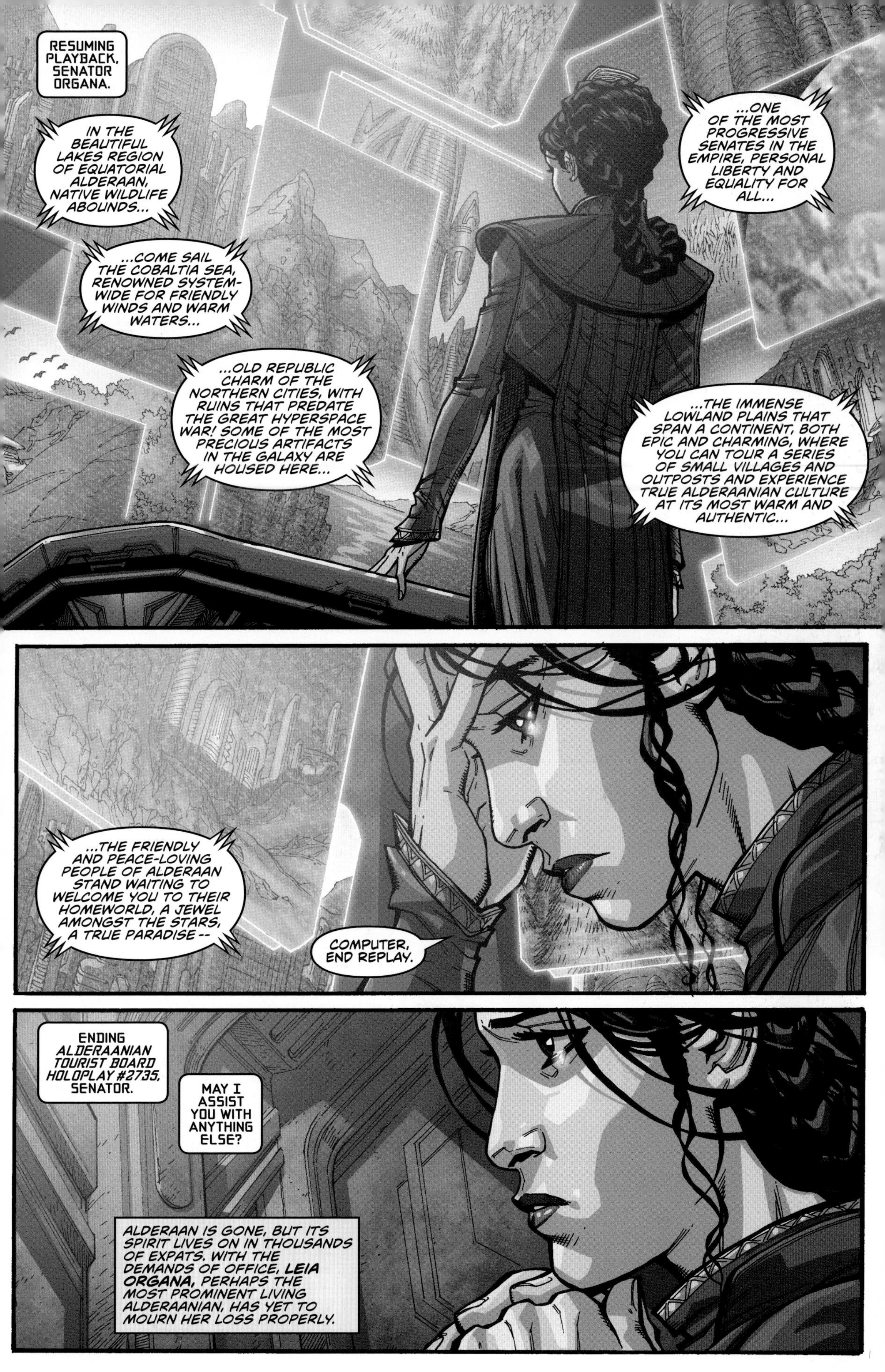
RESUMING PLAYBACK, SENATOR ORGANA.
IN THE BEAUTIFUL LAKES REGION OF EQUATORIAL ALDERAAN, NATIVE WILDLIFE ABOUNDS...
...COME SAIL THE COBALTIA SEA, RENOWNED SYSTEM-WIDE FOR FRIENDLY WINDS AND WARM WATERS...
...OLD REPUBLIC CHARM OF THE NORTHERN CITIES, WITH RUINS THAT PREDATE THE GREAT HYPERSPACE WAR! SOME OF THE MOST PRECIOUS ARTIFACTS IN THE GALAXY ARE HOUSED HERE...
...ONE OF THE MOST PROGRESSIVE SENATES IN THE EMPIRE, PERSONAL LIBERTY AND EQUALITY FOR ALL...
...THE IMMENSE LOWLAND PLAINS THAT SPAN A CONTINENT, BOTH EPIC AND CHARMING, WHERE YOU CAN TOUR A SERIES OF SMALL VILLAGES AND OUTPOSTS AND EXPERIENCE TRUE ALDERAANIAN CULTURE AT ITS MOST WARM AND AUTHENTIC...
...THE FRIENDLY AND PEACE-LOVING PEOPLE OF ALDERAAN STAND WAITING TO WELCOME YOU TO THEIR HOMEWORLD, A JEWEL AMONGST THE STARS, A TRUE PARADISE --
COMPUTER, END REPLAY.
ENDING ALDERAANIAN TOURIST BOARD HOLOPLAY #2735, SENATOR.
MAY I ASSIST YOU WITH ANYTHING ELSE?
ALDERAAN IS GONE, BUT ITS SPIRIT LIVES ON IN THOUSANDS OF EXPATS. WITH THE DEMANDS OF OFFICE, LEIA ORGANA, PERHAPS THE MOST PROMINENT LIVING ALDERAANIAN, HAS YET TO MOURN HER LOSS PROPERLY.

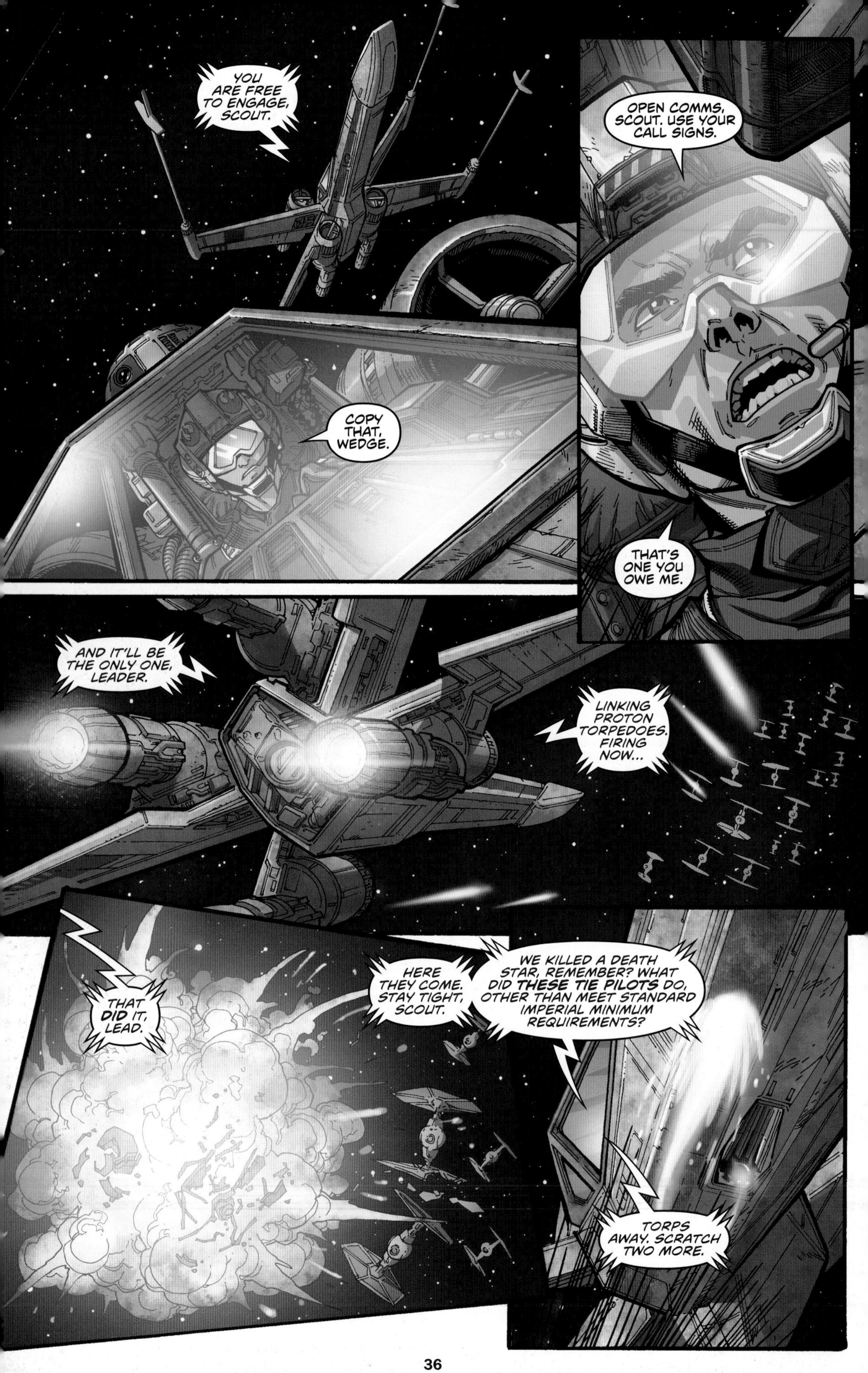
YOU ARE FREE TO ENGAGE, SCOUT.
OPEN COMMS, SCOUT. USE YOUR CALL SIGNS.
COPY THAT, WEDGE.
THAT'S ONE YOU OWE ME.
AND IT'LL BE THE ONLY ONE, LEADER.
LINKING PROTON TORPEDOES. FIRING NOW...
THAT DID IT, LEAD.
HERE THEY COME. STAY TIGHT, SCOUT.
WE KILLED A DEATH STAR, REMEMBER? WHAT DID THESE TIE PILOTS DO, OTHER THAN MEET STANDARD IMPERIAL MINIMUM REQUIREMENTS?
TORPS AWAY. SCRATCH TWO MORE.

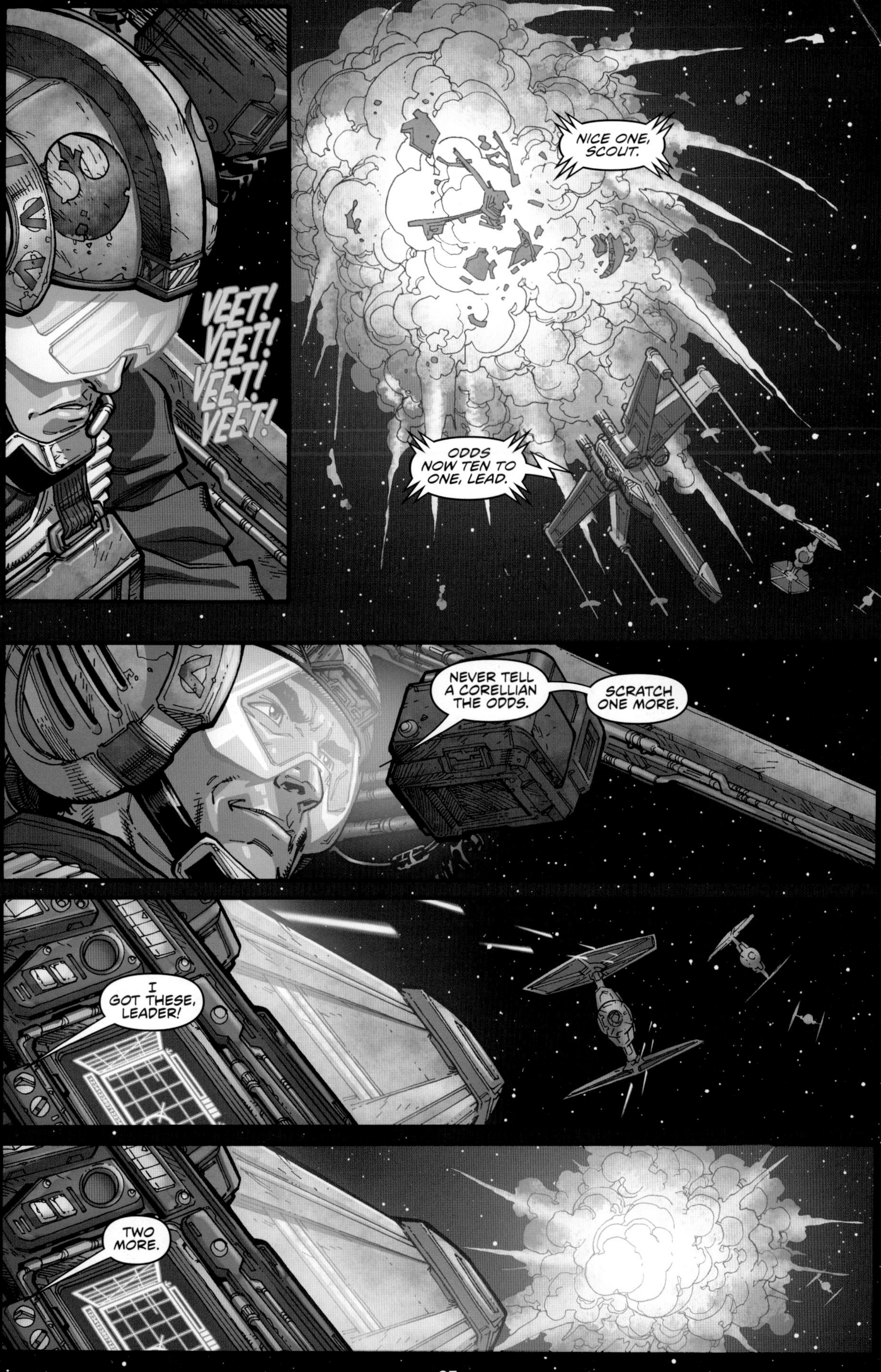
VEET! VEET! VEET! VEET!
NICE ONE, SCOUT.
ODDS NOW TEN TO ONE, LEAD.
NEVER TELL A CORELLIAN THE ODDS.
SCRATCH ONE MORE.
I GOT THESE, LEADER!
TWO MORE.

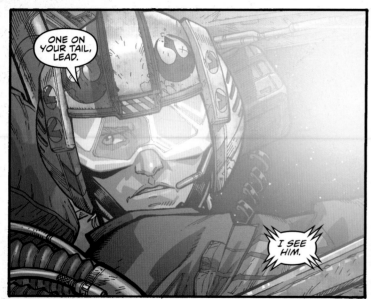

ONE ON YOUR TAIL, LEAD.

I SEE HIM.

CHECK YOUR SCANNER... THEY'RE STARTING TO BUG OUT.

THANKS FOR THE HEADS-UP, SCOUT.

NOT ON MY WATCH.

LEAD, I HAVE A MISSILE LOCK ON ONE OF THE GROUP. SLAVE YOUR TARGETING TO MINE, AND SET YOUR TORPS TO PROXIMITY DETONATION.

DONE, SCOUT.

FIRING...

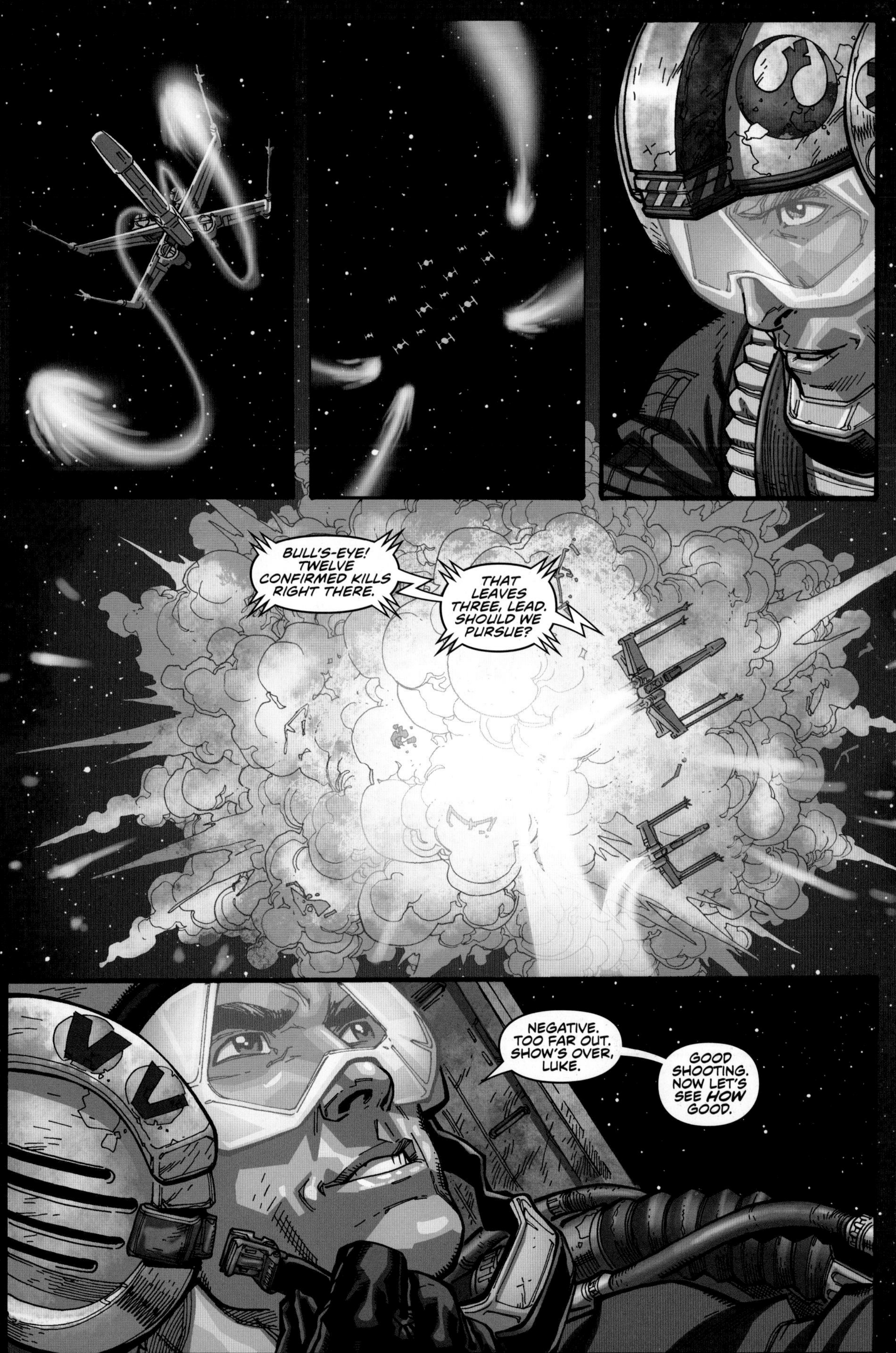
BULL'S-EYE! TWELVE CONFIRMED KILLS RIGHT THERE.
THAT LEAVES THREE, LEAD. SHOULD WE PURSUE?
NEGATIVE. TOO FAR OUT. SHOW'S OVER, LUKE.
GOOD SHOOTING. NOW LET'S SEE *HOW* GOOD.

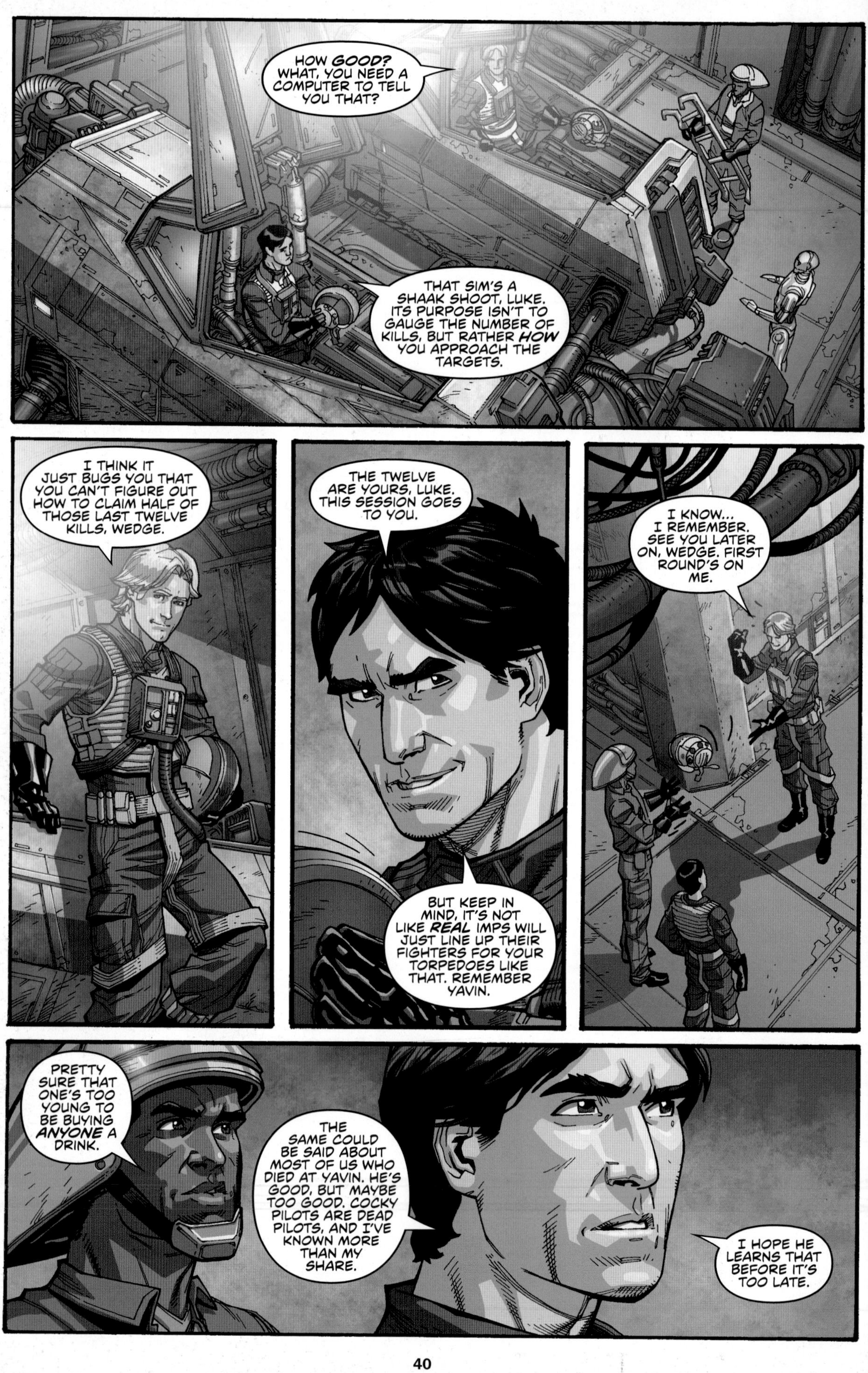
HOW GOOD? WHAT, YOU NEED A COMPUTER TO TELL YOU THAT?
THAT SIM'S A SHAAK SHOOT, LUKE. ITS PURPOSE ISN'T TO GAUGE THE NUMBER OF KILLS, BUT RATHER HOW YOU APPROACH THE TARGETS.
I THINK IT JUST BUGS YOU THAT YOU CAN'T FIGURE OUT HOW TO CLAIM HALF OF THOSE LAST TWELVE KILLS, WEDGE.
THE TWELVE ARE YOURS, LUKE. THIS SESSION GOES TO YOU.
BUT KEEP IN MIND, IT'S NOT LIKE REAL IMPS WILL JUST LINE UP THEIR FIGHTERS FOR YOUR TORPEDOES LIKE THAT. REMEMBER YAVIN.
I KNOW... I REMEMBER. SEE YOU LATER ON, WEDGE. FIRST ROUND'S ON ME.
PRETTY SURE THAT ONE'S TOO YOUNG TO BE BUYING ANYONE A DRINK.
THE SAME COULD BE SAID ABOUT MOST OF US WHO DIED AT YAVIN. HE'S GOOD, BUT MAYBE TOO GOOD. COCKY PILOTS ARE DEAD PILOTS, AND I'VE KNOWN MORE THAN MY SHARE.
I HOPE HE LEARNS THAT BEFORE IT'S TOO LATE.

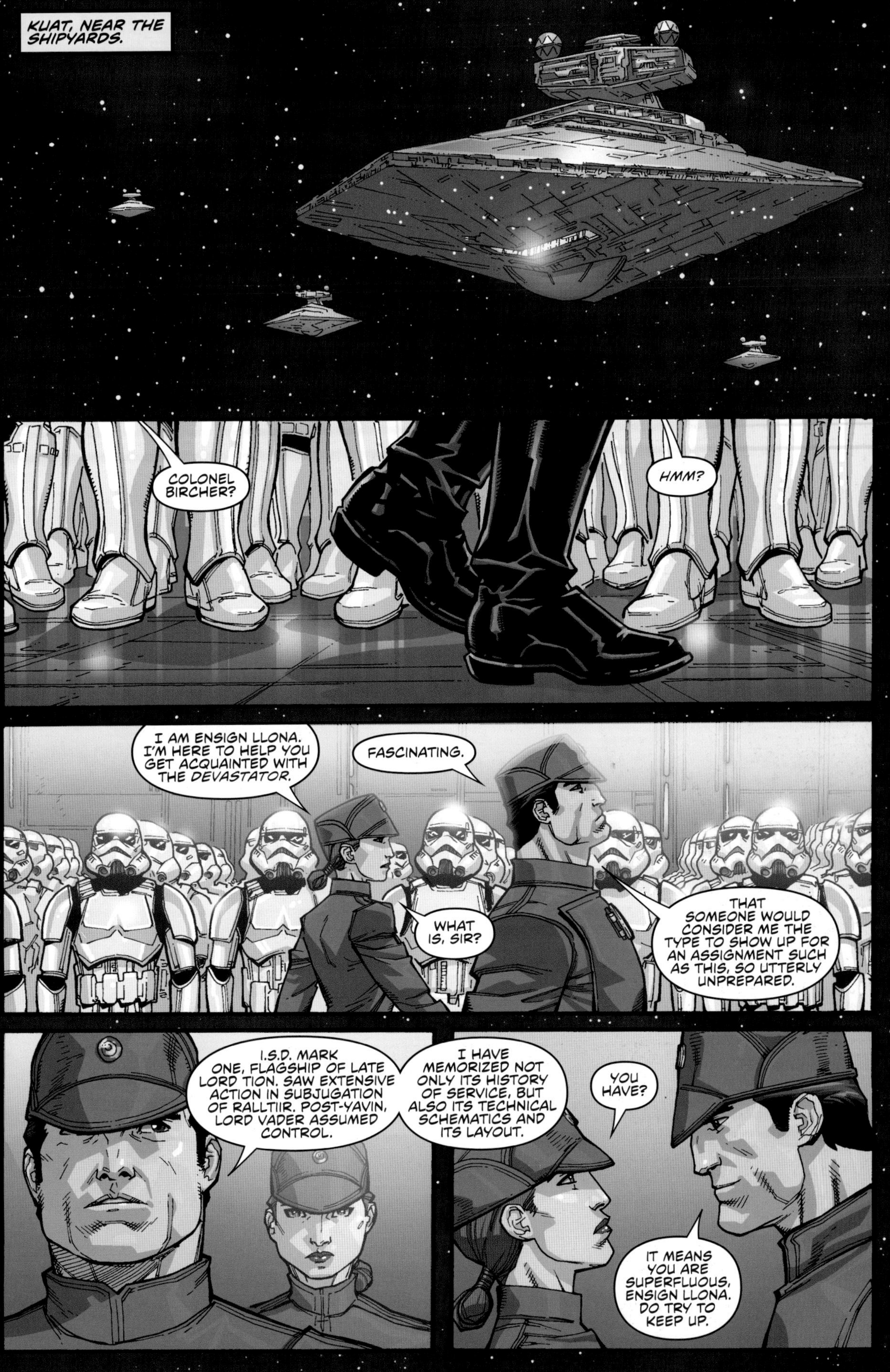
KUAT, NEAR THE SHIPYARDS.
COLONEL BIRCHER?
HMM?
I AM ENSIGN LLONA. I'M HERE TO HELP YOU GET ACQUAINTED WITH THE DEVASTATOR.
FASCINATING.
WHAT IS, SIR?
THAT SOMEONE WOULD CONSIDER ME THE TYPE TO SHOW UP FOR AN ASSIGNMENT SUCH AS THIS, SO UTTERLY UNPREPARED.
I.S.D. MARK ONE, FLAGSHIP OF LATE LORD TION. SAW EXTENSIVE ACTION IN SUBJUGATION OF RALLTIIR. POST-YAVIN, LORD VADER ASSUMED CONTROL.
I HAVE MEMORIZED NOT ONLY ITS HISTORY OF SERVICE, BUT ALSO ITS TECHNICAL SCHEMATICS AND ITS LAYOUT.
YOU HAVE?
IT MEANS YOU ARE SUPERFLUOUS, ENSIGN LLONA. DO TRY TO KEEP UP.

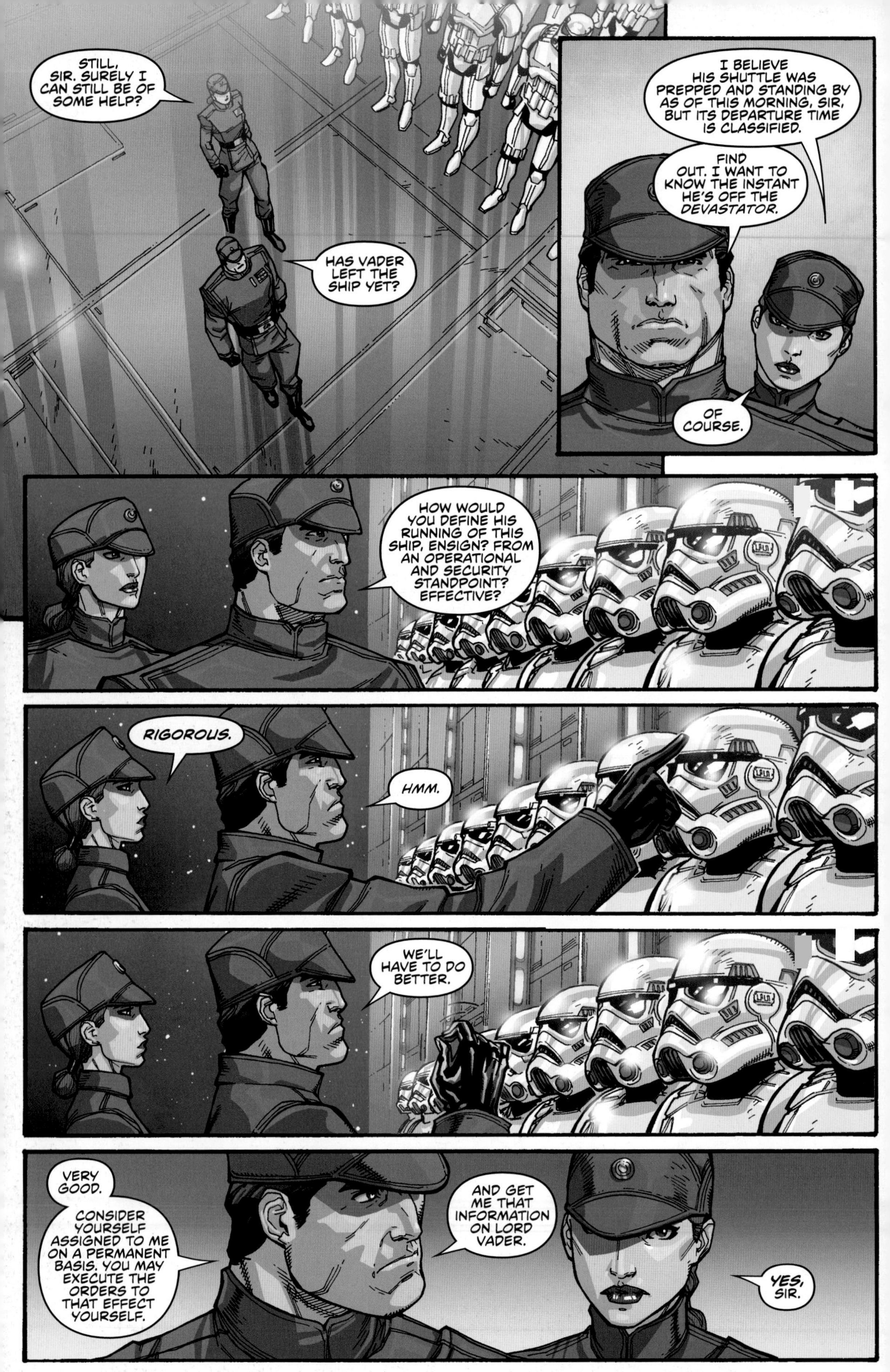
STILL, SIR. SURELY I CAN STILL BE OF SOME HELP?
HAS VADER LEFT THE SHIP YET?
I BELIEVE HIS SHUTTLE WAS PREPPED AND STANDING BY AS OF THIS MORNING, SIR, BUT ITS DEPARTURE TIME IS CLASSIFIED.
FIND OUT. I WANT TO KNOW THE INSTANT HE'S OFF THE *DEVASTATOR*.
OF COURSE.
HOW WOULD YOU DEFINE HIS RUNNING OF THIS SHIP, ENSIGN? FROM AN OPERATIONAL AND SECURITY STANDPOINT? EFFECTIVE?
RIGOROUS.
HMM.
WE'LL HAVE TO DO BETTER.
VERY GOOD.
CONSIDER YOURSELF ASSIGNED TO ME ON A PERMANENT BASIS. YOU MAY EXECUTE THE ORDERS TO THAT EFFECT YOURSELF.
AND GET ME THAT INFORMATION ON LORD VADER.
YES, SIR.

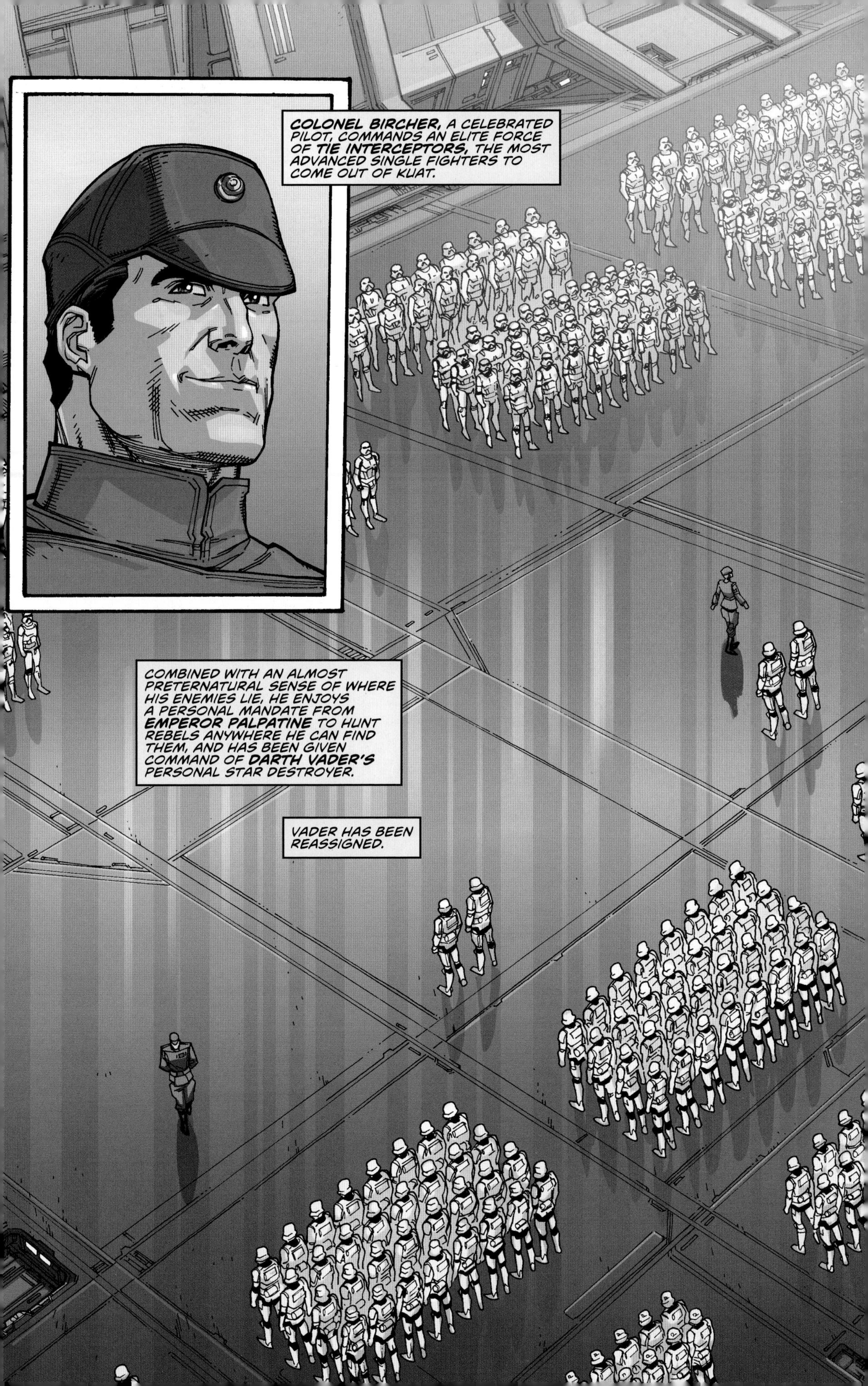
COLONEL BIRCHER, A CELEBRATED PILOT, COMMANDS AN ELITE FORCE OF TIE INTERCEPTORS, THE MOST ADVANCED SINGLE FIGHTERS TO COME OUT OF KUAT.
COMBINED WITH AN ALMOST PRETERNATURAL SENSE OF WHERE HIS ENEMIES LIE, HE ENJOYS A PERSONAL MANDATE FROM EMPEROR PALPATINE TO HUNT REBELS ANYWHERE HE CAN FIND THEM, AND HAS BEEN GIVEN COMMAND OF DARTH VADER'S PERSONAL STAR DESTROYER.
VADER HAS BEEN REASSIGNED.

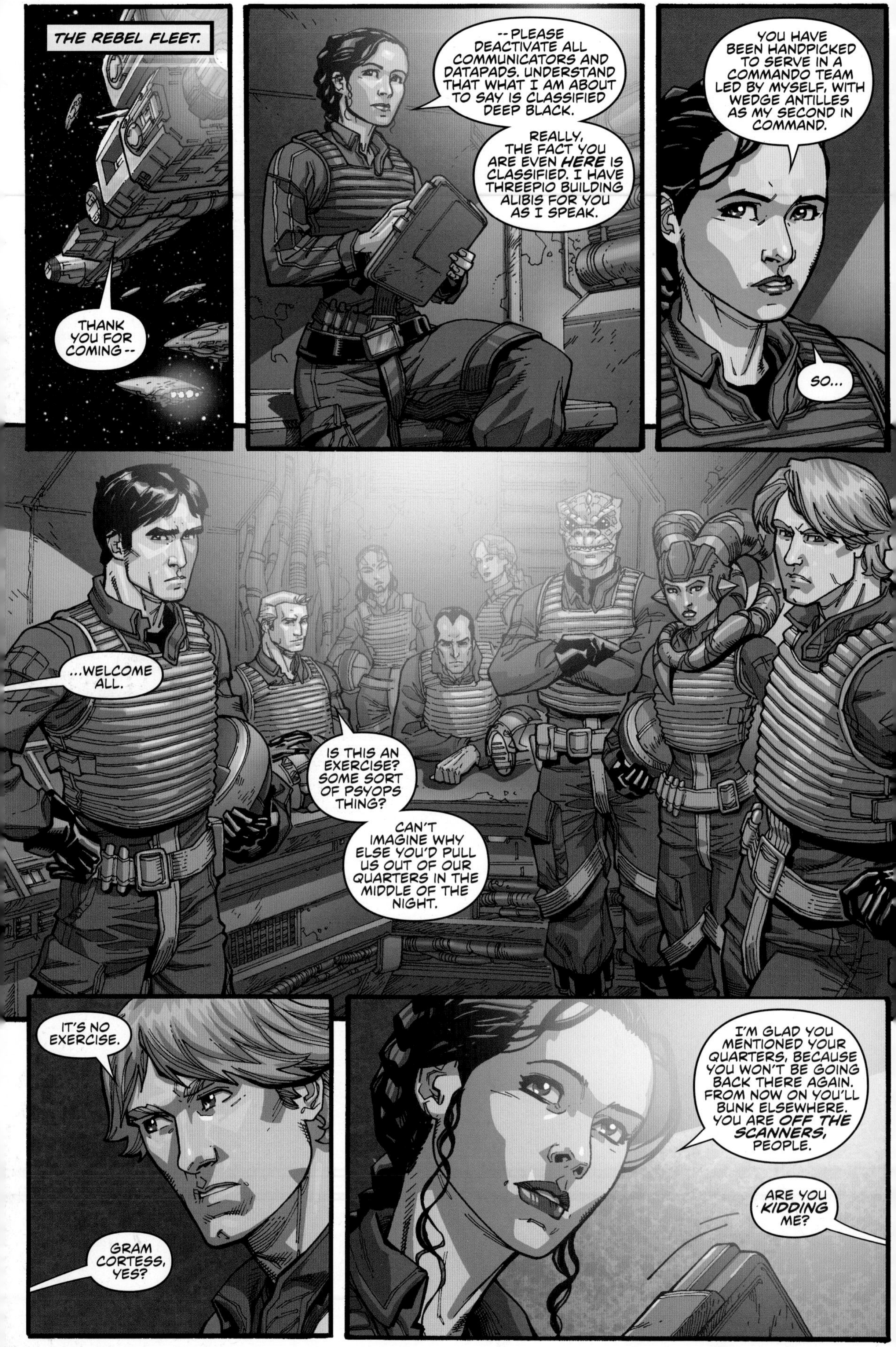
THE REBEL FLEET.
THANK YOU FOR COMING--
--PLEASE DEACTIVATE ALL COMMUNICATORS AND DATAPADS. UNDERSTAND THAT WHAT I AM ABOUT TO SAY IS CLASSIFIED DEEP BLACK.
REALLY, THE FACT YOU ARE EVEN HERE IS CLASSIFIED. I HAVE THREEPIO BUILDING ALIBIS FOR YOU AS I SPEAK.
YOU HAVE BEEN HANDPICKED TO SERVE IN A COMMANDO TEAM LED BY MYSELF, WITH WEDGE ANTILLES AS MY SECOND IN COMMAND.
SO...
...WELCOME ALL.
IS THIS AN EXERCISE? SOME SORT OF PSYOPS THING?
CAN'T IMAGINE WHY ELSE YOU'D PULL US OUT OF OUR QUARTERS IN THE MIDDLE OF THE NIGHT.
IT'S NO EXERCISE.
GRAM CORTESS, YES?
I'M GLAD YOU MENTIONED YOUR QUARTERS, BECAUSE YOU WON'T BE GOING BACK THERE AGAIN. FROM NOW ON YOU'LL BUNK ELSEWHERE. YOU ARE OFF THE SCANNERS, PEOPLE.
ARE YOU KIDDING ME?

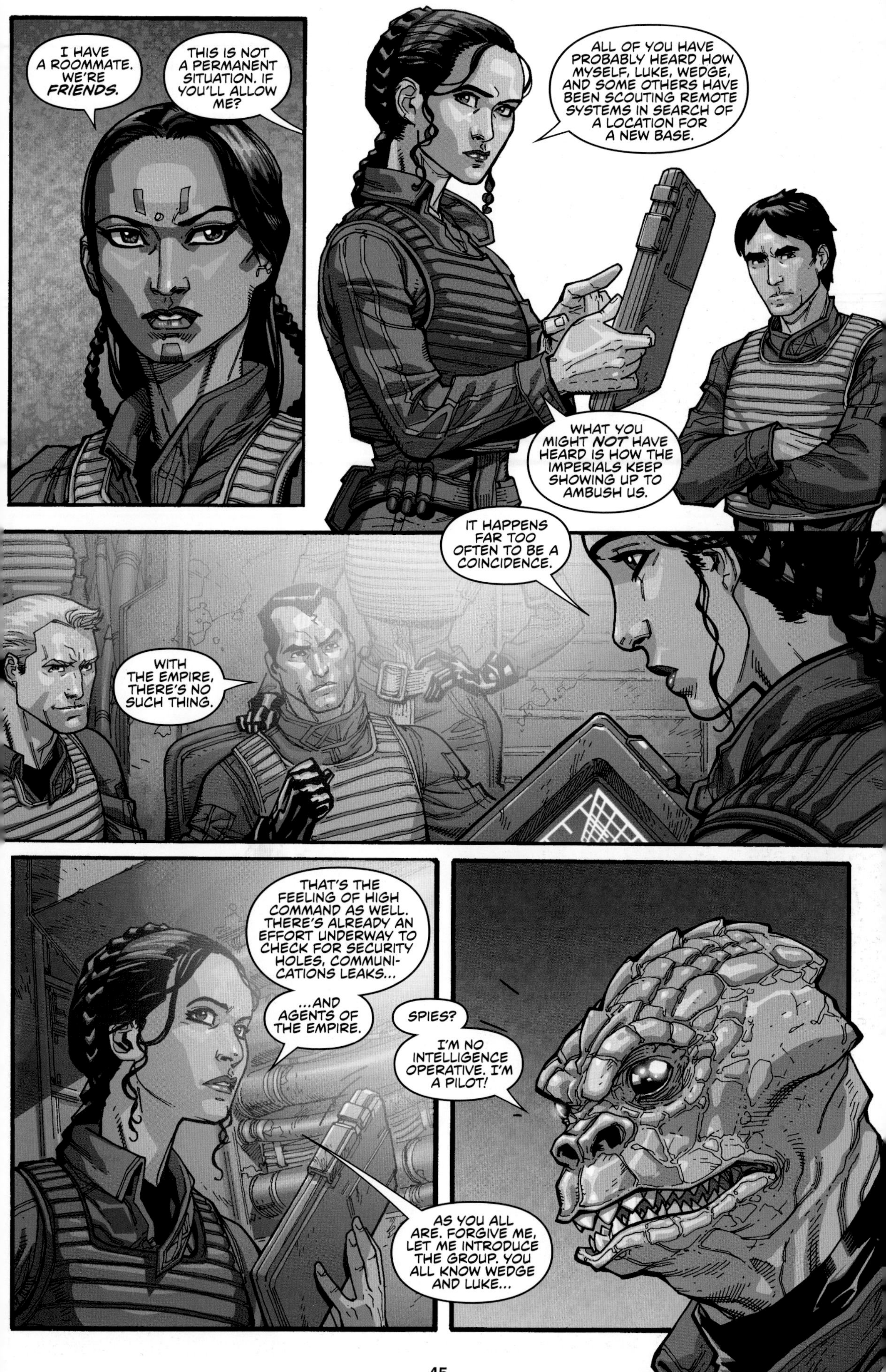
I HAVE A ROOMMATE. WE'RE *FRIENDS*.
THIS IS NOT A PERMANENT SITUATION. IF YOU'LL ALLOW ME?
ALL OF YOU HAVE PROBABLY HEARD HOW MYSELF, LUKE, WEDGE, AND SOME OTHERS HAVE BEEN SCOUTING REMOTE SYSTEMS IN SEARCH OF A LOCATION FOR A NEW BASE.
WHAT YOU MIGHT ***NOT*** HAVE HEARD IS HOW THE IMPERIALS KEEP SHOWING UP TO AMBUSH US.
IT HAPPENS FAR TOO OFTEN TO BE A COINCIDENCE.
WITH THE EMPIRE, THERE'S NO SUCH THING.
THAT'S THE FEELING OF HIGH COMMAND AS WELL. THERE'S ALREADY AN EFFORT UNDERWAY TO CHECK FOR SECURITY HOLES, COMMUNICATIONS LEAKS...
...AND AGENTS OF THE EMPIRE.
SPIES?
I'M NO INTELLIGENCE OPERATIVE. I'M A PILOT!
AS YOU ALL ARE. FORGIVE ME, LET ME INTRODUCE THE GROUP. YOU ALL KNOW WEDGE AND LUKE...

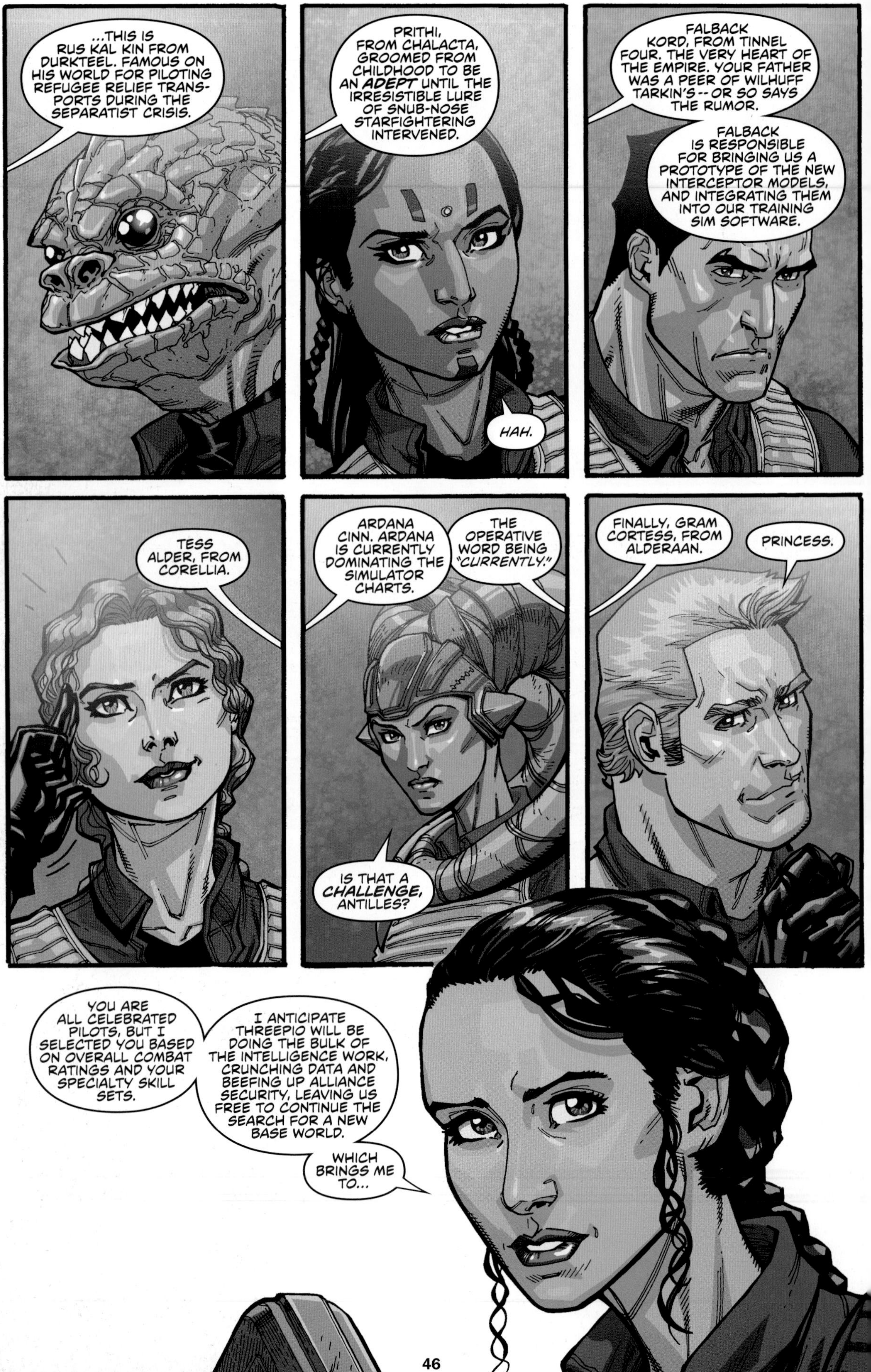
...THIS IS RUS KAL KIN FROM DURKTEEL. FAMOUS ON HIS WORLD FOR PILOTING REFUGEE RELIEF TRANS-PORTS DURING THE SEPARATIST CRISIS.
PRITHI, FROM CHALACTA, GROOMED FROM CHILDHOOD TO BE AN *ADEPT* UNTIL THE IRRESISTIBLE LURE OF SNUB-NOSE STARFIGHTERING INTERVENED.
HAH.
FALBACK KORD, FROM TINNEL FOUR. THE VERY HEART OF THE EMPIRE. YOUR FATHER WAS A PEER OF WILHUFF TARKIN'S--OR SO SAYS THE RUMOR.
FALBACK IS RESPONSIBLE FOR BRINGING US A PROTOTYPE OF THE NEW INTERCEPTOR MODELS, AND INTEGRATING THEM INTO OUR TRAINING SIM SOFTWARE.
TESS ALDER, FROM CORELLIA.
ARDANA CINN. ARDANA IS CURRENTLY DOMINATING THE SIMULATOR CHARTS.
THE OPERATIVE WORD BEING *"CURRENTLY."*
IS THAT A *CHALLENGE*, ANTILLES?
FINALLY, GRAM CORTESS, FROM ALDERAAN.
PRINCESS.
YOU ARE ALL CELEBRATED PILOTS, BUT I SELECTED YOU BASED ON OVERALL COMBAT RATINGS AND YOUR SPECIALTY SKILL SETS.
I ANTICIPATE THREEPIO WILL BE DOING THE BULK OF THE INTELLIGENCE WORK, CRUNCHING DATA AND BEEFING UP ALLIANCE SECURITY, LEAVING US FREE TO CONTINUE THE SEARCH FOR A NEW BASE WORLD.
WHICH BRINGS ME TO...

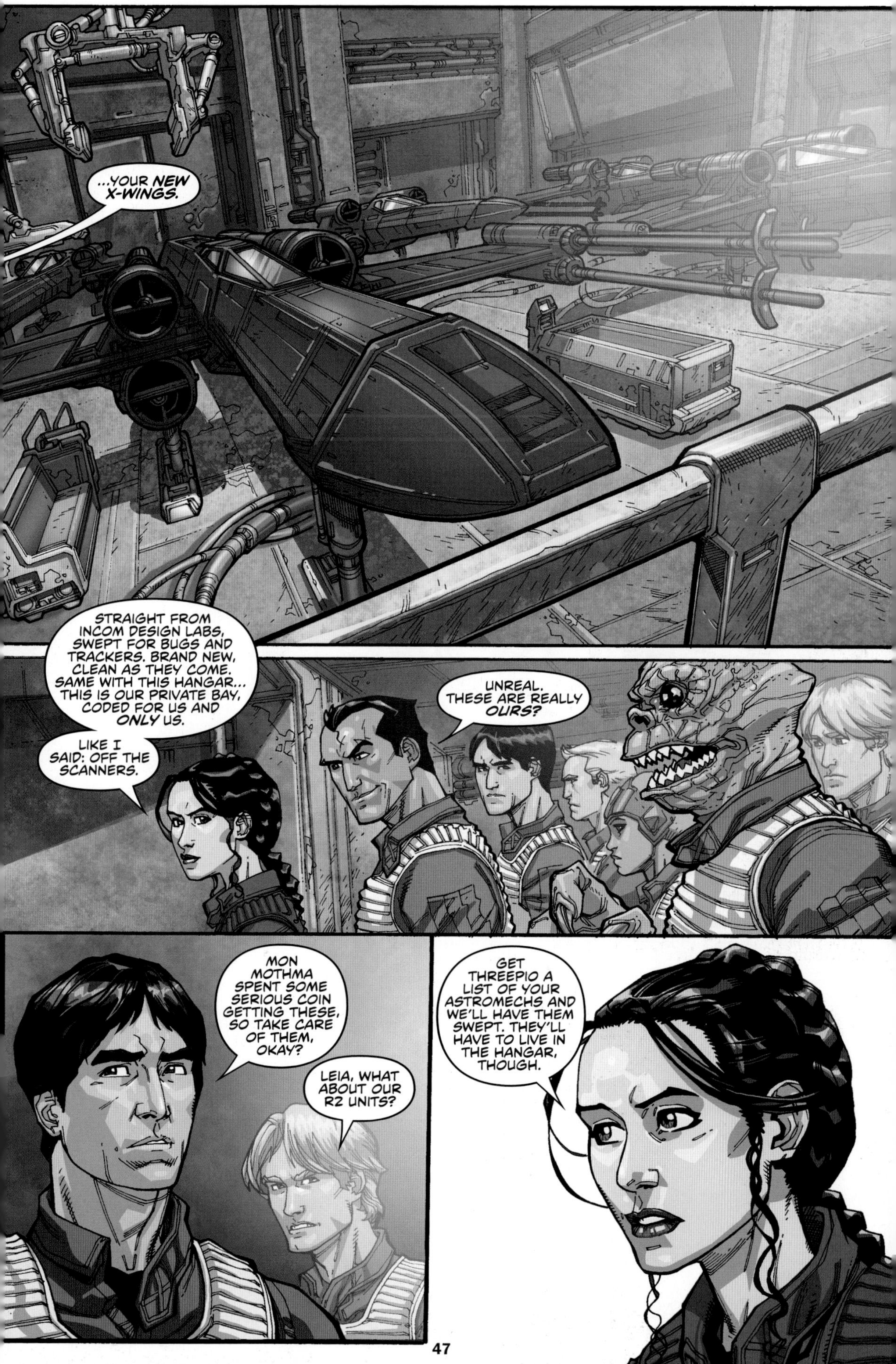
...YOUR *NEW* *X-WINGS.*
STRAIGHT FROM INCOM DESIGN LABS, SWEPT FOR BUGS AND TRACKERS. BRAND NEW, CLEAN AS THEY COME. SAME WITH THIS HANGAR... THIS IS OUR PRIVATE BAY, CODED FOR US AND *ONLY* US.
LIKE I SAID: OFF THE SCANNERS.
UNREAL. THESE ARE REALLY *OURS?*
MON MOTHMA SPENT SOME SERIOUS COIN GETTING THESE, SO TAKE CARE OF THEM, OKAY?
LEIA, WHAT ABOUT OUR R2 UNITS?
GET THREEPIO A LIST OF YOUR ASTROMECHS AND WE'LL HAVE THEM SWEPT. THEY'LL HAVE TO LIVE IN THE HANGAR, THOUGH.

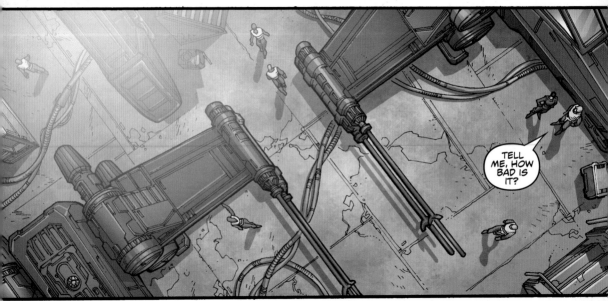

TELL ME, HOW BAD IS IT?

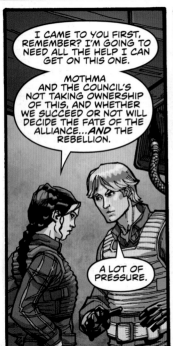

I CAME TO YOU FIRST, REMEMBER? I'M GOING TO NEED ALL THE HELP I CAN GET ON THIS ONE.

MOTHMA AND THE COUNCIL'S NOT TAKING OWNERSHIP OF THIS, AND WHETHER WE SUCCEED OR NOT WILL DECIDE THE FATE OF THE ALLIANCE...*AND* THE REBELLION.

A LOT OF PRESSURE.

I'M USED TO IT.

ARE YOU?

DOES IT MATTER? I HAVE A JOB TO DO, REGARDLESS.

WELL, WEDGE'LL HELP YOU OUT.

I NEED *YOUR* HELP TOO, LUKE. WEDGE AS SECOND IN COMMAND...IT'S NOT A COMPETITION. HE'S GOT SENIORITY.

YOU'RE MY *FRIEND,* LUKE. I *NEED* YOU WITH ME ON THIS.

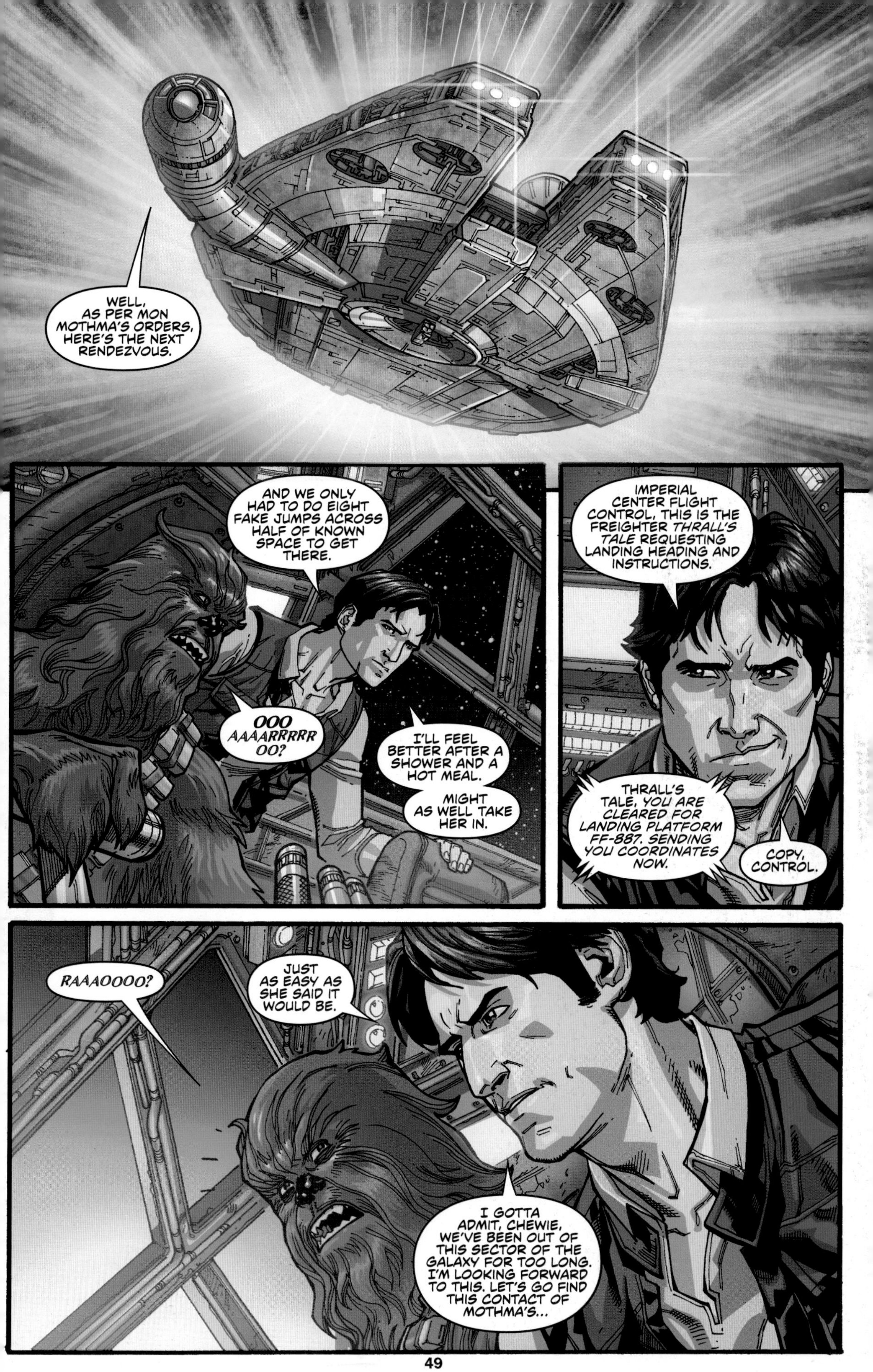
WELL, AS PER MON MOTHMA'S ORDERS, HERE'S THE NEXT RENDEZVOUS.
AND WE ONLY HAD TO DO EIGHT FAKE JUMPS ACROSS HALF OF KNOWN SPACE TO GET THERE.
OOO AAAARRRRR OO?
I'LL FEEL BETTER AFTER A SHOWER AND A HOT MEAL.
MIGHT AS WELL TAKE HER IN.
IMPERIAL CENTER FLIGHT CONTROL, THIS IS THE FREIGHTER *THRALL'S TALE* REQUESTING LANDING HEADING AND INSTRUCTIONS.
THRALL'S TALE, YOU ARE CLEARED FOR LANDING PLATFORM FF-887. SENDING YOU COORDINATES NOW.
COPY, CONTROL.
RAAAOOOO?
JUST AS EASY AS SHE SAID IT WOULD BE.
I GOTTA ADMIT, CHEWIE, WE'VE BEEN OUT OF THIS SECTOR OF THE GALAXY FOR TOO LONG. I'M LOOKING FORWARD TO THIS. LET'S GO FIND THIS CONTACT OF MOTHMA'S...

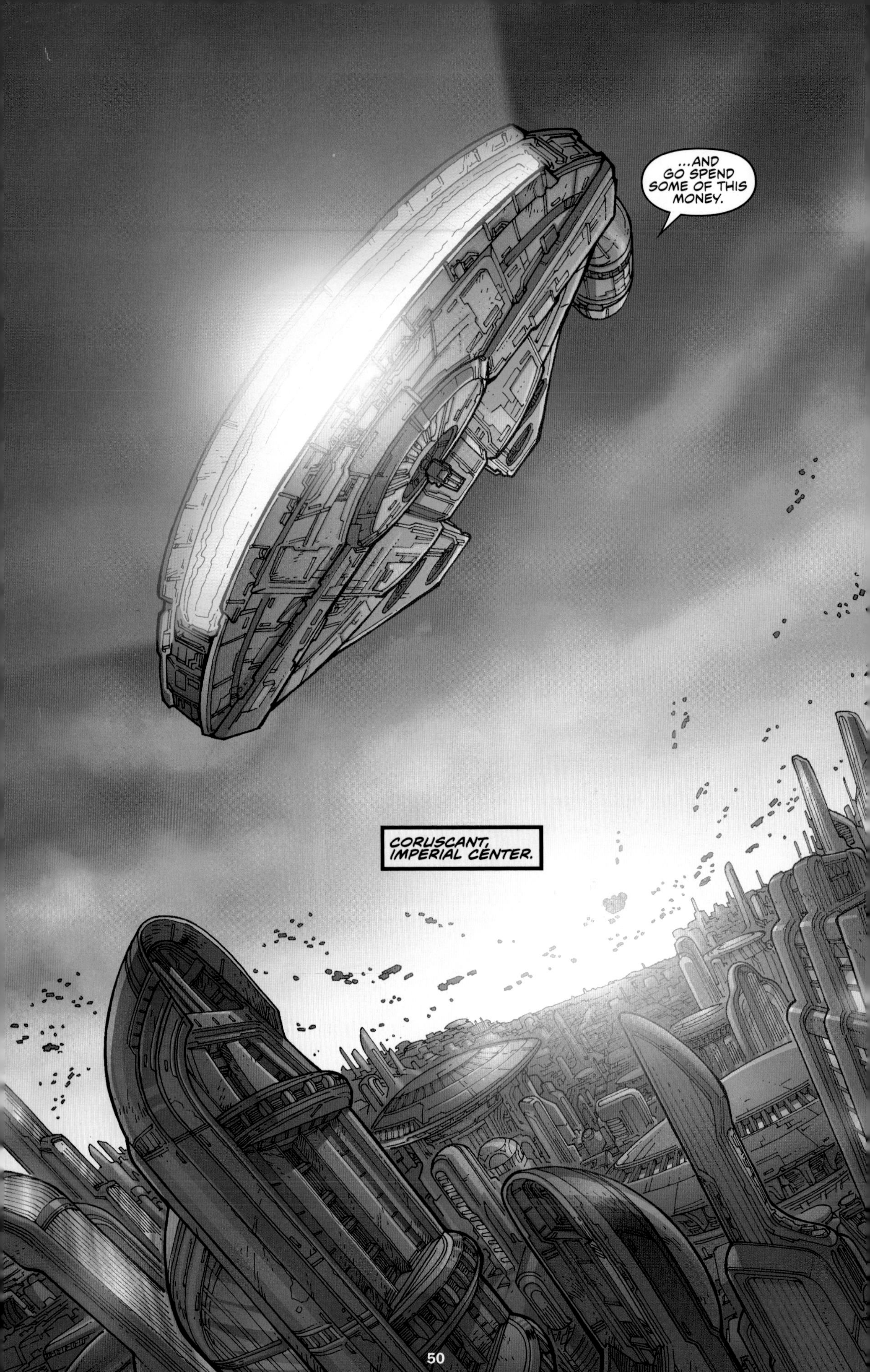
...AND GO SPEND SOME OF THIS MONEY.
CORUSCANT, IMPERIAL CENTER.

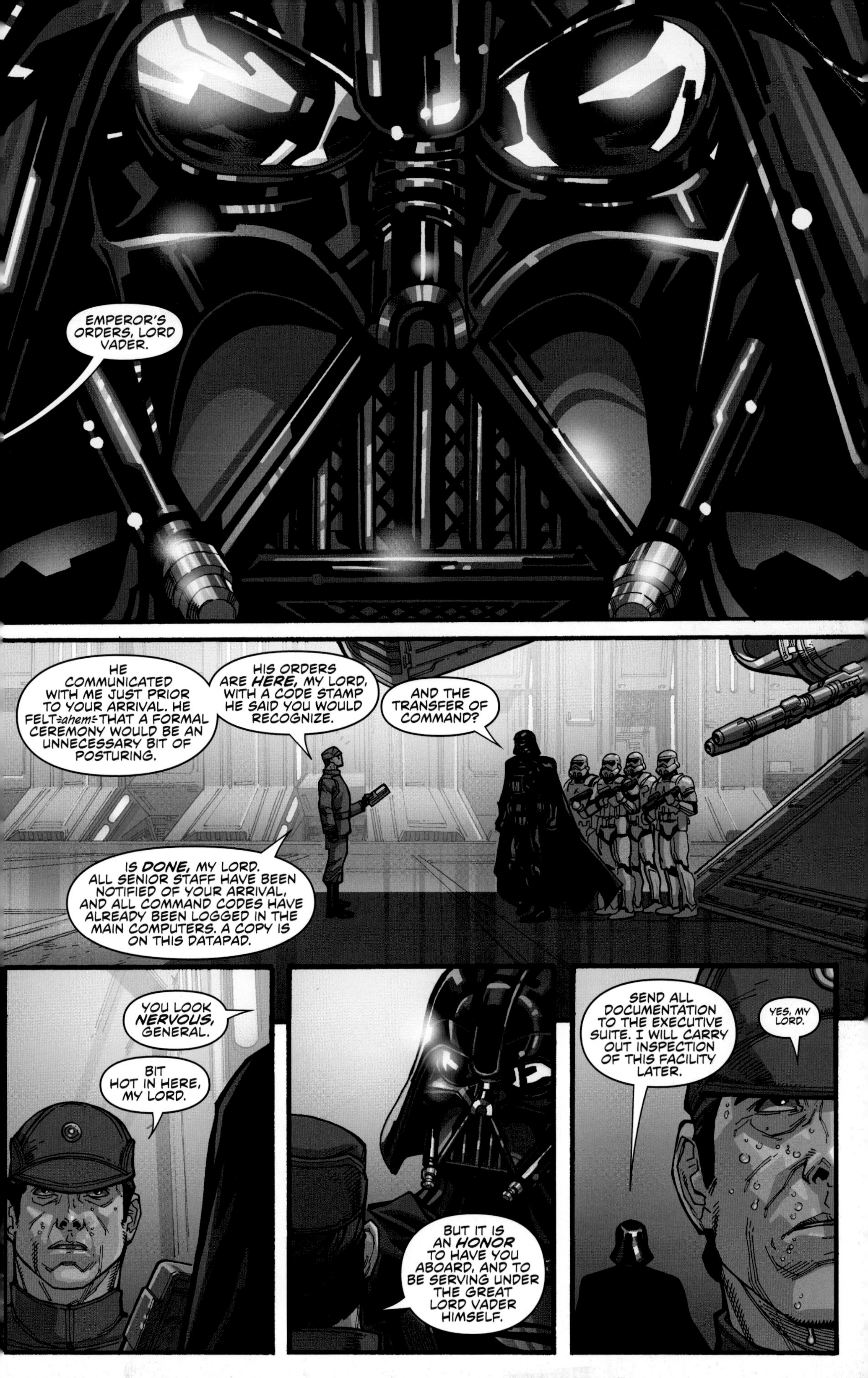
EMPEROR'S ORDERS, LORD VADER.
HE COMMUNICATED WITH ME JUST PRIOR TO YOUR ARRIVAL. HE FELT--ahem--THAT A FORMAL CEREMONY WOULD BE AN UNNECESSARY BIT OF POSTURING.
HIS ORDERS ARE HERE, MY LORD, WITH A CODE STAMP HE SAID YOU WOULD RECOGNIZE.
AND THE TRANSFER OF COMMAND?
IS DONE, MY LORD. ALL SENIOR STAFF HAVE BEEN NOTIFIED OF YOUR ARRIVAL, AND ALL COMMAND CODES HAVE ALREADY BEEN LOGGED IN THE MAIN COMPUTERS. A COPY IS ON THIS DATAPAD.
YOU LOOK NERVOUS, GENERAL.
BIT HOT IN HERE, MY LORD.
BUT IT IS AN HONOR TO HAVE YOU ABOARD, AND TO BE SERVING UNDER THE GREAT LORD VADER HIMSELF.
SEND ALL DOCUMENTATION TO THE EXECUTIVE SUITE. I WILL CARRY OUT INSPECTION OF THIS FACILITY LATER.
YES, MY LORD.

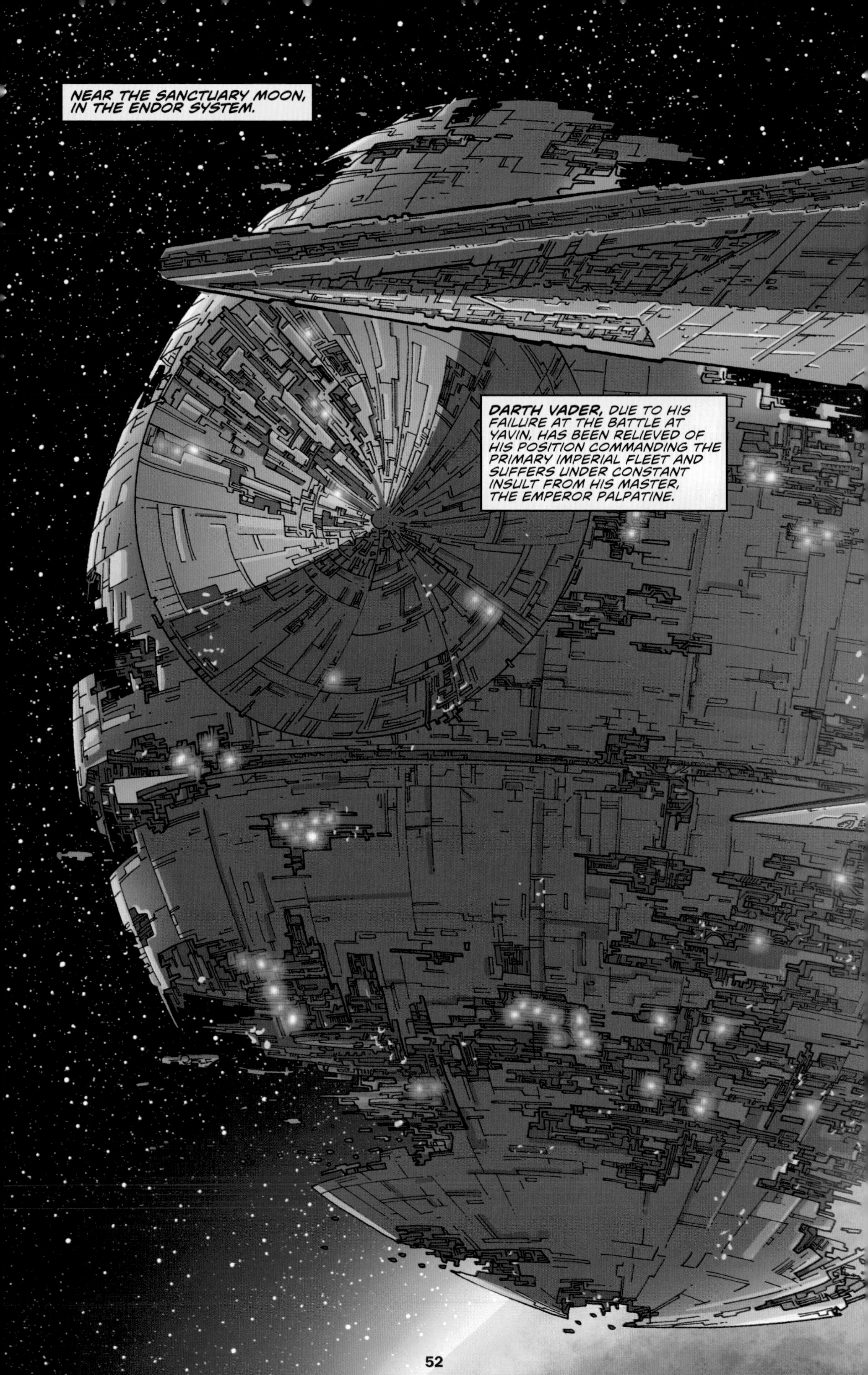
NEAR THE SANCTUARY MOON, IN THE ENDOR SYSTEM.
DARTH VADER, DUE TO HIS FAILURE AT THE BATTLE AT YAVIN, HAS BEEN RELIEVED OF HIS POSITION COMMANDING THE PRIMARY IMPERIAL FLEET AND SUFFERS UNDER CONSTANT INSULT FROM HIS MASTER, THE EMPEROR PALPATINE.

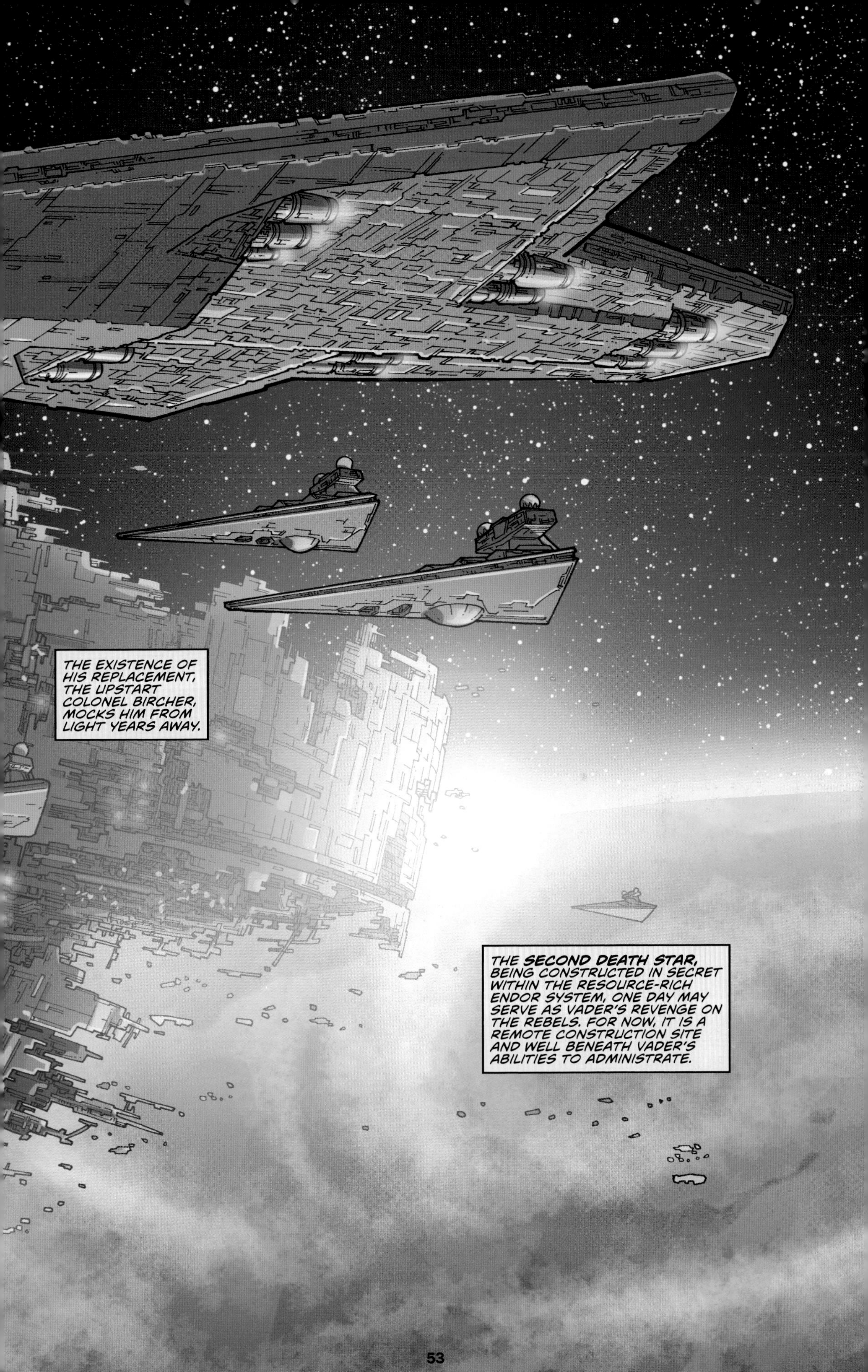
THE EXISTENCE OF HIS REPLACEMENT, THE UPSTART COLONEL BIRCHER, MOCKS HIM FROM LIGHT YEARS AWAY.
THE SECOND DEATH STAR, BEING CONSTRUCTED IN SECRET WITHIN THE RESOURCE-RICH ENDOR SYSTEM, ONE DAY MAY SERVE AS VADER'S REVENGE ON THE REBELS. FOR NOW, IT IS A REMOTE CONSTRUCTION SITE AND WELL BENEATH VADER'S ABILITIES TO ADMINISTRATE.

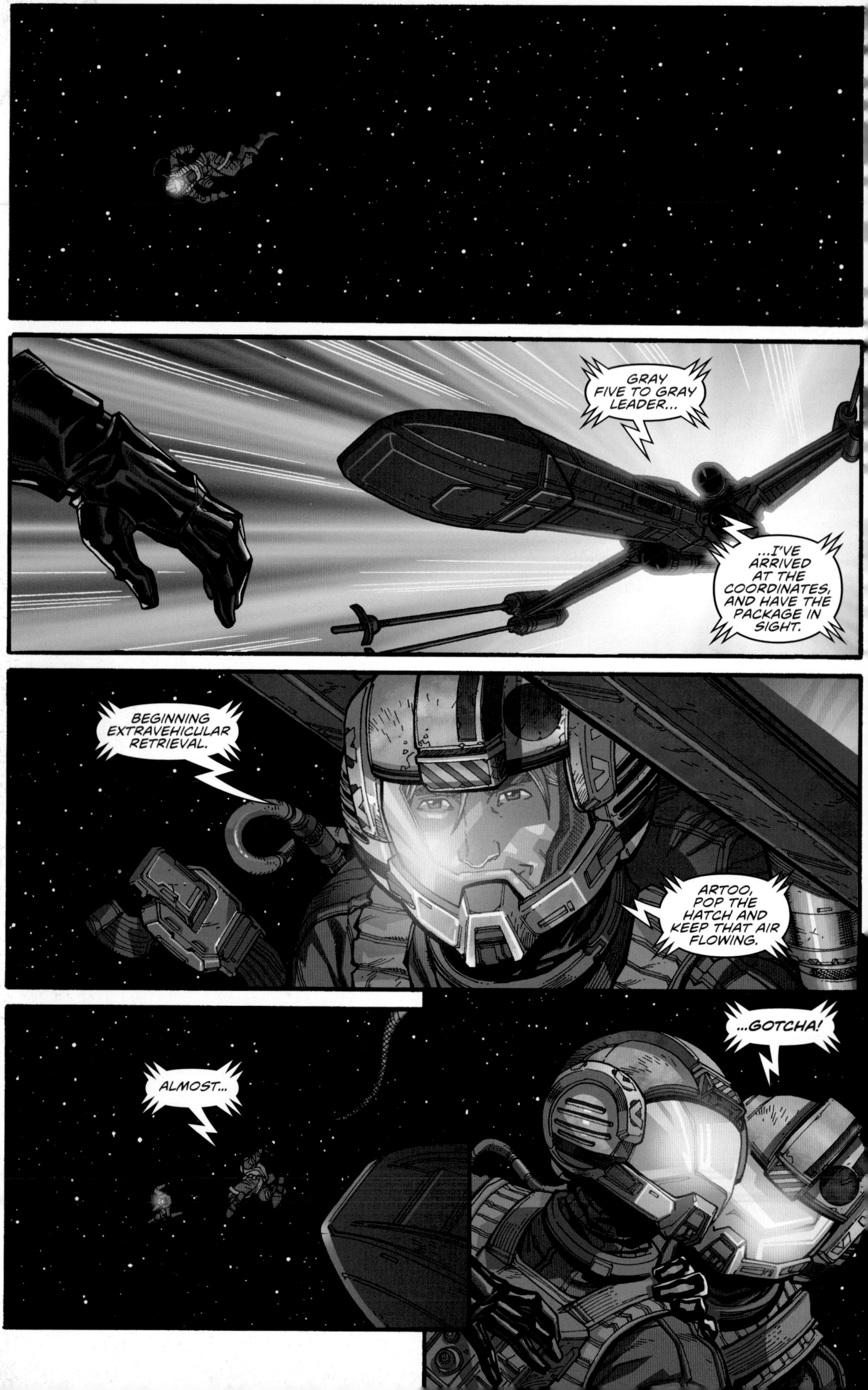
GRAY FIVE TO GRAY LEADER...
...I'VE ARRIVED AT THE COORDINATES, AND HAVE THE PACKAGE IN SIGHT.
BEGINNING EXTRAVEHICULAR RETRIEVAL.
ARTOO, POP THE HATCH AND KEEP THAT AIR FLOWING.
ALMOST...
...GOTCHA!

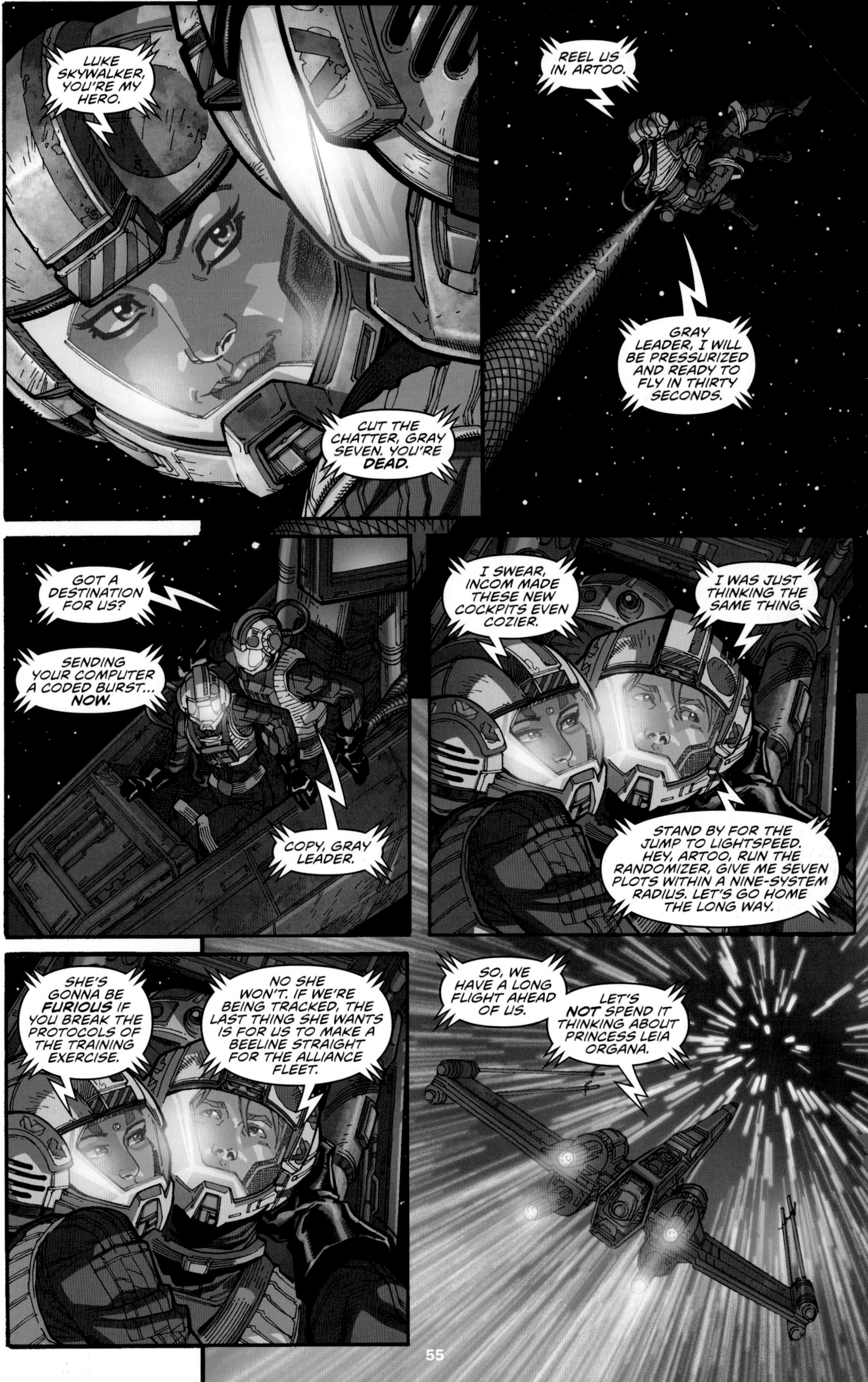

LUKE SKYWALKER, YOU'RE MY HERO.
CUT THE CHATTER, GRAY SEVEN. YOU'RE **DEAD.**
REEL US IN, ARTOO.
GRAY LEADER, I WILL BE PRESSURIZED AND READY TO FLY IN THIRTY SECONDS.
GOT A DESTINATION FOR US?
SENDING YOUR COMPUTER A CODED BURST... **NOW.**
COPY, GRAY LEADER.
I SWEAR, INCOM MADE THESE NEW COCKPITS EVEN COZIER.
I WAS JUST THINKING THE SAME THING.
STAND BY FOR THE JUMP TO LIGHTSPEED. HEY, ARTOO, RUN THE RANDOMIZER, GIVE ME SEVEN PLOTS WITHIN A NINE-SYSTEM RADIUS. LET'S GO HOME THE LONG WAY.
SHE'S GONNA BE **FURIOUS** IF YOU BREAK THE PROTOCOLS OF THE TRAINING EXERCISE.
NO SHE WON'T. IF WE'RE BEING TRACKED, THE LAST THING SHE WANTS IS FOR US TO MAKE A BEELINE STRAIGHT FOR THE ALLIANCE FLEET.
SO, WE HAVE A LONG FLIGHT AHEAD OF US.
LET'S **NOT** SPEND IT THINKING ABOUT PRINCESS LEIA ORGANA.

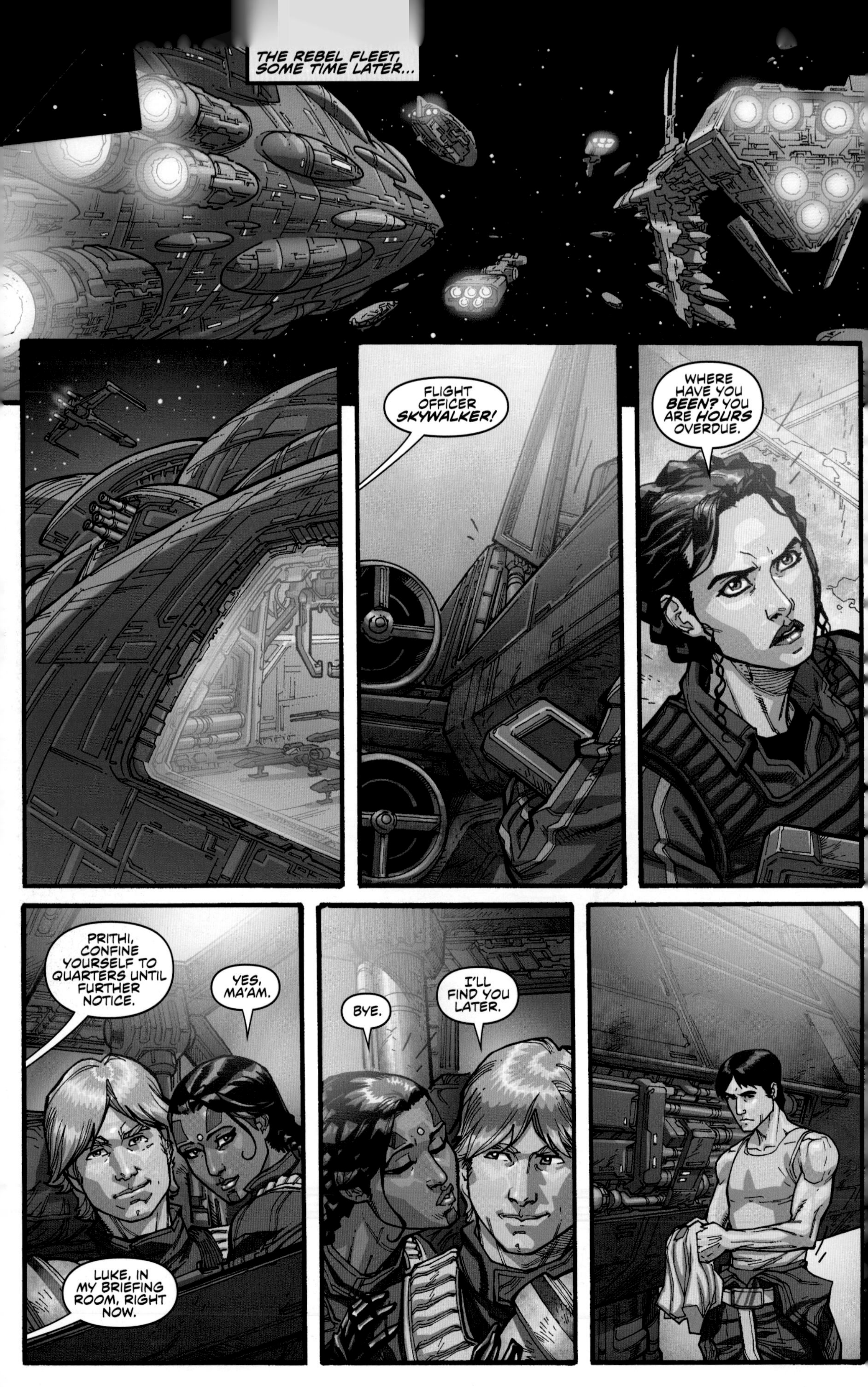
THE REBEL FLEET, SOME TIME LATER...
FLIGHT OFFICER SKYWALKER!
WHERE HAVE YOU BEEN? YOU ARE HOURS OVERDUE.
PRITHI, CONFINE YOURSELF TO QUARTERS UNTIL FURTHER NOTICE.
YES, MA'AM.
LUKE, IN MY BRIEFING ROOM, RIGHT NOW.
BYE.
I'LL FIND YOU LATER.

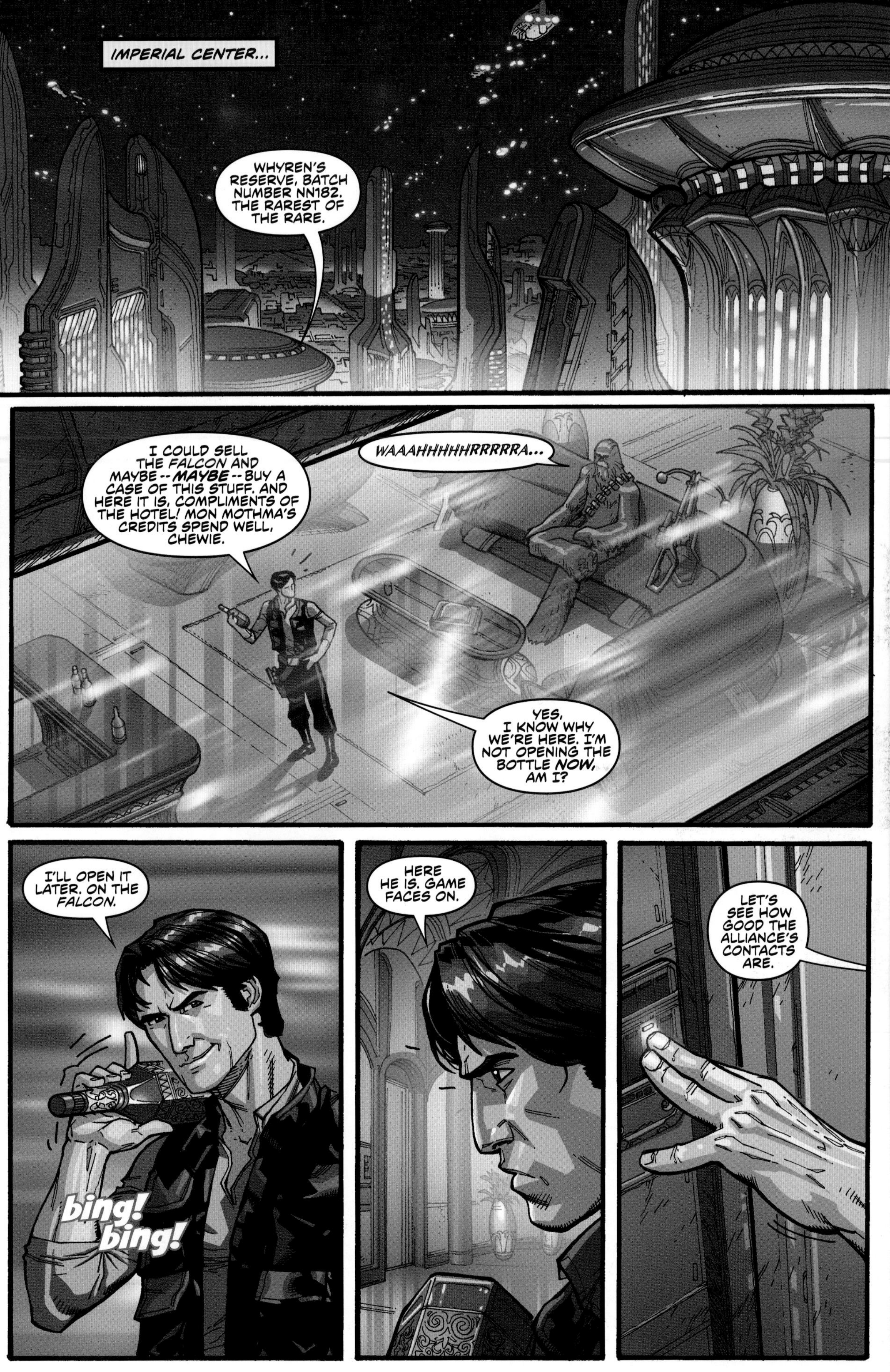
IMPERIAL CENTER...
WHYREN'S RESERVE, BATCH NUMBER NN182. THE RAREST OF THE RARE.
I COULD SELL THE FALCON AND MAYBE -- MAYBE -- BUY A CASE OF THIS STUFF. AND HERE IT IS, COMPLIMENTS OF THE HOTEL! MON MOTHMA'S CREDITS SPEND WELL, CHEWIE.
WAAAHHHHHRRRRRA...
YES, I KNOW WHY WE'RE HERE. I'M NOT OPENING THE BOTTLE NOW, AM I?
I'LL OPEN IT LATER. ON THE FALCON.
bing! bing!
HERE HE IS. GAME FACES ON.
LET'S SEE HOW GOOD THE ALLIANCE'S CONTACTS ARE.

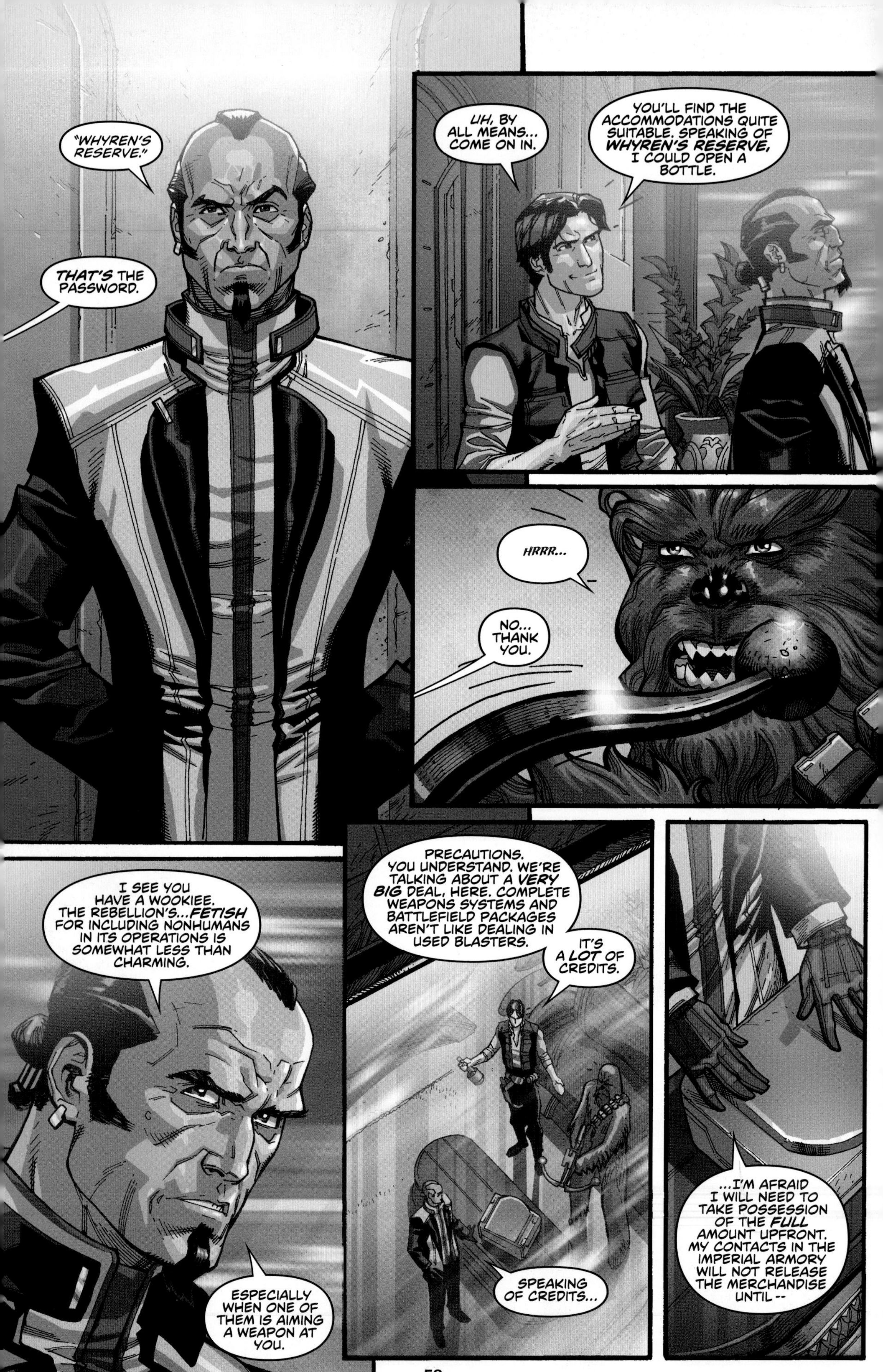
"WHYREN'S RESERVE."
THAT'S THE PASSWORD.
UH, BY ALL MEANS... COME ON IN.
YOU'LL FIND THE ACCOMMODATIONS QUITE SUITABLE. SPEAKING OF WHYREN'S RESERVE, I COULD OPEN A BOTTLE.
HRRR...
NO... THANK YOU.
I SEE YOU HAVE A WOOKIEE. THE REBELLION'S...FETISH FOR INCLUDING NONHUMANS IN ITS OPERATIONS IS SOMEWHAT LESS THAN CHARMING.
ESPECIALLY WHEN ONE OF THEM IS AIMING A WEAPON AT YOU.
PRECAUTIONS. YOU UNDERSTAND. WE'RE TALKING ABOUT A VERY BIG DEAL, HERE. COMPLETE WEAPONS SYSTEMS AND BATTLEFIELD PACKAGES AREN'T LIKE DEALING IN USED BLASTERS.
IT'S A LOT OF CREDITS.
SPEAKING OF CREDITS...
...I'M AFRAID I WILL NEED TO TAKE POSSESSION OF THE FULL AMOUNT UPFRONT. MY CONTACTS IN THE IMPERIAL ARMORY WILL NOT RELEASE THE MERCHANDISE UNTIL --

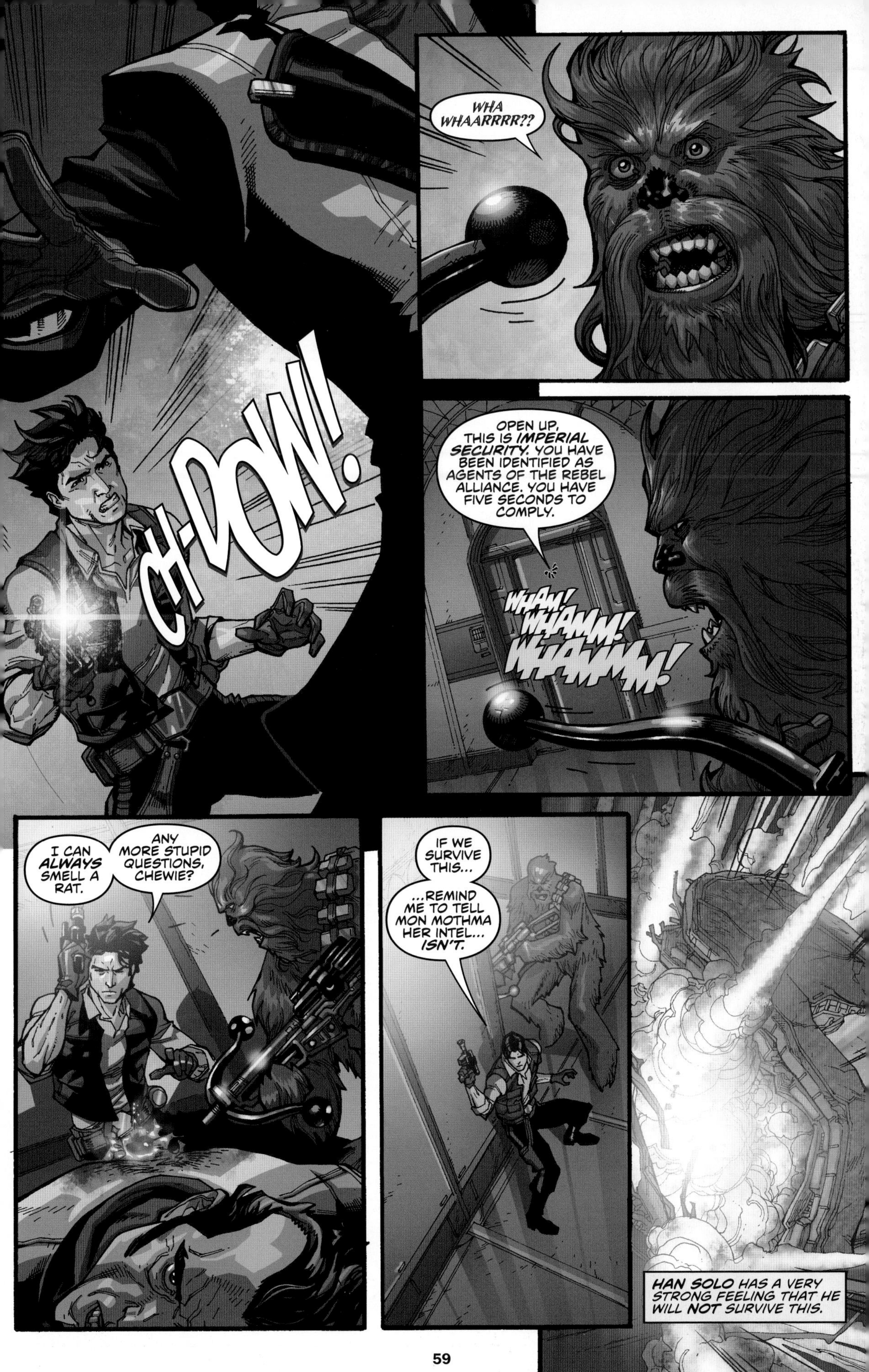
WHA WHAARRRR??
CH-DOW!
OPEN UP, THIS IS IMPERIAL SECURITY. YOU HAVE BEEN IDENTIFIED AS AGENTS OF THE REBEL ALLIANCE. YOU HAVE FIVE SECONDS TO COMPLY.
WHAM! WHAMM! WHAMMM!
I CAN ALWAYS SMELL A RAT.
ANY MORE STUPID QUESTIONS, CHEWIE?
IF WE SURVIVE THIS...
...REMIND ME TO TELL MON MOTHMA HER INTEL... ISN'T.
HAN SOLO HAS A VERY STRONG FEELING THAT HE WILL NOT SURVIVE THIS.

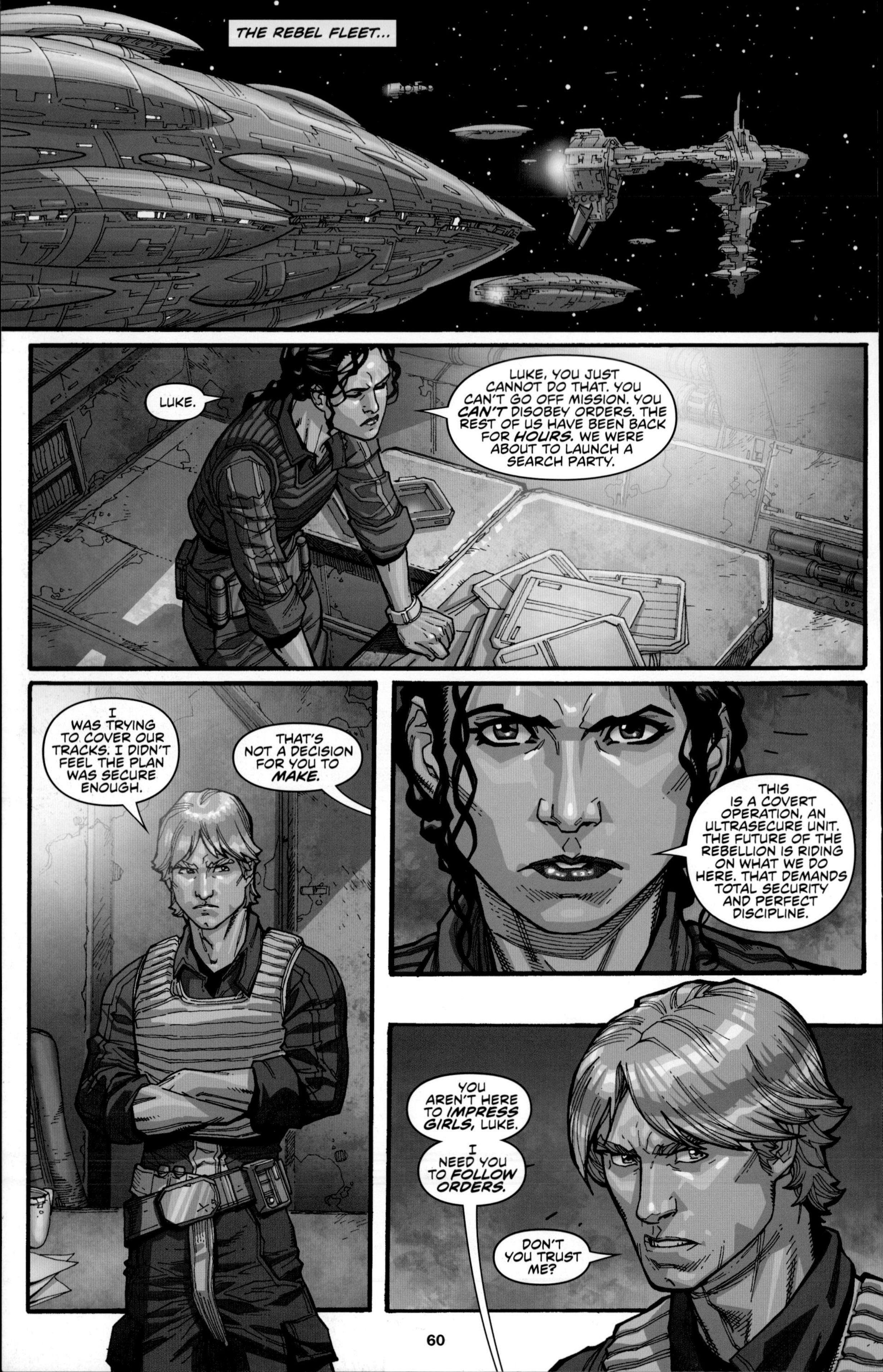
THE REBEL FLEET...
LUKE.
LUKE, YOU JUST CANNOT DO THAT. YOU CAN'T GO OFF MISSION. YOU CAN'T DISOBEY ORDERS. THE REST OF US HAVE BEEN BACK FOR HOURS. WE WERE ABOUT TO LAUNCH A SEARCH PARTY.
I WAS TRYING TO COVER OUR TRACKS. I DIDN'T FEEL THE PLAN WAS SECURE ENOUGH.
THAT'S NOT A DECISION FOR YOU TO MAKE.
THIS IS A COVERT OPERATION, AN ULTRASECURE UNIT. THE FUTURE OF THE REBELLION IS RIDING ON WHAT WE DO HERE. THAT DEMANDS TOTAL SECURITY AND PERFECT DISCIPLINE.
YOU AREN'T HERE TO IMPRESS GIRLS, LUKE.
I NEED YOU TO FOLLOW ORDERS.
DON'T YOU TRUST ME?

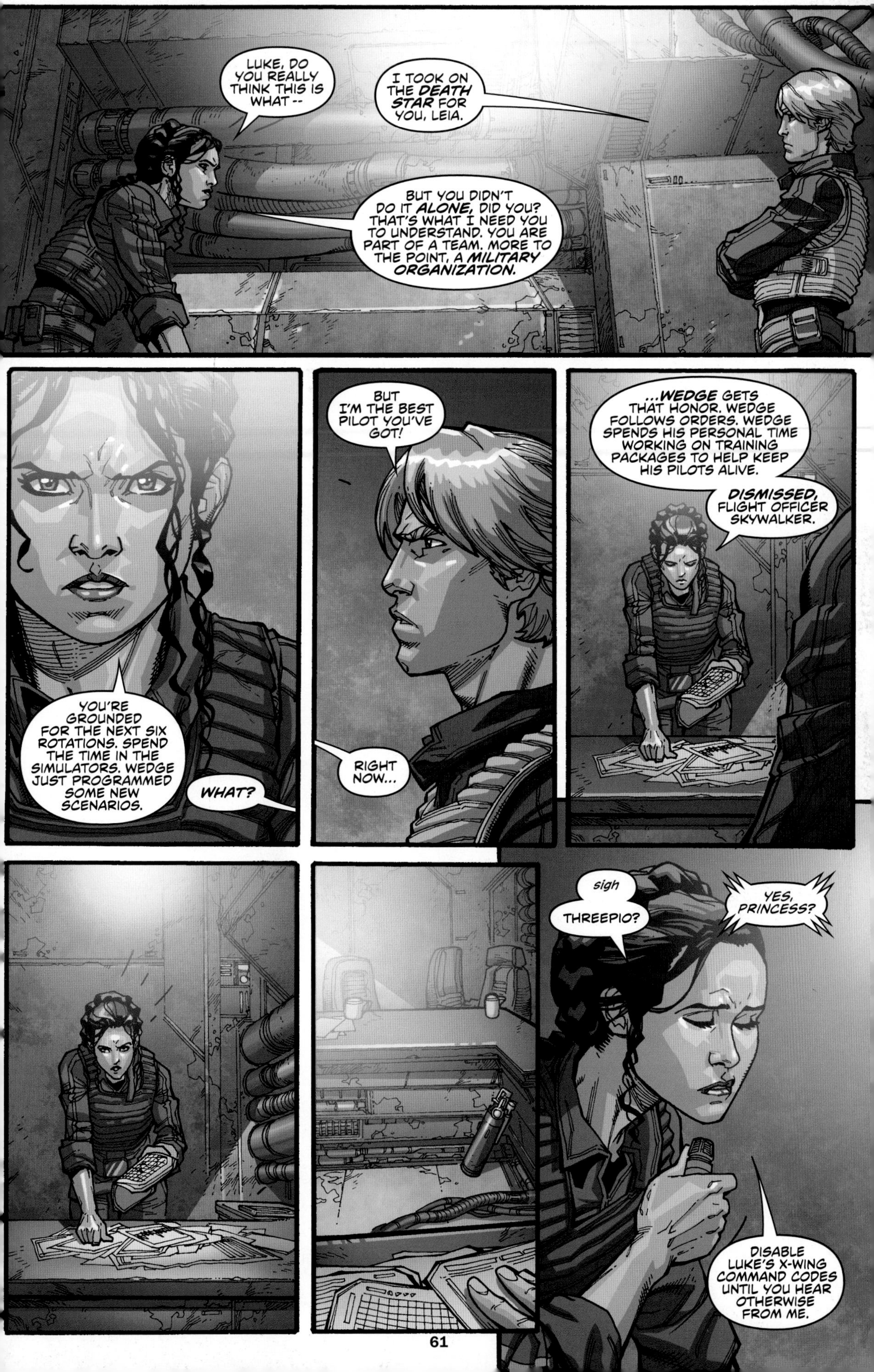

LUKE, DO YOU REALLY THINK THIS IS WHAT --
I TOOK ON THE DEATH STAR FOR YOU, LEIA.
BUT YOU DIDN'T DO IT ALONE, DID YOU? THAT'S WHAT I NEED YOU TO UNDERSTAND. YOU ARE PART OF A TEAM. MORE TO THE POINT, A MILITARY ORGANIZATION.
YOU'RE GROUNDED FOR THE NEXT SIX ROTATIONS. SPEND THE TIME IN THE SIMULATORS. WEDGE JUST PROGRAMMED SOME NEW SCENARIOS.
WHAT?
BUT I'M THE BEST PILOT YOU'VE GOT!
RIGHT NOW...
...WEDGE GETS THAT HONOR. WEDGE FOLLOWS ORDERS. WEDGE SPENDS HIS PERSONAL TIME WORKING ON TRAINING PACKAGES TO HELP KEEP HIS PILOTS ALIVE.
DISMISSED, FLIGHT OFFICER SKYWALKER.
sigh
THREEPIO?
YES, PRINCESS?
DISABLE LUKE'S X-WING COMMAND CODES UNTIL YOU HEAR OTHERWISE FROM ME.

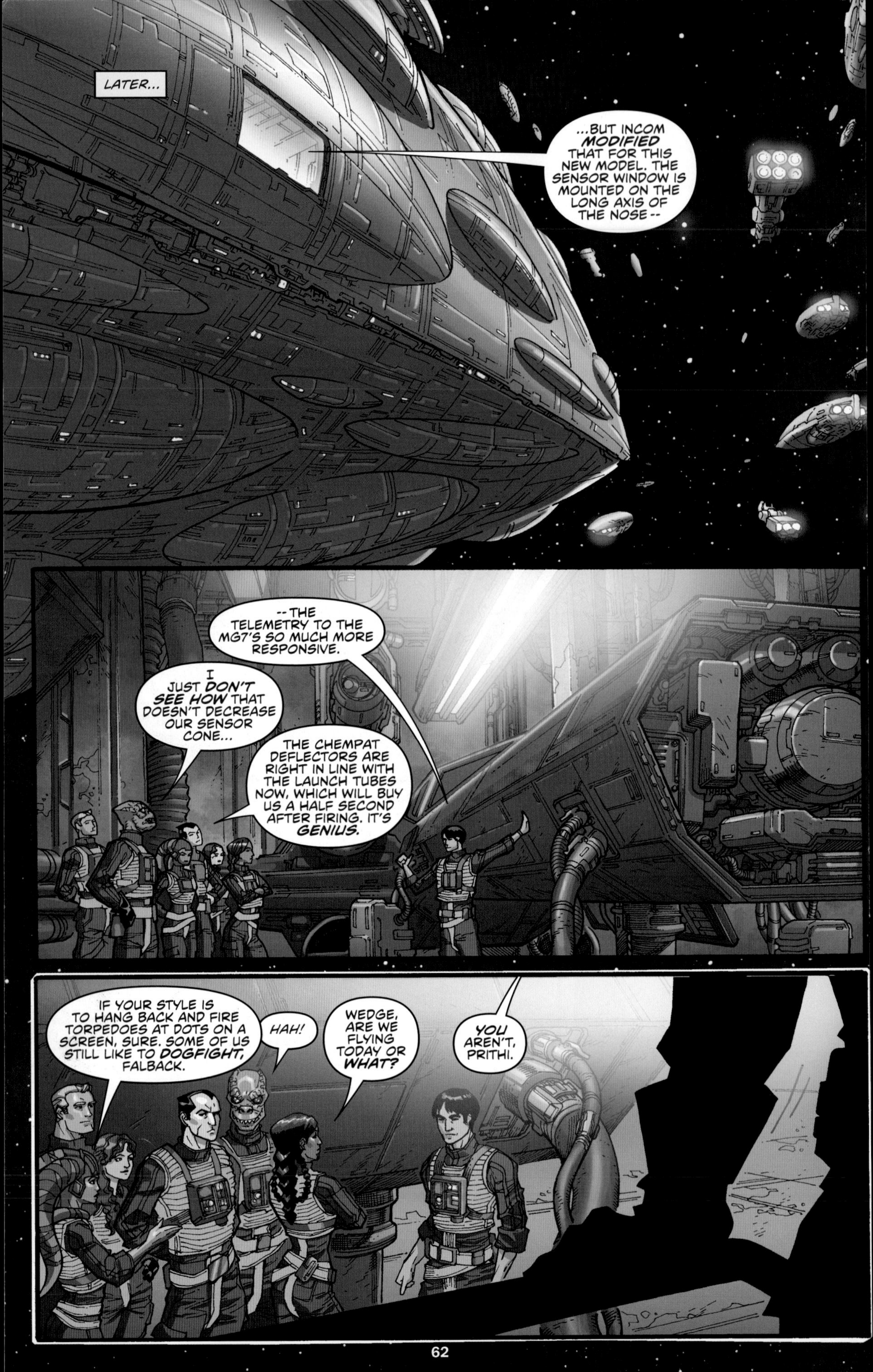
LATER...
...BUT INCOM MODIFIED THAT FOR THIS NEW MODEL. THE SENSOR WINDOW IS MOUNTED ON THE LONG AXIS OF THE NOSE --
-- THE TELEMETRY TO THE MG7'S SO MUCH MORE RESPONSIVE.
I JUST DON'T SEE HOW THAT DOESN'T DECREASE OUR SENSOR CONE...
THE CHEMPAT DEFLECTORS ARE RIGHT IN LINE WITH THE LAUNCH TUBES NOW, WHICH WILL BUY US A HALF SECOND AFTER FIRING. IT'S GENIUS.
IF YOUR STYLE IS TO HANG BACK AND FIRE TORPEDOES AT DOTS ON A SCREEN, SURE. SOME OF US STILL LIKE TO DOGFIGHT, FALBACK.
HAH!
WEDGE, ARE WE FLYING TODAY OR WHAT?
YOU AREN'T, PRITHI.

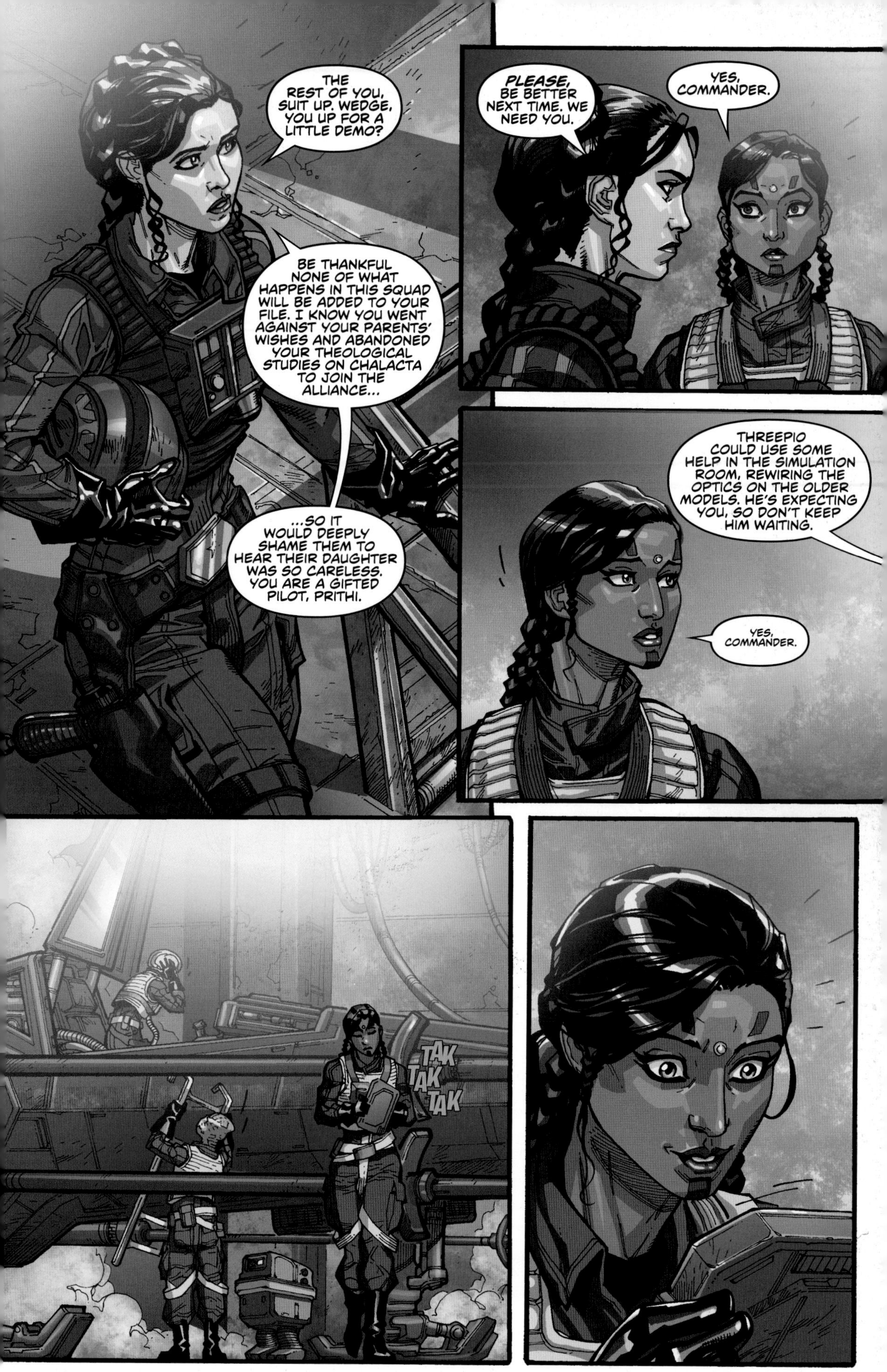
THE REST OF YOU, SUIT UP. WEDGE, YOU UP FOR A LITTLE DEMO?
BE THANKFUL NONE OF WHAT HAPPENS IN THIS SQUAD WILL BE ADDED TO YOUR FILE. I KNOW YOU WENT AGAINST YOUR PARENTS' WISHES AND ABANDONED YOUR THEOLOGICAL STUDIES ON CHALACTA TO JOIN THE ALLIANCE...
...SO IT WOULD DEEPLY SHAME THEM TO HEAR THEIR DAUGHTER WAS SO CARELESS. YOU ARE A GIFTED PILOT, PRITHI.
PLEASE, BE BETTER NEXT TIME. WE NEED YOU.
YES, COMMANDER.
THREEPIO COULD USE SOME HELP IN THE SIMULATION ROOM, REWIRING THE OPTICS ON THE OLDER MODELS. HE'S EXPECTING YOU, SO DON'T KEEP HIM WAITING.
YES, COMMANDER.
TAK TAK TAK

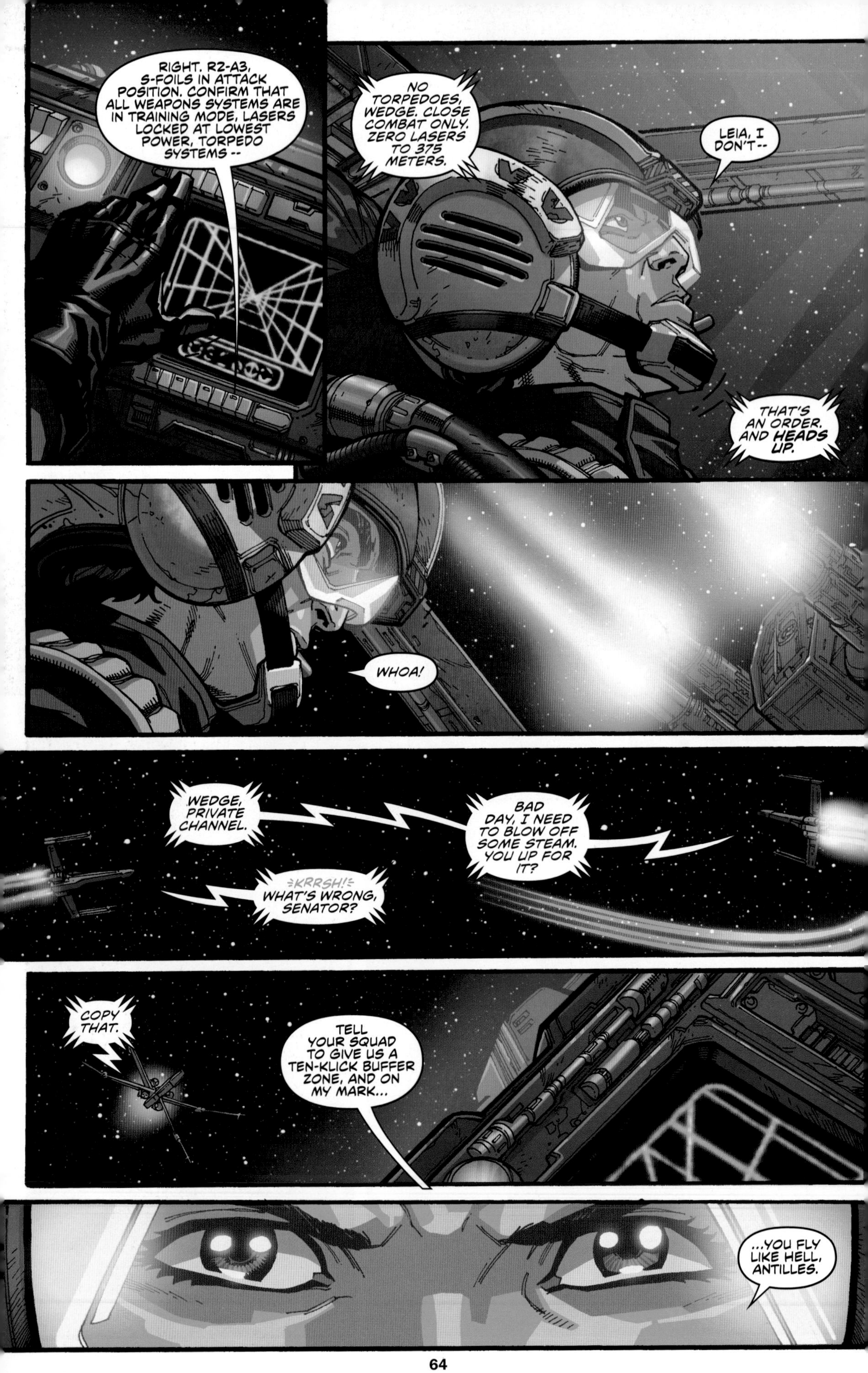
RIGHT. R2-A3, S-FOILS IN ATTACK POSITION. CONFIRM THAT ALL WEAPONS SYSTEMS ARE IN TRAINING MODE, LASERS LOCKED AT LOWEST POWER, TORPEDO SYSTEMS --
NO TORPEDOES, WEDGE. CLOSE COMBAT ONLY. ZERO LASERS TO 375 METERS.
LEIA, I DON'T --
THAT'S AN ORDER. AND **HEADS UP.**
WHOA!
WEDGE, PRIVATE CHANNEL.
KRRSH! WHAT'S WRONG, SENATOR?
BAD DAY, I NEED TO BLOW OFF SOME STEAM. YOU UP FOR IT?
COPY THAT.
TELL YOUR SQUAD TO GIVE US A TEN-KLICK BUFFER ZONE, AND ON MY MARK...
...YOU FLY LIKE HELL, ANTILLES.

"I TOOK ON THE **DEATH STAR** FOR YOU, LEIA." LUKE'S WORDS HANG IN HER THOUGHTS, THE PETULANCE OF A FARM BOY ADDRESSING A YOUNG WOMAN WHO SPENT DAYS UNDER THE BRUTAL ADMINISTRATIONS OF AN IMPERIAL INTERROGATION DROID...

...GRAND MOFF TARKIN'S BARELY CONTAINED GLEE AS HE ORDERED THE DESTRUCTION OF HER HOMEWORLD...

...AND VADER'S HANDS GRIPPING HER FOREARMS SO HARD AS HE FORCED HER TO WATCH THAT SHE WAS BRUISED FOR WEEKS.

PRINCESS LEIA ORGANA, SENATOR FROM ALDERAAN, NOTED DIPLOMAT, AND KEY PLAYER IN THE ALLIANCE TO RESTORE THE REPUBLIC, HAS LITTLE PATIENCE FOR THOSE WHO CONDESCEND TO HER.

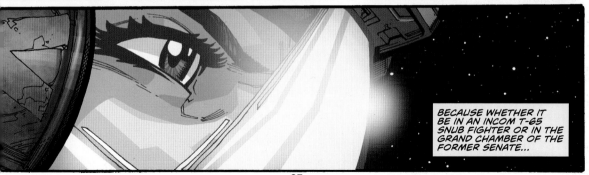

BECAUSE WHETHER IT BE IN AN INCOM T-65 SNUB FIGHTER OR IN THE GRAND CHAMBER OF THE FORMER SENATE...

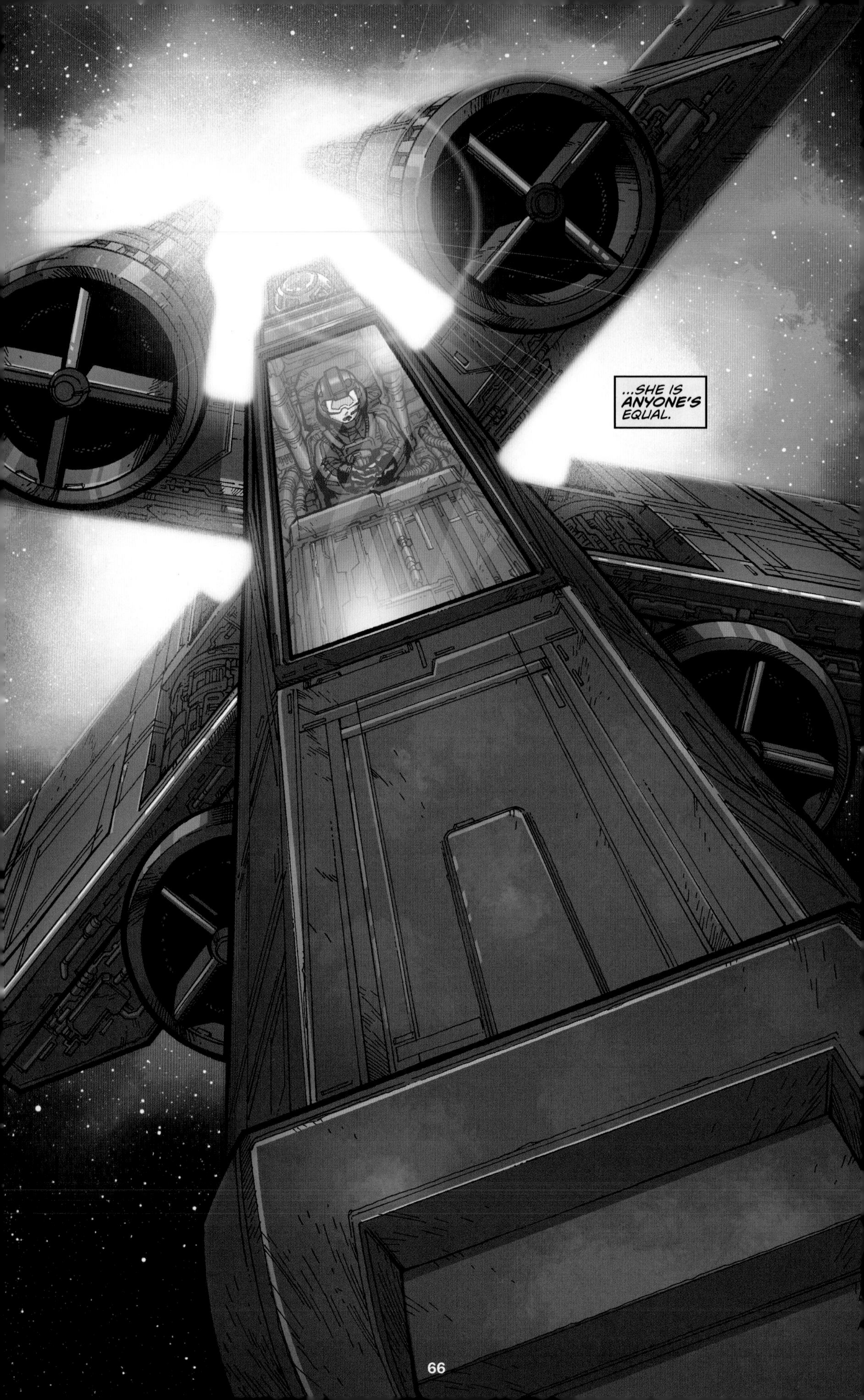
...SHE IS ANYONE'S EQUAL.

IMPERIAL CENTER.

CHOOOM!

WAHHHHOOOOOOOOOARROOOU?

HOW AM *I* SUPPOSED TO KNOW?

HE WAS *MON MOTHMA'S* CONTACT!

CHOOM! CHOOM!

BDOW! BDOW!

DOW!

DOW! DOW!

C'MON CHEWIE, THERE'S TOO MANY OF THEM!

I'M NOT DYING HERE!

67

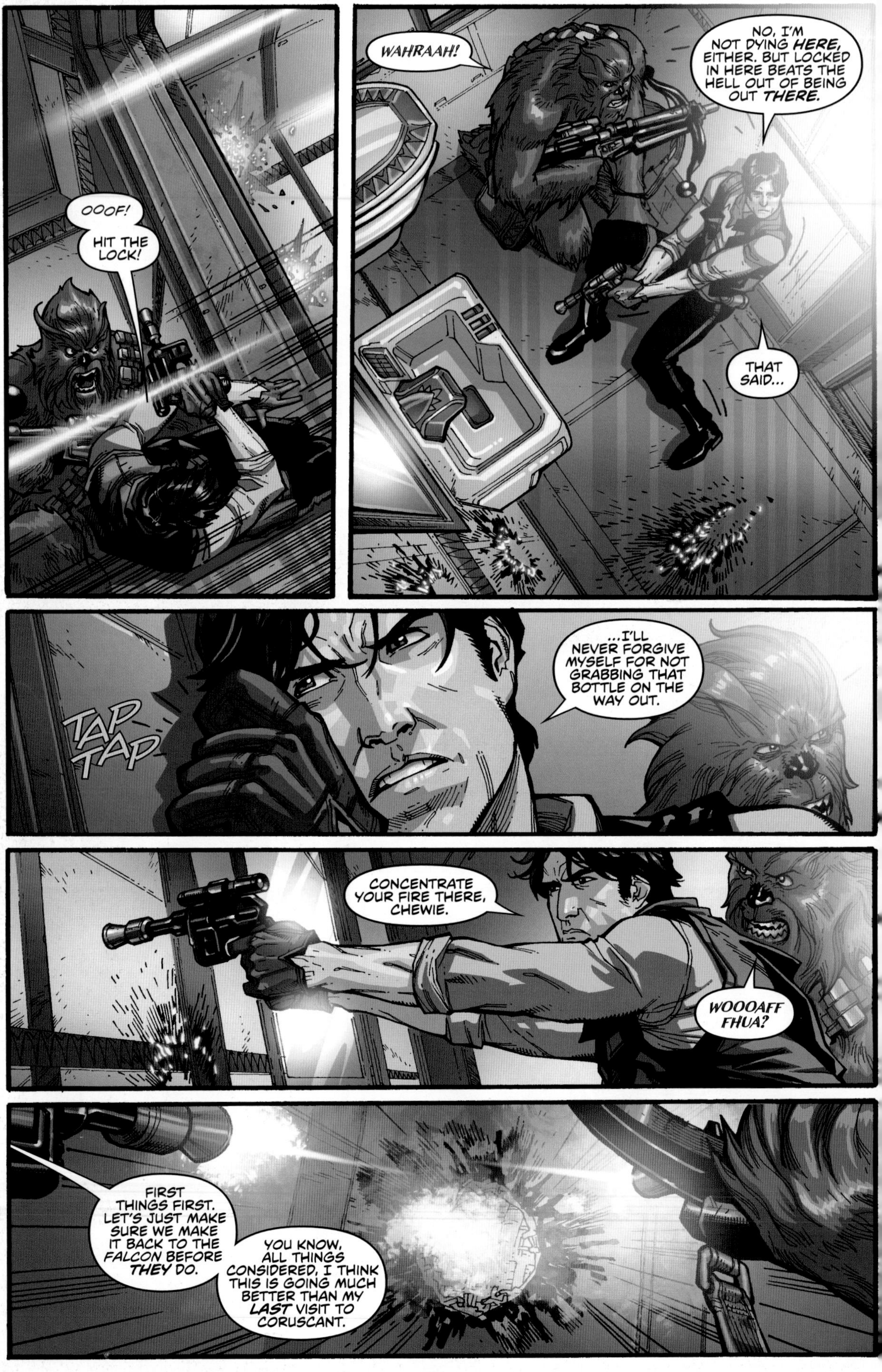
OOOF!
HIT THE LOCK!
WAHRAAH!
NO, I'M NOT DYING HERE, EITHER. BUT LOCKED IN HERE BEATS THE HELL OUT OF BEING OUT THERE.
THAT SAID...
TAP TAP
...I'LL NEVER FORGIVE MYSELF FOR NOT GRABBING THAT BOTTLE ON THE WAY OUT.
CONCENTRATE YOUR FIRE THERE, CHEWIE.
WOOOAFF FHUA?
FIRST THINGS FIRST. LET'S JUST MAKE SURE WE MAKE IT BACK TO THE FALCON BEFORE THEY DO.
YOU KNOW, ALL THINGS CONSIDERED, I THINK THIS IS GOING MUCH BETTER THAN MY LAST VISIT TO CORUSCANT.

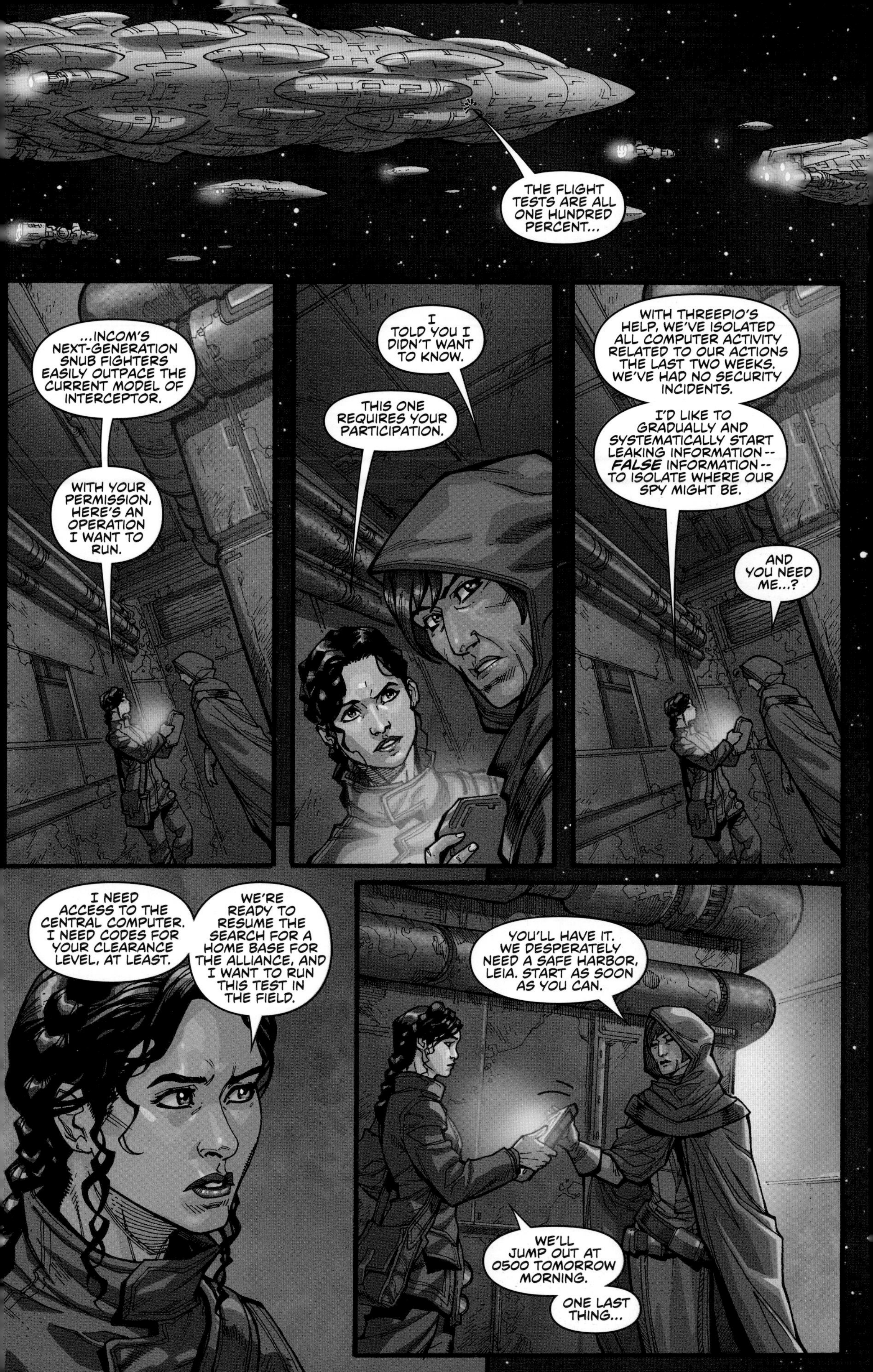

THE FLIGHT TESTS ARE ALL ONE HUNDRED PERCENT...
...INCOM'S NEXT-GENERATION SNUB FIGHTERS EASILY OUTPACE THE CURRENT MODEL OF INTERCEPTOR.
WITH YOUR PERMISSION, HERE'S AN OPERATION I WANT TO RUN.
I TOLD YOU I DIDN'T WANT TO KNOW.
THIS ONE REQUIRES YOUR PARTICIPATION.
WITH THREEPIO'S HELP, WE'VE ISOLATED ALL COMPUTER ACTIVITY RELATED TO OUR ACTIONS THE LAST TWO WEEKS. WE'VE HAD NO SECURITY INCIDENTS.
I'D LIKE TO GRADUALLY AND SYSTEMATICALLY START LEAKING INFORMATION-- *FALSE* INFORMATION-- TO ISOLATE WHERE OUR SPY MIGHT BE.
AND YOU NEED ME...?
I NEED ACCESS TO THE CENTRAL COMPUTER. I NEED CODES FOR YOUR CLEARANCE LEVEL, AT LEAST.
WE'RE READY TO RESUME THE SEARCH FOR A HOME BASE FOR THE ALLIANCE, AND I WANT TO RUN THIS TEST IN THE FIELD.
YOU'LL HAVE IT. WE DESPERATELY NEED A SAFE HARBOR, LEIA. START AS SOON AS YOU CAN.
WE'LL JUMP OUT AT 0500 TOMORROW MORNING.
ONE LAST THING...

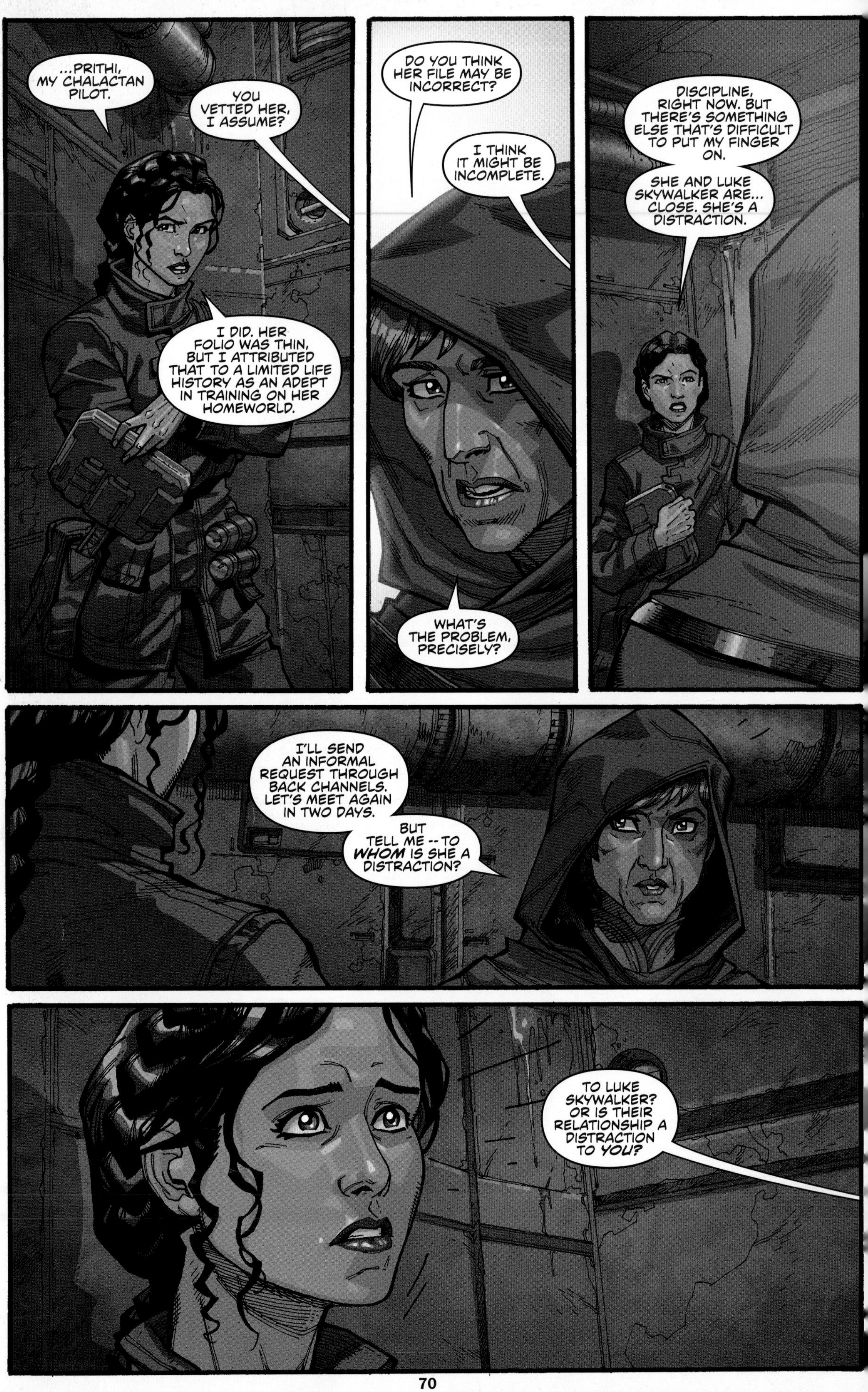
...PRITHI, MY CHALACTAN PILOT.
YOU VETTED HER, I ASSUME?
I DID. HER FOLIO WAS THIN, BUT I ATTRIBUTED THAT TO A LIMITED LIFE HISTORY AS AN ADEPT IN TRAINING ON HER HOMEWORLD.
DO YOU THINK HER FILE MAY BE INCORRECT?
I THINK IT MIGHT BE INCOMPLETE.
WHAT'S THE PROBLEM, PRECISELY?
DISCIPLINE, RIGHT NOW. BUT THERE'S SOMETHING ELSE THAT'S DIFFICULT TO PUT MY FINGER ON.
SHE AND LUKE SKYWALKER ARE... CLOSE. SHE'S A DISTRACTION.
I'LL SEND AN INFORMAL REQUEST THROUGH BACK CHANNELS. LET'S MEET AGAIN IN TWO DAYS.
BUT TELL ME -- TO *WHOM* IS SHE A DISTRACTION?
TO LUKE SKYWALKER? OR IS THEIR RELATIONSHIP A DISTRACTION TO *YOU*?

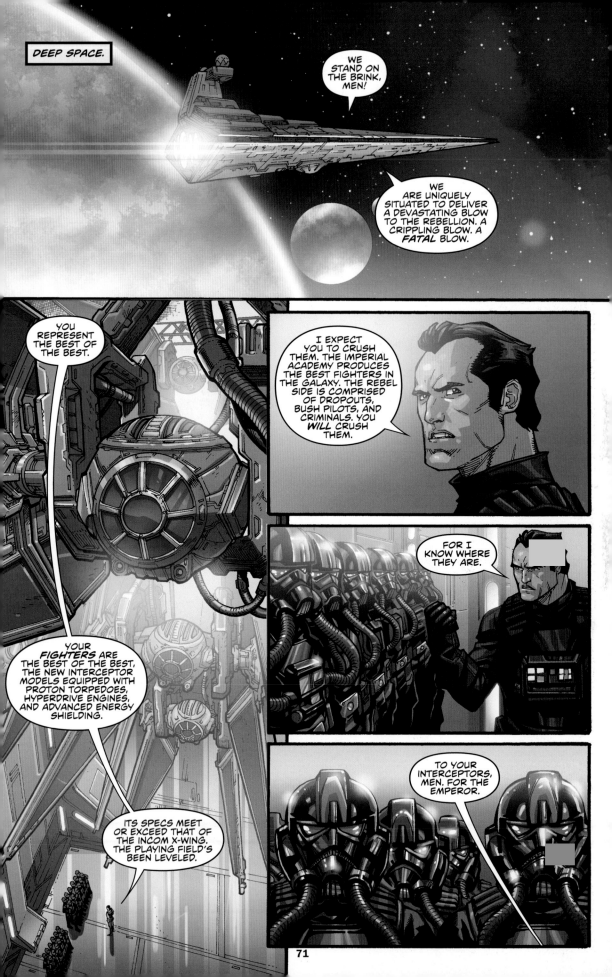

DEEP SPACE.

WE STAND ON THE BRINK, MEN!

WE ARE UNIQUELY SITUATED TO DELIVER A DEVASTATING BLOW TO THE REBELLION. A CRIPPLING BLOW. A *FATAL* BLOW.

YOU REPRESENT THE BEST OF THE BEST.

I EXPECT YOU TO CRUSH THEM. THE IMPERIAL ACADEMY PRODUCES THE BEST FIGHTERS IN THE GALAXY. THE REBEL SIDE IS COMPRISED OF DROPOUTS, BUSH PILOTS, AND CRIMINALS. YOU *WILL* CRUSH THEM.

YOUR *FIGHTERS* ARE THE BEST OF THE BEST, THE NEW INTERCEPTOR MODELS EQUIPPED WITH PROTON TORPEDOES, HYPERDRIVE ENGINES, AND ADVANCED ENERGY SHIELDING.

FOR I KNOW WHERE THEY ARE.

ITS SPECS MEET OR EXCEED THAT OF THE INCOM X-WING. THE PLAYING FIELD'S BEEN LEVELED.

TO YOUR INTERCEPTORS, MEN. FOR THE EMPEROR.

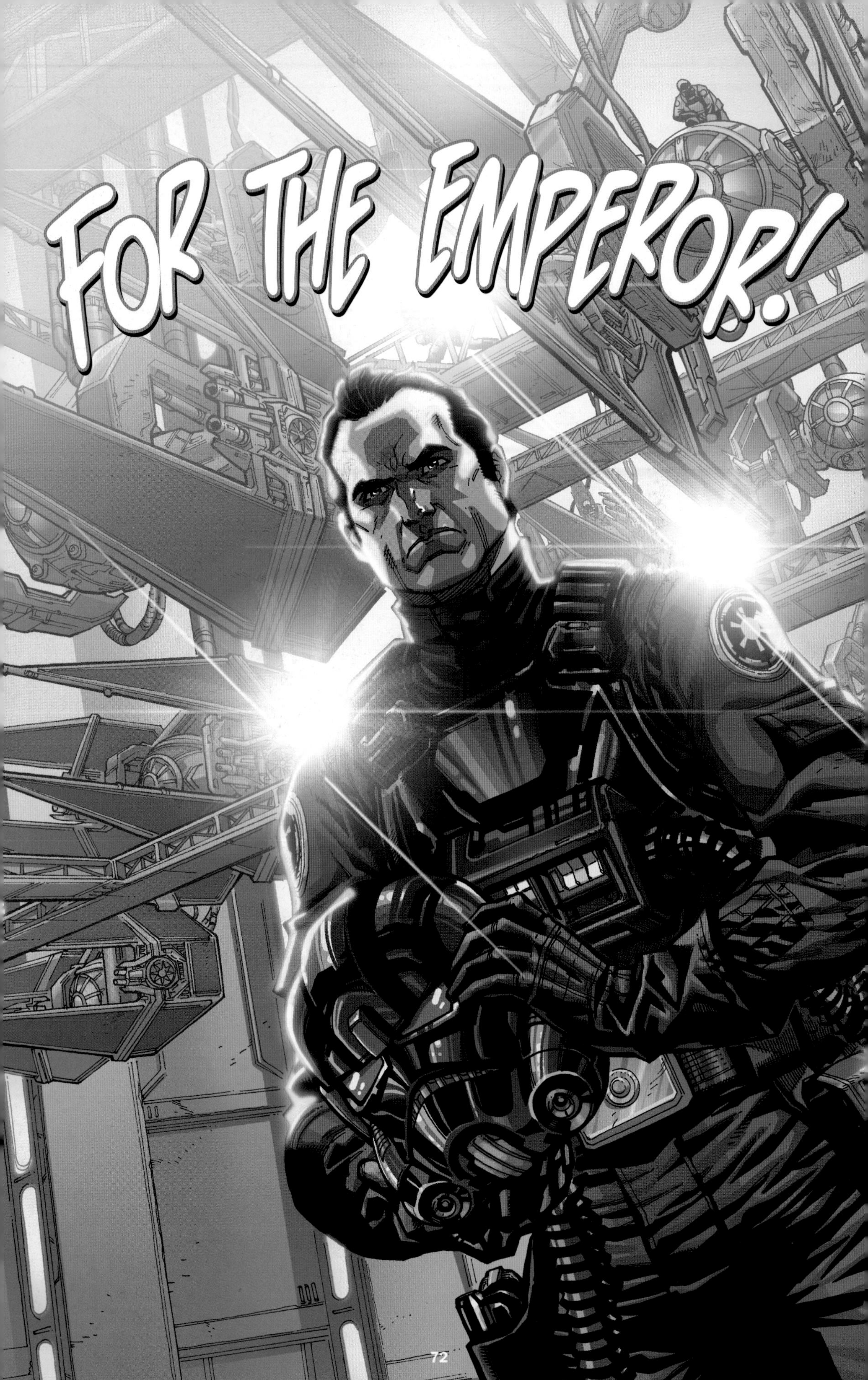
FOR THE EMPEROR!

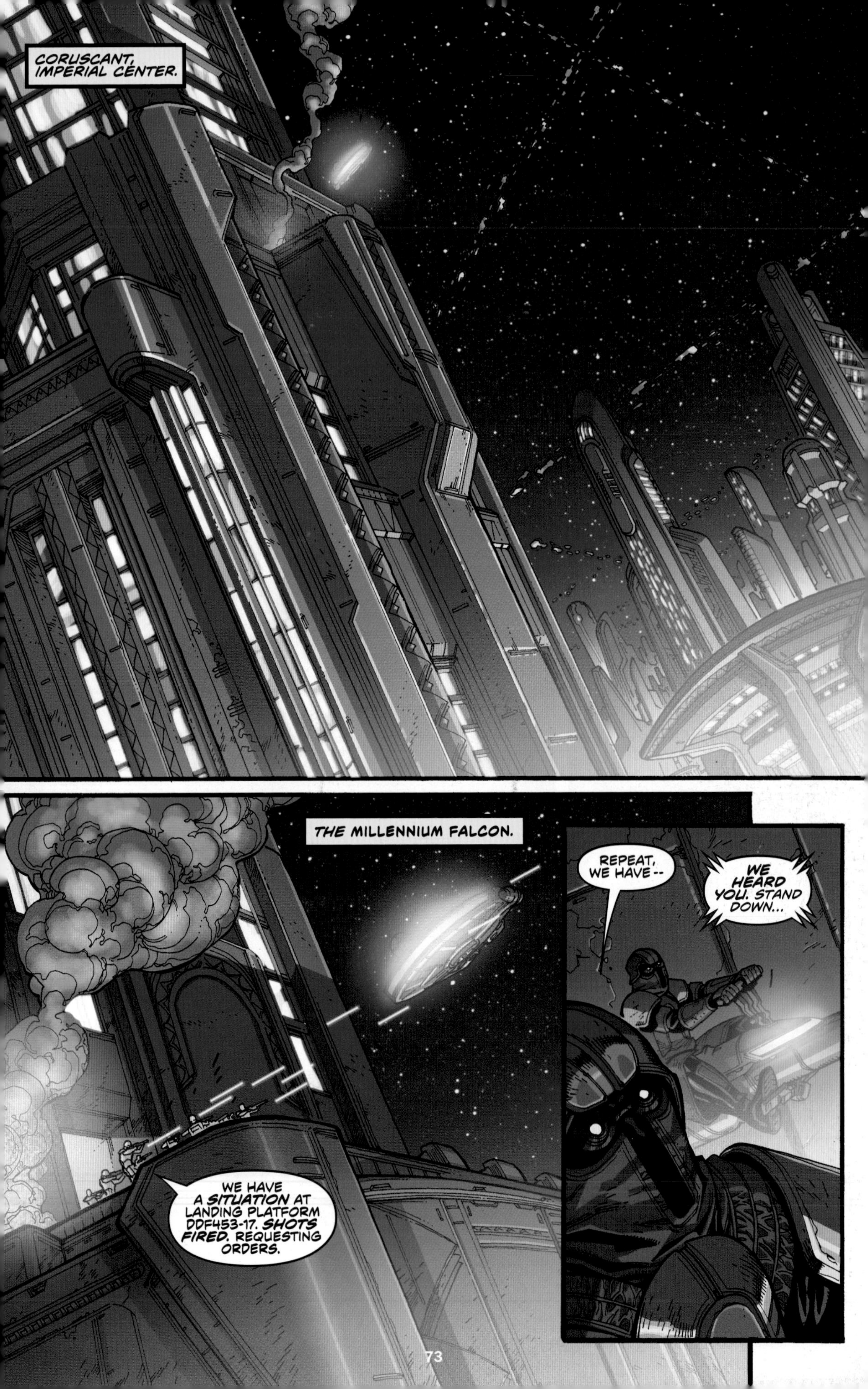

CORUSCANT, IMPERIAL CENTER.
THE MILLENNIUM FALCON.
WE HAVE A SITUATION AT LANDING PLATFORM DDF453-17. SHOTS FIRED. REQUESTING ORDERS.
REPEAT, WE HAVE --
WE HEARD YOU. STAND DOWN...

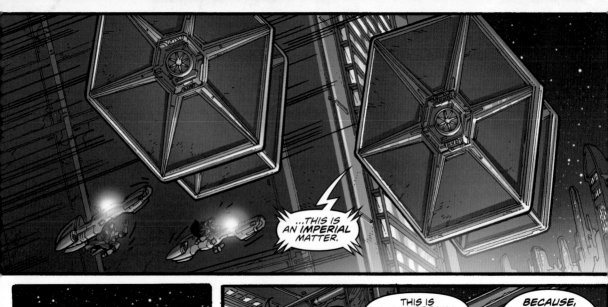

...THIS IS AN *IMPERIAL* MATTER.

WRAHH!

WHAT?

THIS IS JUST *TERRIFIC.* CHEWIE, I'M TAKING US DOWN.

WFHUA??

BECAUSE, THOSE THREE FIGHTERS BACK THERE WILL HAVE ALREADY TOLD THE *TWO DOZEN* OR SO CAPITAL SHIPS IN ORBIT THAT WE'RE HEADED THEIR WAY.

AND THAT'S *ASSUMING* WE MAKE IT PAST THE *GOLAN* DEFENSE NET.

I'M NO FOOL. AND BEING SNEAKY IS *WAY* UNDERRATED.

HOLD ON, CHEWIE...

...I *THINK* I REMEMBER THIS SECTOR FROM MY ACADEMY DAYS.

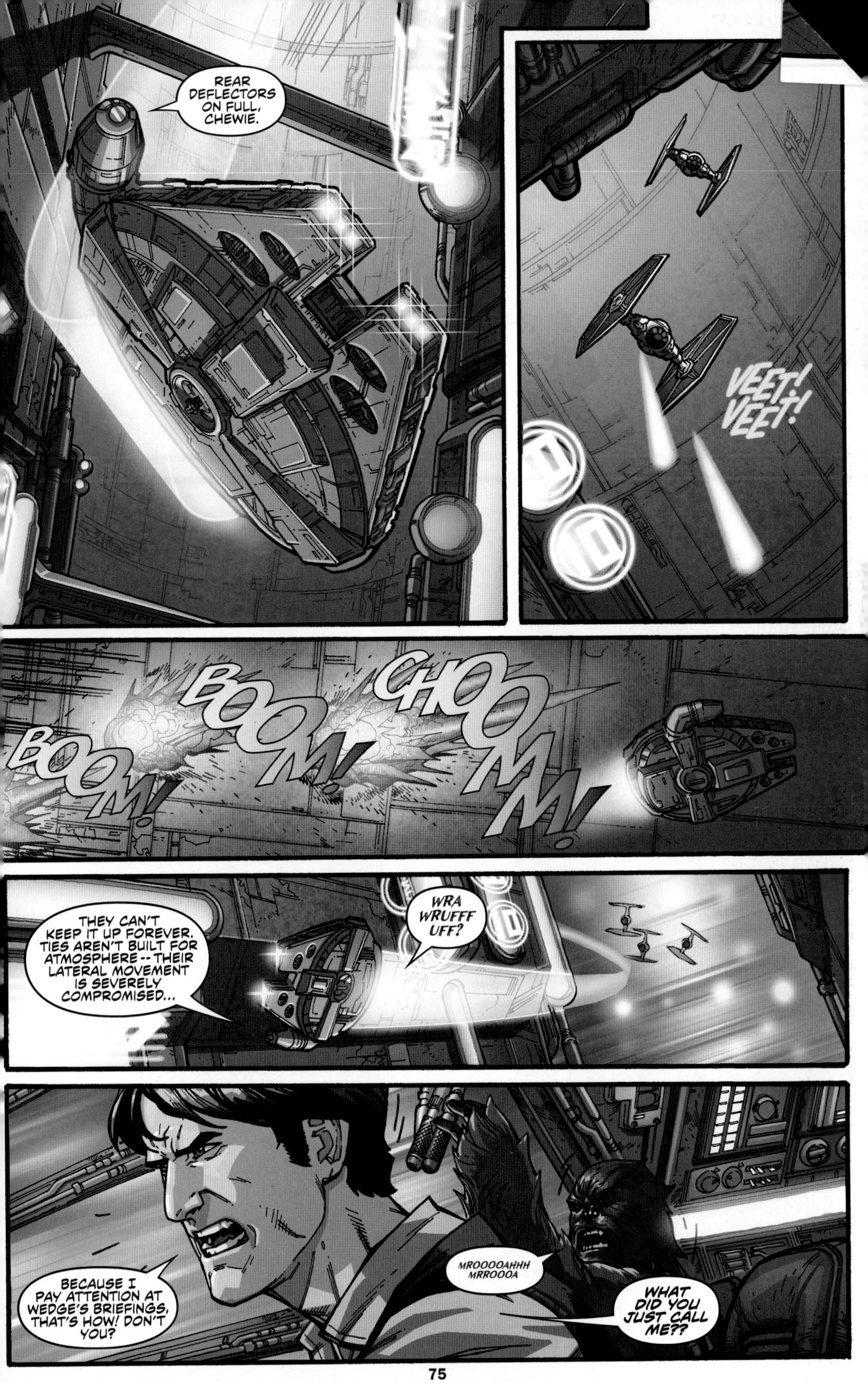

REAR DEFLECTORS ON FULL, CHEWIE.
VEET! VEET!
BOOM! BOOM! CHOOMM!
THEY CAN'T KEEP IT UP FOREVER. TIES AREN'T BUILT FOR ATMOSPHERE -- THEIR LATERAL MOVEMENT IS SEVERELY COMPROMISED...
WRA WRUFFF UFF?
BECAUSE I PAY ATTENTION AT WEDGE'S BRIEFINGS, THAT'S HOW! DON'T YOU?
MROOOOAHHH MRROOOA
WHAT DID YOU JUST CALL ME??

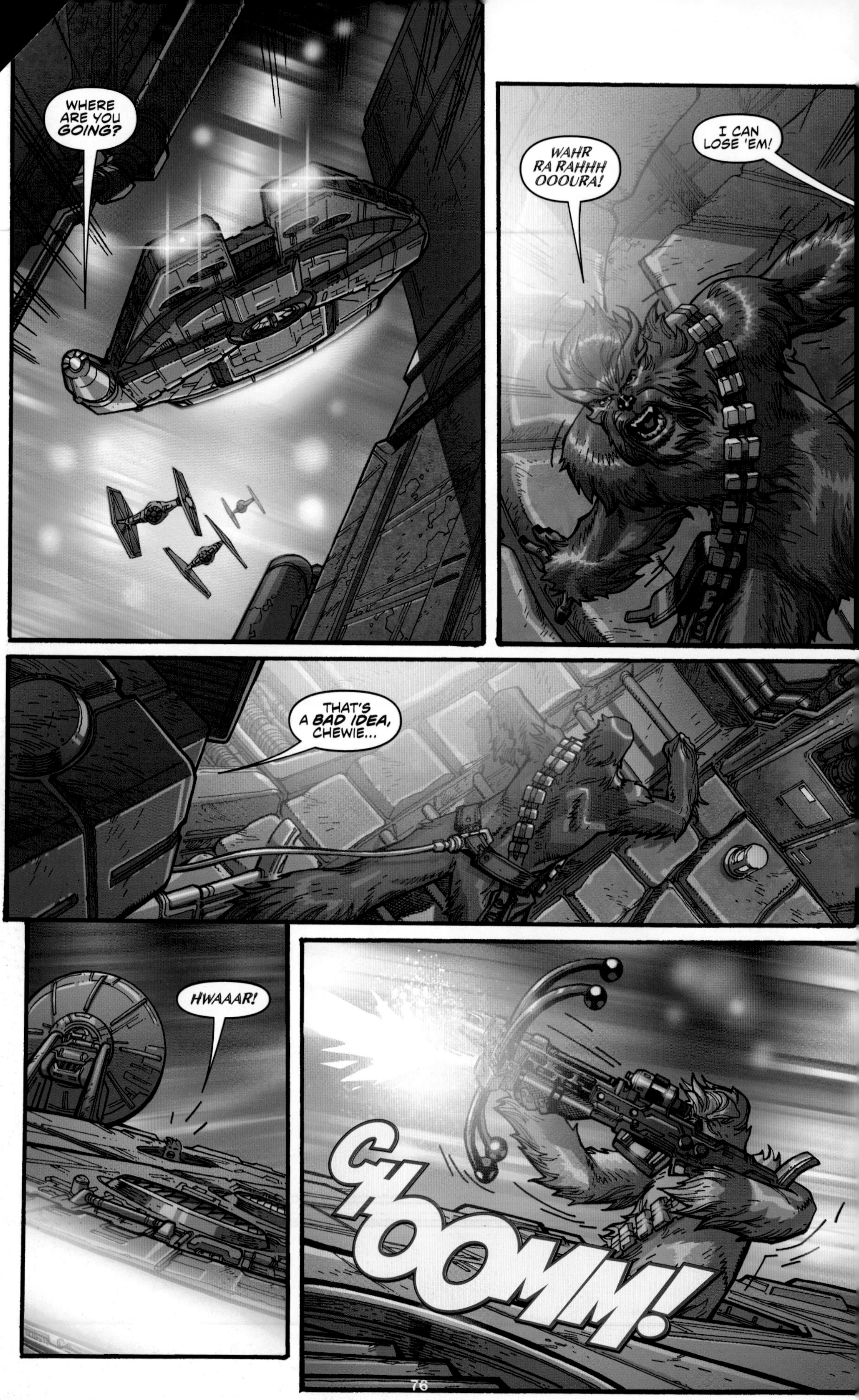
WHERE ARE YOU GOING?
WAHR RA RAHHH OOOURA!
I CAN LOSE 'EM!
THAT'S A BAD IDEA, CHEWIE...
HWAAAR!
CHOOMM!

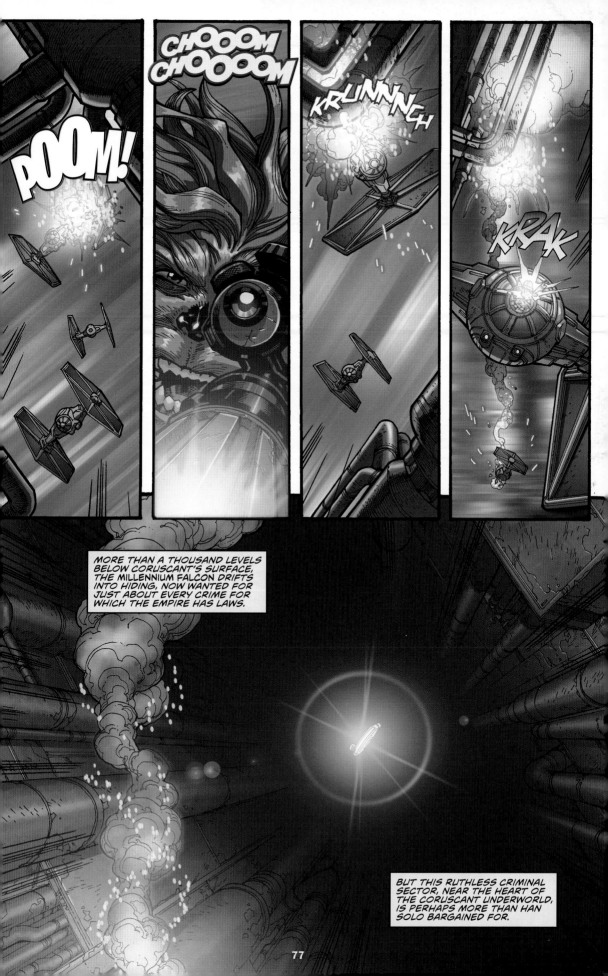

POOM!

CHOOOM CHOOOOM

KRUNNNCH

KRAK

MORE THAN A THOUSAND LEVELS BELOW CORUSCANT'S SURFACE, THE MILLENNIUM FALCON DRIFTS INTO HIDING, NOW WANTED FOR JUST ABOUT EVERY CRIME FOR WHICH THE EMPIRE HAS LAWS.

BUT THIS RUTHLESS CRIMINAL SECTOR, NEAR THE HEART OF THE CORUSCANT UNDERWORLD, IS PERHAPS MORE THAN HAN SOLO BARGAINED FOR.

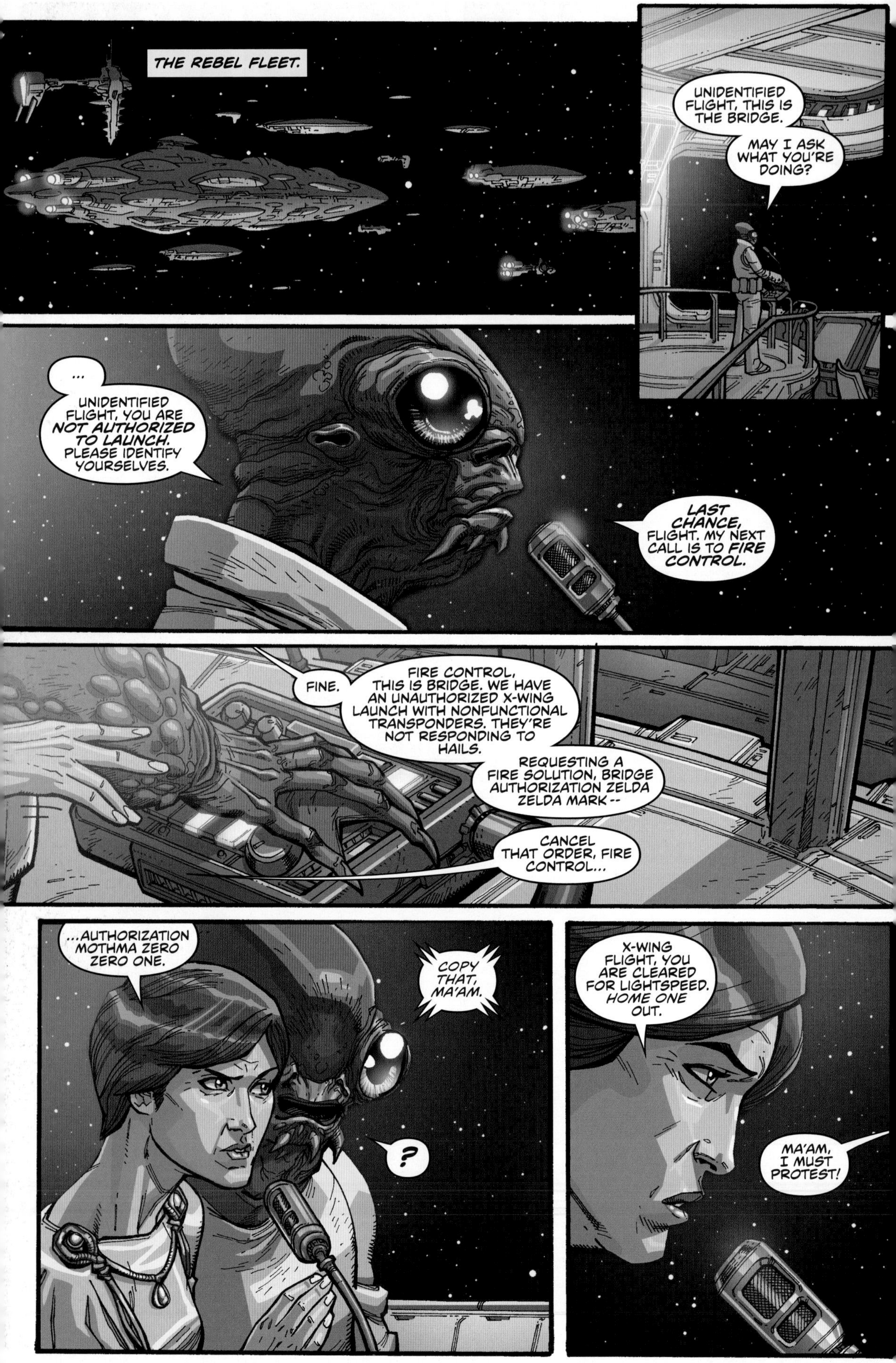
THE REBEL FLEET.
UNIDENTIFIED FLIGHT, THIS IS THE BRIDGE.
MAY I ASK WHAT YOU'RE DOING?
...
UNIDENTIFIED FLIGHT, YOU ARE NOT AUTHORIZED TO LAUNCH. PLEASE IDENTIFY YOURSELVES.
LAST CHANCE, FLIGHT. MY NEXT CALL IS TO FIRE CONTROL.
FINE.
FIRE CONTROL, THIS IS BRIDGE. WE HAVE AN UNAUTHORIZED X-WING LAUNCH WITH NONFUNCTIONAL TRANSPONDERS. THEY'RE NOT RESPONDING TO HAILS.
REQUESTING A FIRE SOLUTION, BRIDGE AUTHORIZATION ZELDA ZELDA MARK--
CANCEL THAT ORDER, FIRE CONTROL...
...AUTHORIZATION MOTHMA ZERO ZERO ONE.
COPY THAT, MA'AM.
?
X-WING FLIGHT, YOU ARE CLEARED FOR LIGHTSPEED. HOME ONE OUT.
MA'AM, I MUST PROTEST!

MUST YOU?

BRIDGE PROTOCOL *CLEARLY* STATES THAT--

YOU WILL LET THAT X-WING FLIGHT GO, AND YOU WILL *NOT* CHALLENGE THEM AGAIN.

YOU WILL ALSO SCRUB *ANY MENTION* OF THOSE FIGHTERS FROM THE BRIDGE LOGS. AND, AS IS MY HOPE, FROM YOUR MIND AS WELL.

DO YOU *COPY*, BRIDGE OFFICER?

COPY, MA'AM...

...BUT AT *LEAST* ASSURE ME THIS IS IN SERVICE OF THE *REBELLION* AGAINST THE *EMPIRE?!?*

EVERY BREATH I *DRAW* IS IN REBELLION TO THE EMPIRE.

NOW FORGET I WAS HERE.

GIVE 'EM HELL, PILOTS.

"GRAY FLIGHT, THIS IS GRAY LEADER. STAND BY."

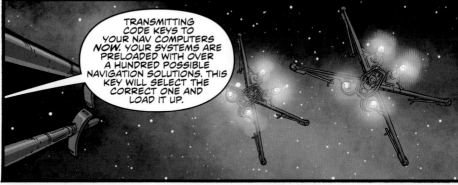

TRANSMITTING CODE KEYS TO YOUR NAV COMPUTERS *NOW.* YOUR SYSTEMS ARE PRELOADED WITH OVER A HUNDRED POSSIBLE NAVIGATION SOLUTIONS. THIS KEY WILL SELECT THE CORRECT ONE AND LOAD IT UP.

THE SECOND KEY WILL GO ACTIVE AT THE PREDETERMINED TIME MARK AND LOAD OUR RENDEZVOUS COORDINATES. THIS IS FOR *SECURITY,* PILOTS, YOURS AND THE FLEET'S.

YOU HAVE YOUR FLIGHT ASSIGNMENTS. WEDGE, TESS, YOU'RE WITH ME. RUS, FALBACK, YOU'RE GRAY TWO. GRAM, ARDANA, GRAY THREE.

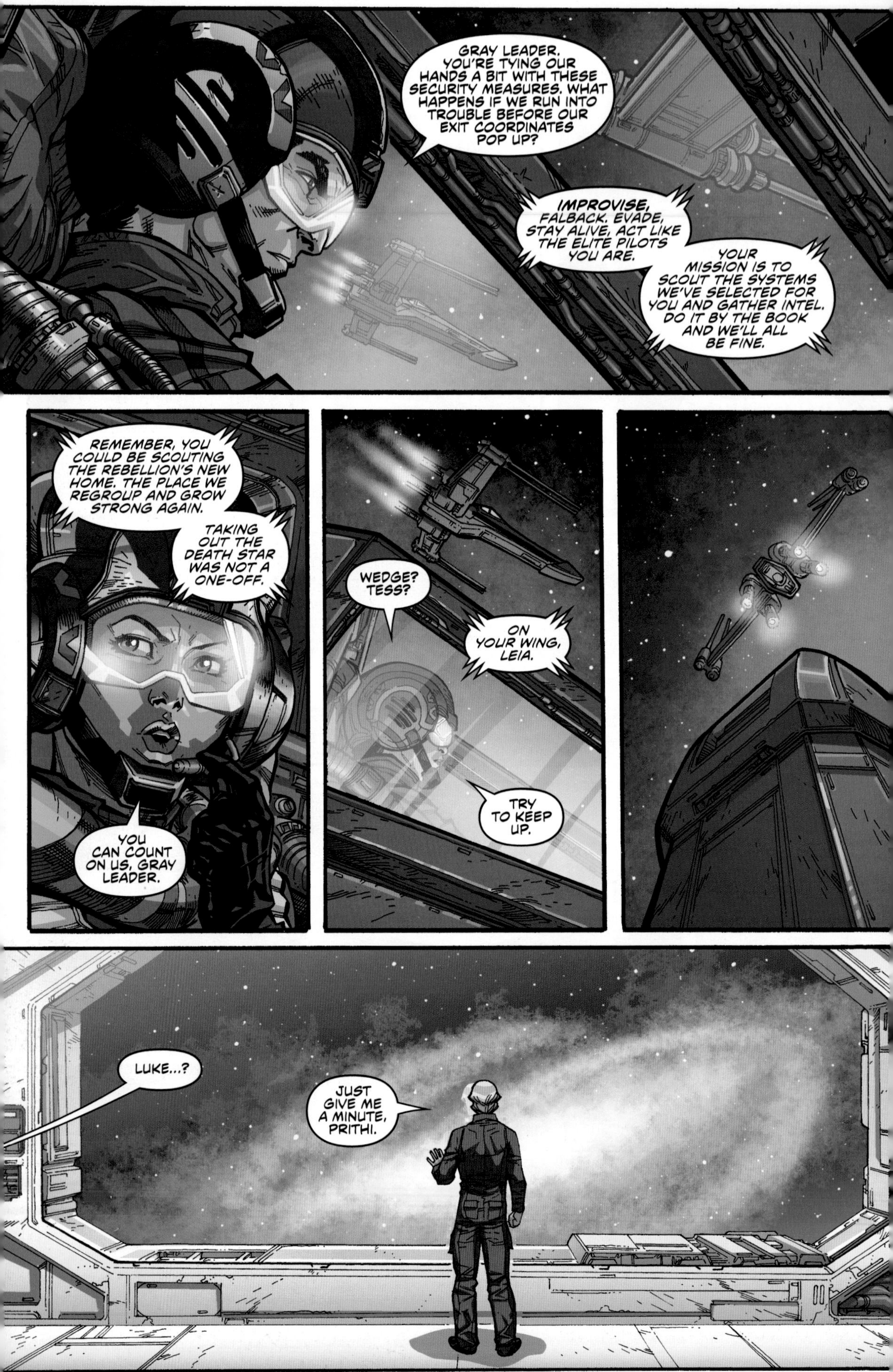
GRAY LEADER. YOU'RE TYING OUR HANDS A BIT WITH THESE SECURITY MEASURES. WHAT HAPPENS IF WE RUN INTO TROUBLE BEFORE OUR EXIT COORDINATES POP UP?
IMPROVISE, FALBACK. EVADE, STAY ALIVE, ACT LIKE THE ELITE PILOTS YOU ARE.
YOUR MISSION IS TO SCOUT THE SYSTEMS WE'VE SELECTED FOR YOU AND GATHER INTEL. DO IT BY THE BOOK AND WE'LL ALL BE FINE.
REMEMBER, YOU COULD BE SCOUTING THE REBELLION'S NEW HOME. THE PLACE WE REGROUP AND GROW STRONG AGAIN.
TAKING OUT THE DEATH STAR WAS NOT A ONE-OFF.
YOU CAN COUNT ON US, GRAY LEADER.
WEDGE? TESS?
ON YOUR WING, LEIA.
TRY TO KEEP UP.
LUKE...?
JUST GIVE ME A MINUTE, PRITHI.

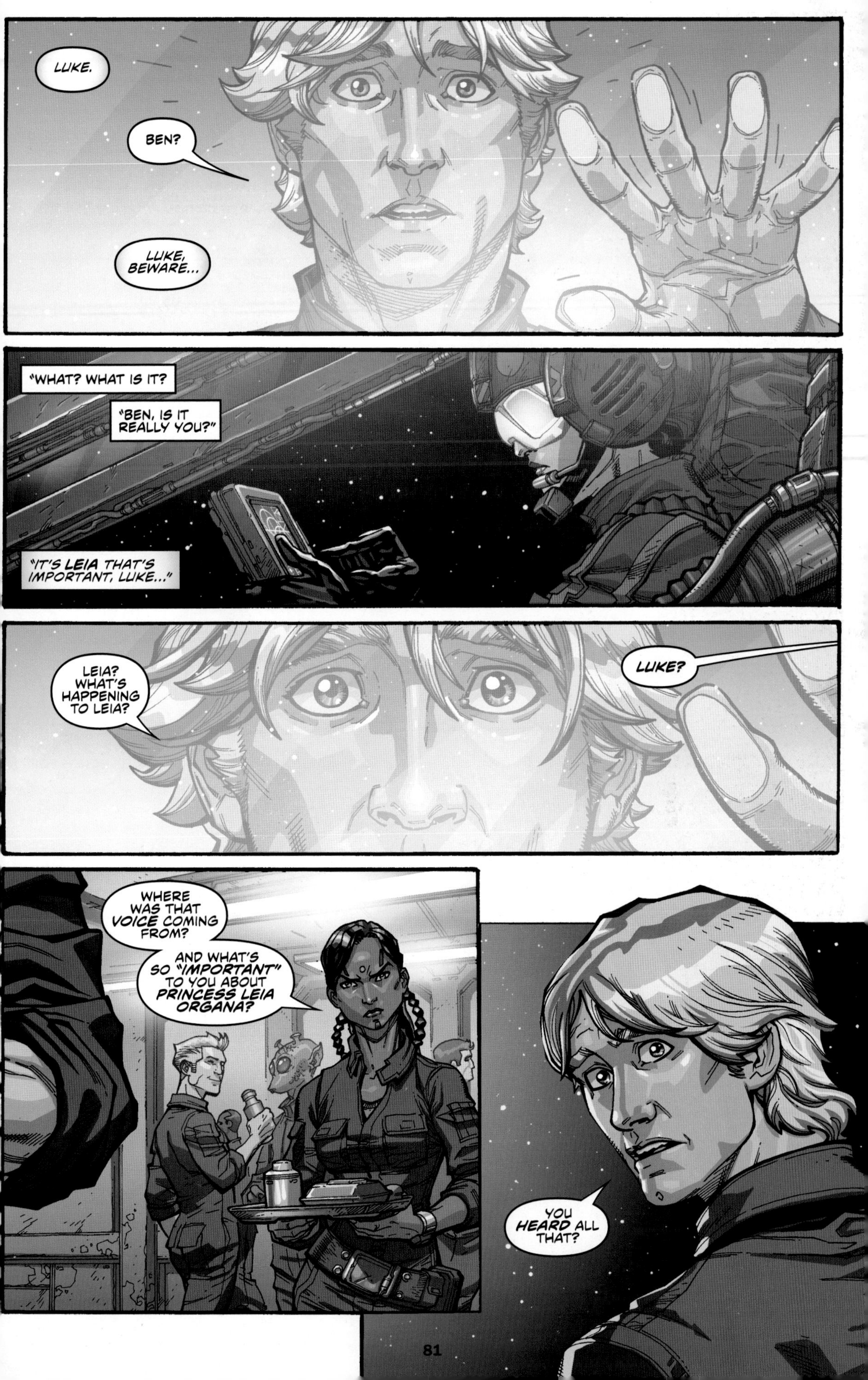
LUKE.
BEN?
LUKE, BEWARE...
"WHAT? WHAT IS IT?
"BEN, IS IT REALLY YOU?"
"IT'S LEIA THAT'S IMPORTANT, LUKE..."
LEIA? WHAT'S HAPPENING TO LEIA?
LUKE?
WHERE WAS THAT VOICE COMING FROM?
AND WHAT'S SO "IMPORTANT" TO YOU ABOUT PRINCESS LEIA ORGANA?
YOU HEARD ALL THAT?

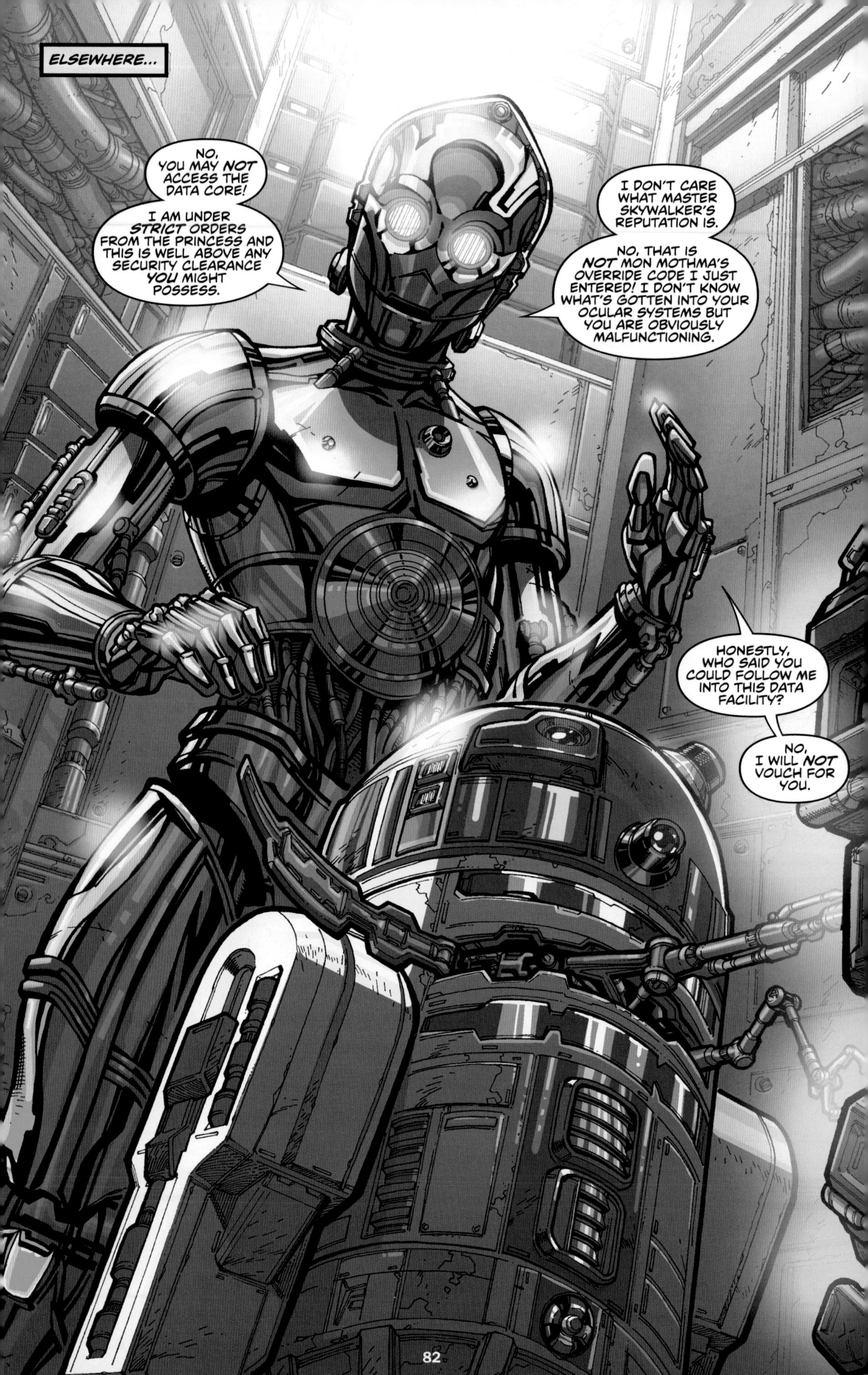
ELSEWHERE...
NO, YOU MAY NOT ACCESS THE DATA CORE!
I AM UNDER STRICT ORDERS FROM THE PRINCESS AND THIS IS WELL ABOVE ANY SECURITY CLEARANCE YOU MIGHT POSSESS.
I DON'T CARE WHAT MASTER SKYWALKER'S REPUTATION IS.
NO, THAT IS NOT MON MOTHMA'S OVERRIDE CODE I JUST ENTERED! I DON'T KNOW WHAT'S GOTTEN INTO YOUR OCULAR SYSTEMS BUT YOU ARE OBVIOUSLY MALFUNCTIONING.
HONESTLY, WHO SAID YOU COULD FOLLOW ME INTO THIS DATA FACILITY?
NO, I WILL NOT VOUCH FOR YOU.

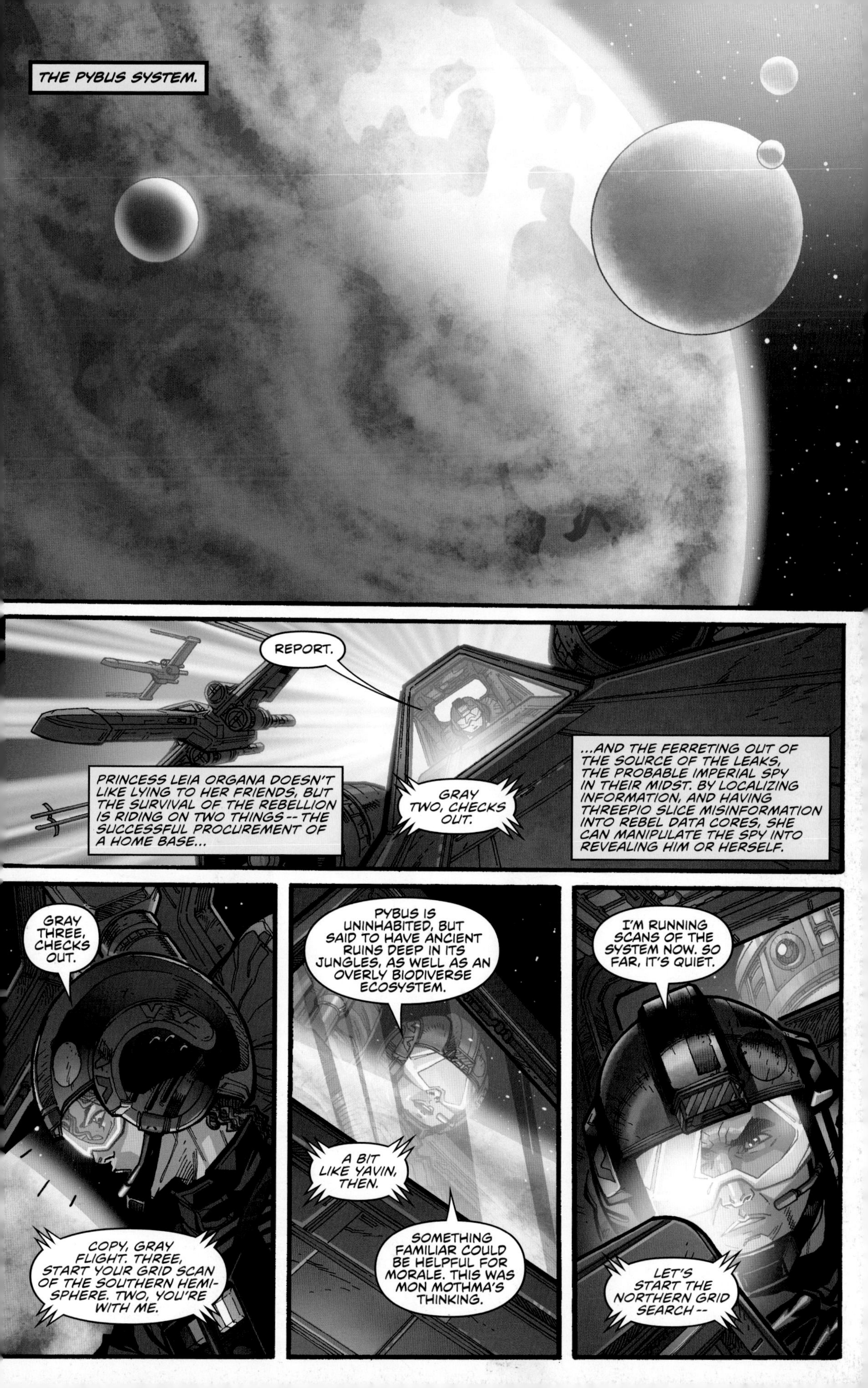
THE PYBUS SYSTEM.
REPORT.
PRINCESS LEIA ORGANA DOESN'T LIKE LYING TO HER FRIENDS, BUT THE SURVIVAL OF THE REBELLION IS RIDING ON TWO THINGS -- THE SUCCESSFUL PROCUREMENT OF A HOME BASE...
GRAY TWO, CHECKS OUT.
...AND THE FERRETING OUT OF THE SOURCE OF THE LEAKS, THE PROBABLE IMPERIAL SPY IN THEIR MIDST. BY LOCALIZING INFORMATION, AND HAVING THREEPIO SLICE MISINFORMATION INTO REBEL DATA CORES, SHE CAN MANIPULATE THE SPY INTO REVEALING HIM OR HERSELF.
GRAY THREE, CHECKS OUT.
COPY, GRAY FLIGHT. THREE, START YOUR GRID SCAN OF THE SOUTHERN HEMI-SPHERE. TWO, YOU'RE WITH ME.
PYBUS IS UNINHABITED, BUT SAID TO HAVE ANCIENT RUINS DEEP IN ITS JUNGLES, AS WELL AS AN OVERLY BIODIVERSE ECOSYSTEM.
A BIT LIKE YAVIN, THEN.
SOMETHING FAMILIAR COULD BE HELPFUL FOR MORALE. THIS WAS MON MOTHMA'S THINKING.
I'M RUNNING SCANS OF THE SYSTEM NOW. SO FAR, IT'S QUIET.
LET'S START THE NORTHERN GRID SEARCH --

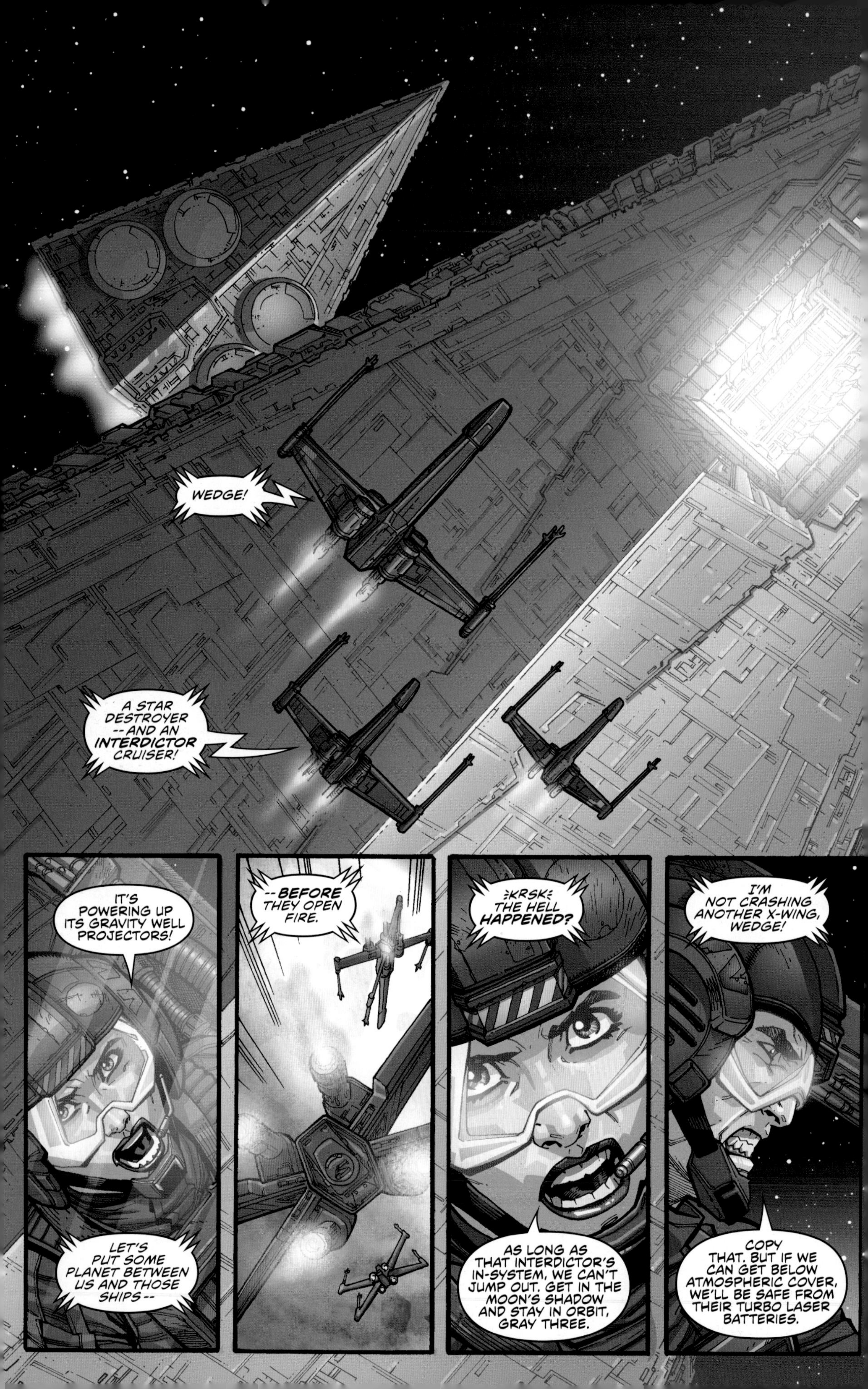
WEDGE!
A STAR DESTROYER --AND AN INTERDICTOR CRUISER!
IT'S POWERING UP ITS GRAVITY WELL PROJECTORS!
LET'S PUT SOME PLANET BETWEEN US AND THOSE SHIPS--
--BEFORE THEY OPEN FIRE.
KRSK THE HELL HAPPENED?
AS LONG AS THAT INTERDICTOR'S IN-SYSTEM, WE CAN'T JUMP OUT. GET IN THE MOON'S SHADOW AND STAY IN ORBIT, GRAY THREE.
I'M NOT CRASHING ANOTHER X-WING, WEDGE!
COPY THAT. BUT IF WE CAN GET BELOW ATMOSPHERIC COVER, WE'LL BE SAFE FROM THEIR TURBO LASER BATTERIES.

SO MUCH FOR OPERATIONAL SECURITY. THOSE SHIPS **KNEW** JUST WHERE TO FIND US--

--JUST LIKE IN THE DOMINUS SECTOR.

I DON'T UNDERSTAND...

WEDGE?

PYBUS WAS **NOT** A LOCATION LISTED IN THE FILES THREEPIO SLICED INTO THE FLEET'S DATA SYSTEM. AND IT WAS JUST ONE OF MANY IN LEIA'S PERSONAL NAVIGATION PACKET.

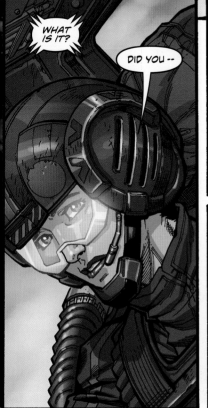

WHAT IS IT?

DID YOU --

POOOOM!

BREAK RIGHT!

POOOOM! POOOM! POOOM!

GRAY THREE! TESS! REGROUP NOW!

THEY'RE BOMBARDING THE SURFACE! WE NEED TO GO ON THE OFFENSIVE, OR THEY'LL BURN THE ENTIRE CONTINENT.

AGAINST TWO CAPITAL SHIPS?

WE KILLED A **DEATH STAR**, LEIA. GET IN UNDER THEIR SHIELDS AND INSIDE THE RANGE OF THEIR BIG GUNS. IT'S OUR ONLY SHOT.

SHIELDS FRONT FULL. GRAVITY DAMPENERS ON MAX.

THE DEATH STAR SENT DOZENS OF TIE FIGHTERS AFTER YOU, WEDGE ...DON'T FORGET ABOUT THAT.

I'LL NEVER FORGET.

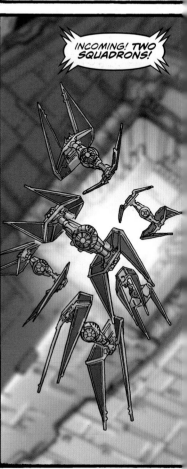

INCOMING! **TWO** SQUADRONS!

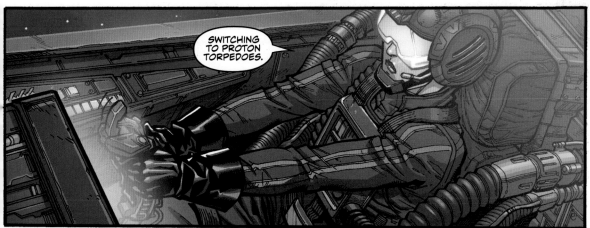

SWITCHING TO PROTON TORPEDOES.

MASTER LUKE! PLEASE, THE DATAPAD!

I'M UNDER *STRICT ORDERS* FROM THE PRINCESS!

SO ARE WE, THREEPIO, BUT RIGHT NOW I CAN'T THINK ABOUT THAT!

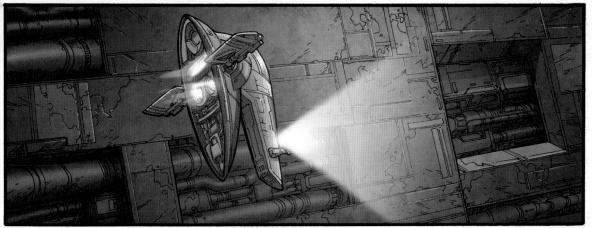

MON MOTHMA? YOU HAVE A PRIORITY INCOMING MESSAGE, MARKED CONFIDENTIAL --

DISREGARD, AND HOLD ALL MY CALLS.

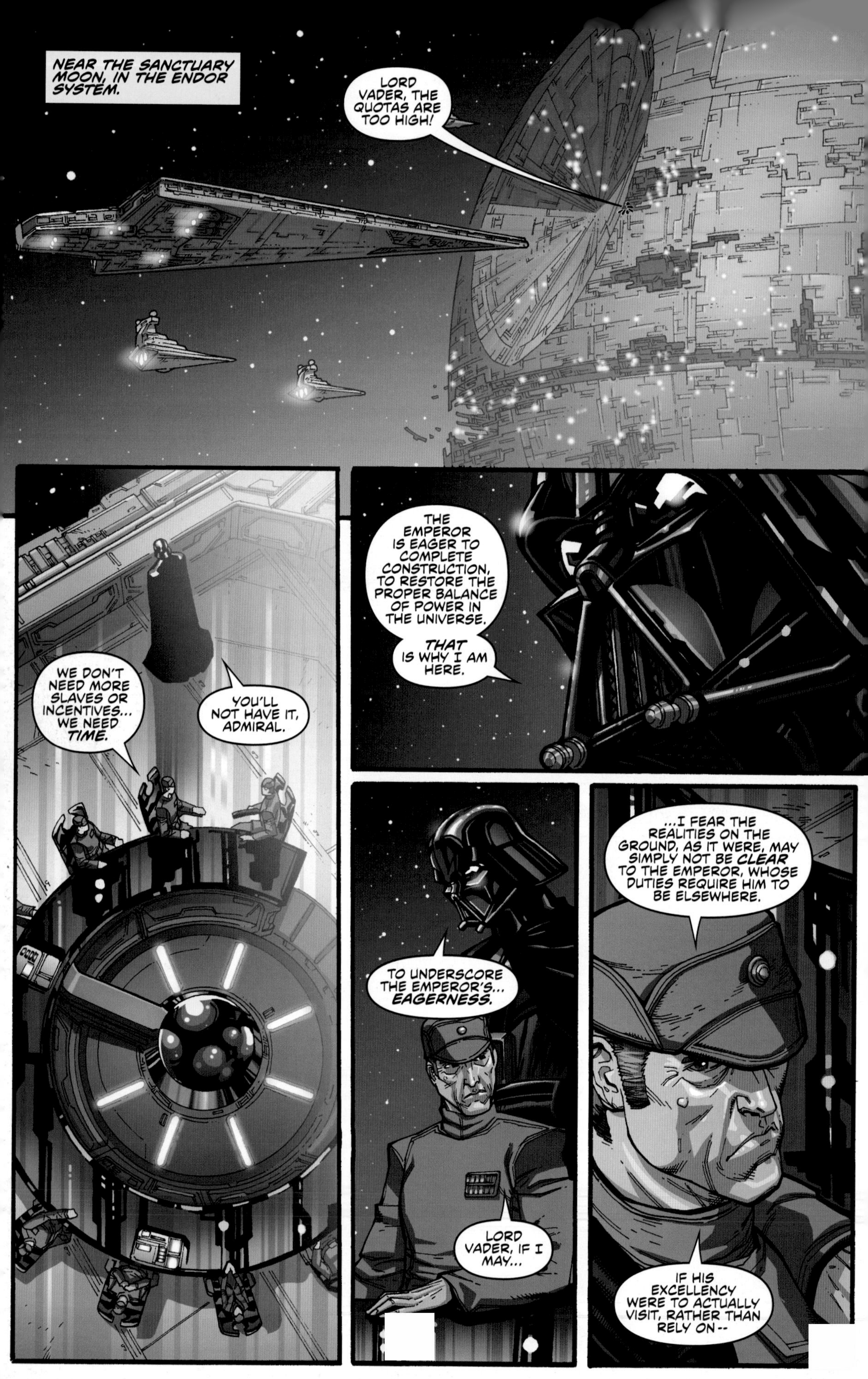
NEAR THE SANCTUARY MOON, IN THE ENDOR SYSTEM.
LORD VADER, THE QUOTAS ARE TOO HIGH!
WE DON'T NEED MORE SLAVES OR INCENTIVES... WE NEED TIME.
YOU'LL NOT HAVE IT, ADMIRAL.
THE EMPEROR IS EAGER TO COMPLETE CONSTRUCTION, TO RESTORE THE PROPER BALANCE OF POWER IN THE UNIVERSE.
THAT IS WHY I AM HERE.
TO UNDERSCORE THE EMPEROR'S... EAGERNESS.
LORD VADER, IF I MAY...
...I FEAR THE REALITIES ON THE GROUND, AS IT WERE, MAY SIMPLY NOT BE CLEAR TO THE EMPEROR, WHOSE DUTIES REQUIRE HIM TO BE ELSEWHERE.
IF HIS EXCELLENCY WERE TO ACTUALLY VISIT, RATHER THAN RELY ON--

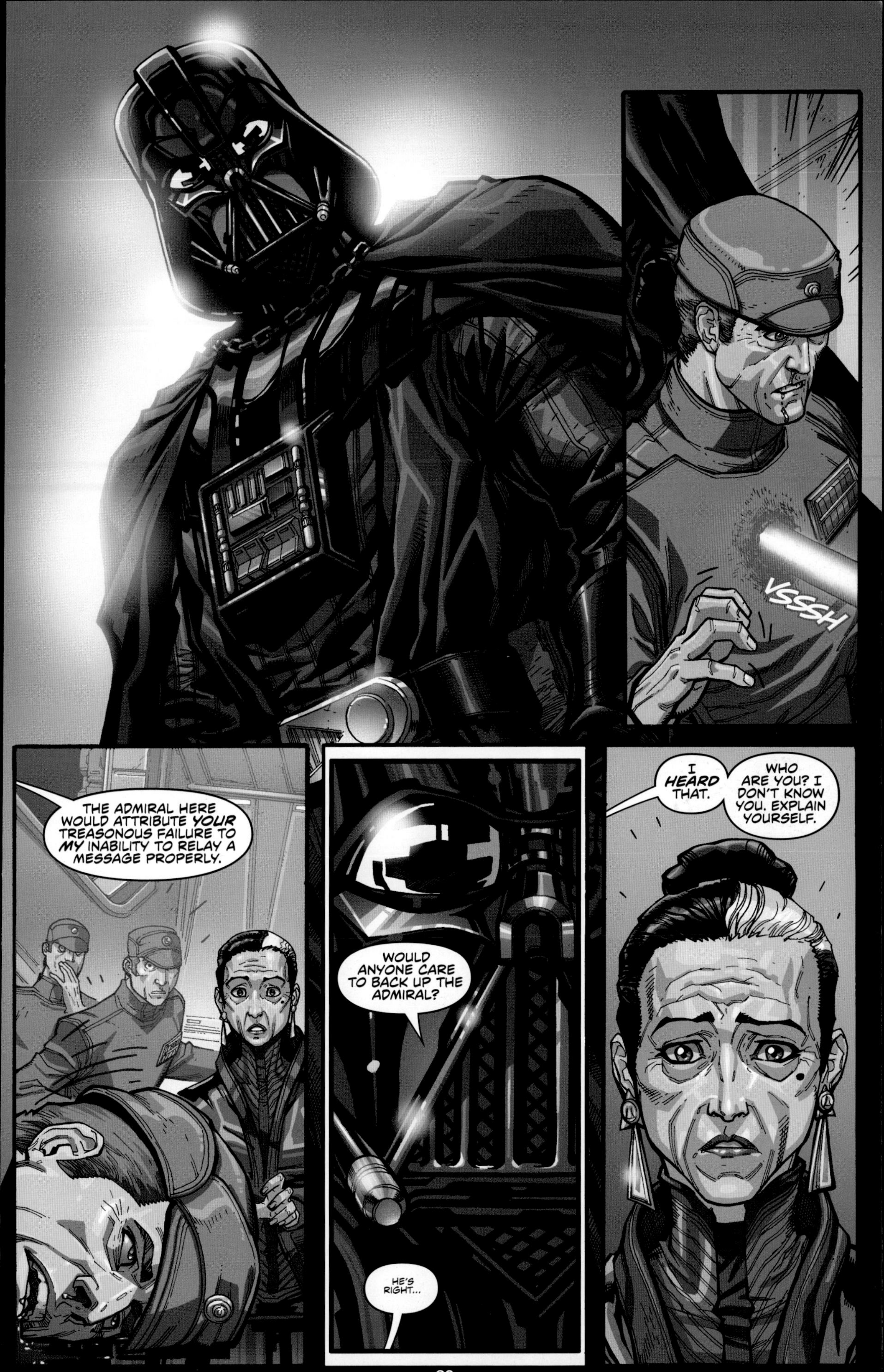
VSSSH
THE ADMIRAL HERE WOULD ATTRIBUTE *YOUR* TREASONOUS FAILURE TO *MY* INABILITY TO RELAY A MESSAGE PROPERLY.
WOULD ANYONE CARE TO BACK UP THE ADMIRAL?
HE'S RIGHT...
I *HEARD* THAT.
WHO ARE YOU? I DON'T KNOW YOU. EXPLAIN YOURSELF.

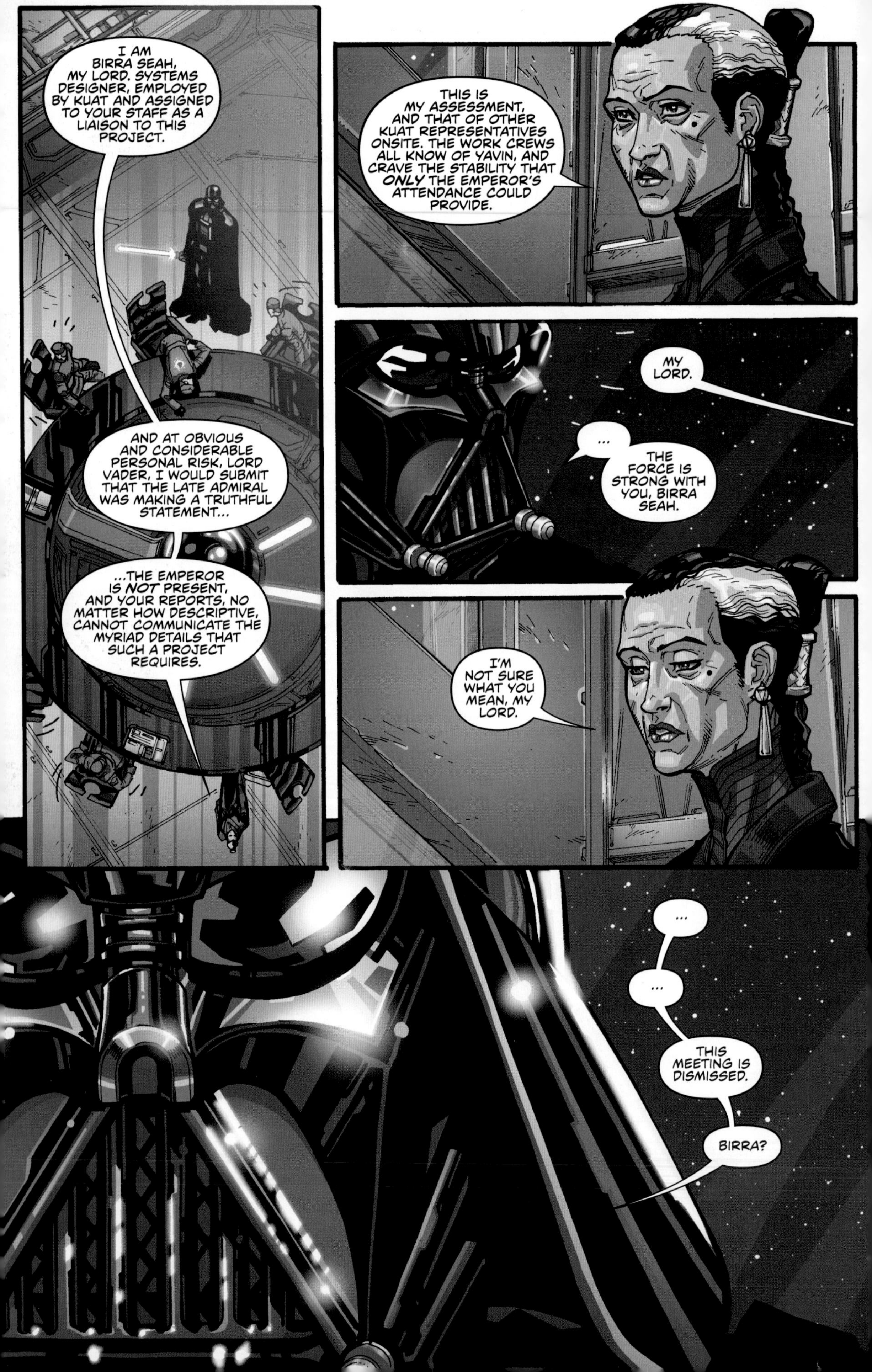
I AM BIRRA SEAH, MY LORD. SYSTEMS DESIGNER, EMPLOYED BY KUAT AND ASSIGNED TO YOUR STAFF AS A LIAISON TO THIS PROJECT.
AND AT OBVIOUS AND CONSIDERABLE PERSONAL RISK, LORD VADER, I WOULD SUBMIT THAT THE LATE ADMIRAL WAS MAKING A TRUTHFUL STATEMENT...
...THE EMPEROR IS NOT PRESENT, AND YOUR REPORTS, NO MATTER HOW DESCRIPTIVE, CANNOT COMMUNICATE THE MYRIAD DETAILS THAT SUCH A PROJECT REQUIRES.
THIS IS MY ASSESSMENT, AND THAT OF OTHER KUAT REPRESENTATIVES ONSITE. THE WORK CREWS ALL KNOW OF YAVIN, AND CRAVE THE STABILITY THAT ONLY THE EMPEROR'S ATTENDANCE COULD PROVIDE.
MY LORD.
...
THE FORCE IS STRONG WITH YOU, BIRRA SEAH.
I'M NOT SURE WHAT YOU MEAN, MY LORD.
...
...
THIS MEETING IS DISMISSED.
BIRRA?

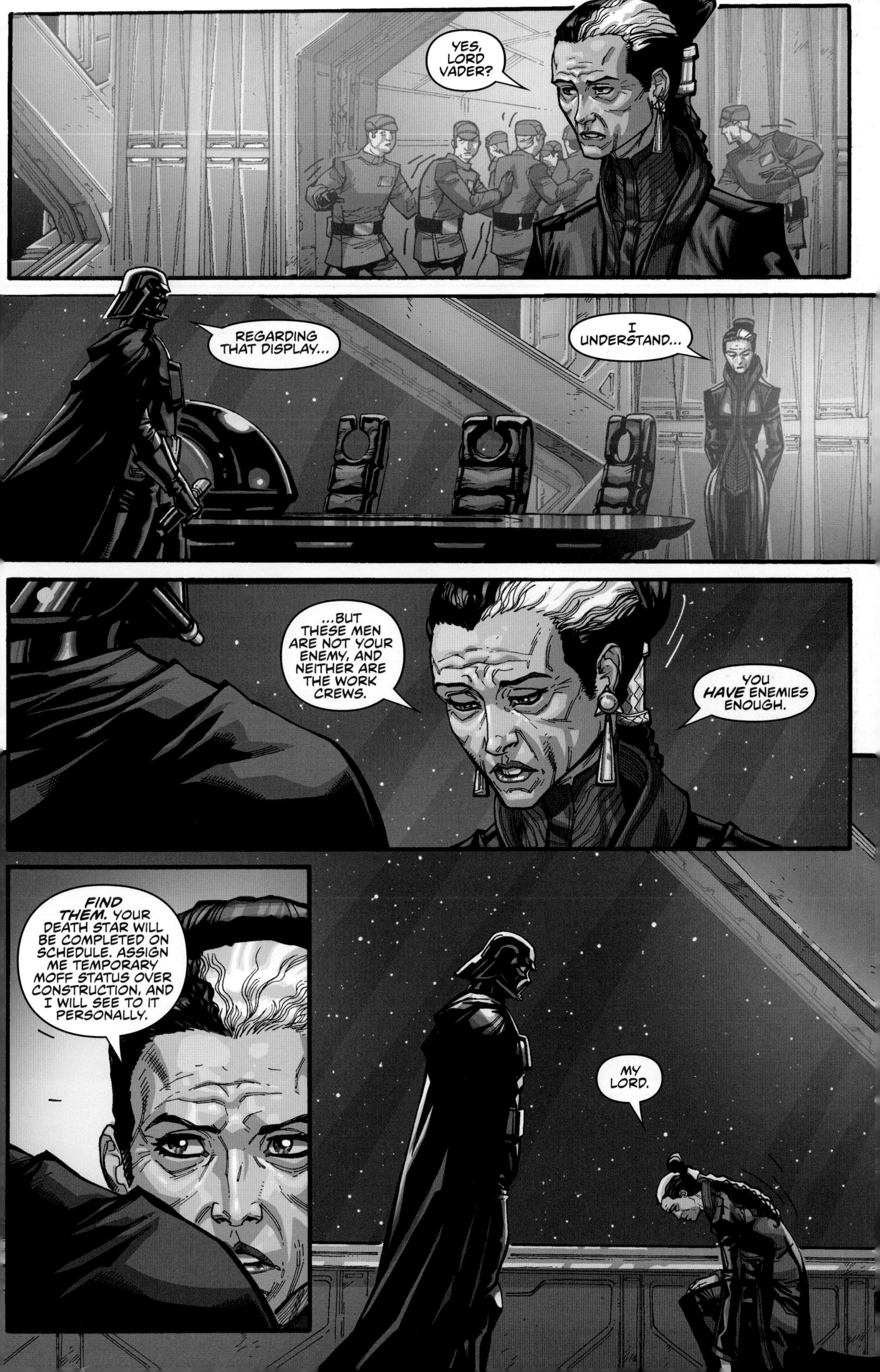
YES, LORD VADER?
REGARDING THAT DISPLAY...
I UNDERSTAND...
...BUT THESE MEN ARE NOT YOUR ENEMY, AND NEITHER ARE THE WORK CREWS.
YOU HAVE ENEMIES ENOUGH.
FIND THEM. YOUR DEATH STAR WILL BE COMPLETED ON SCHEDULE. ASSIGN ME TEMPORARY MOFF STATUS OVER CONSTRUCTION, AND I WILL SEE TO IT PERSONALLY.
MY LORD.

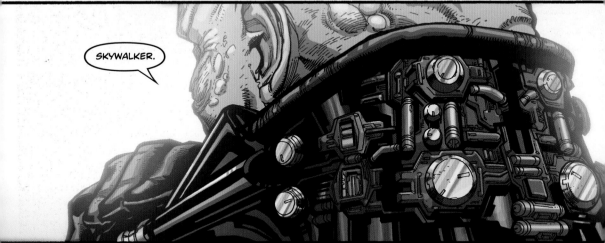

SKYWALKER.

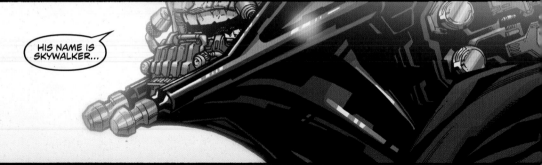

HIS NAME IS SKYWALKER...

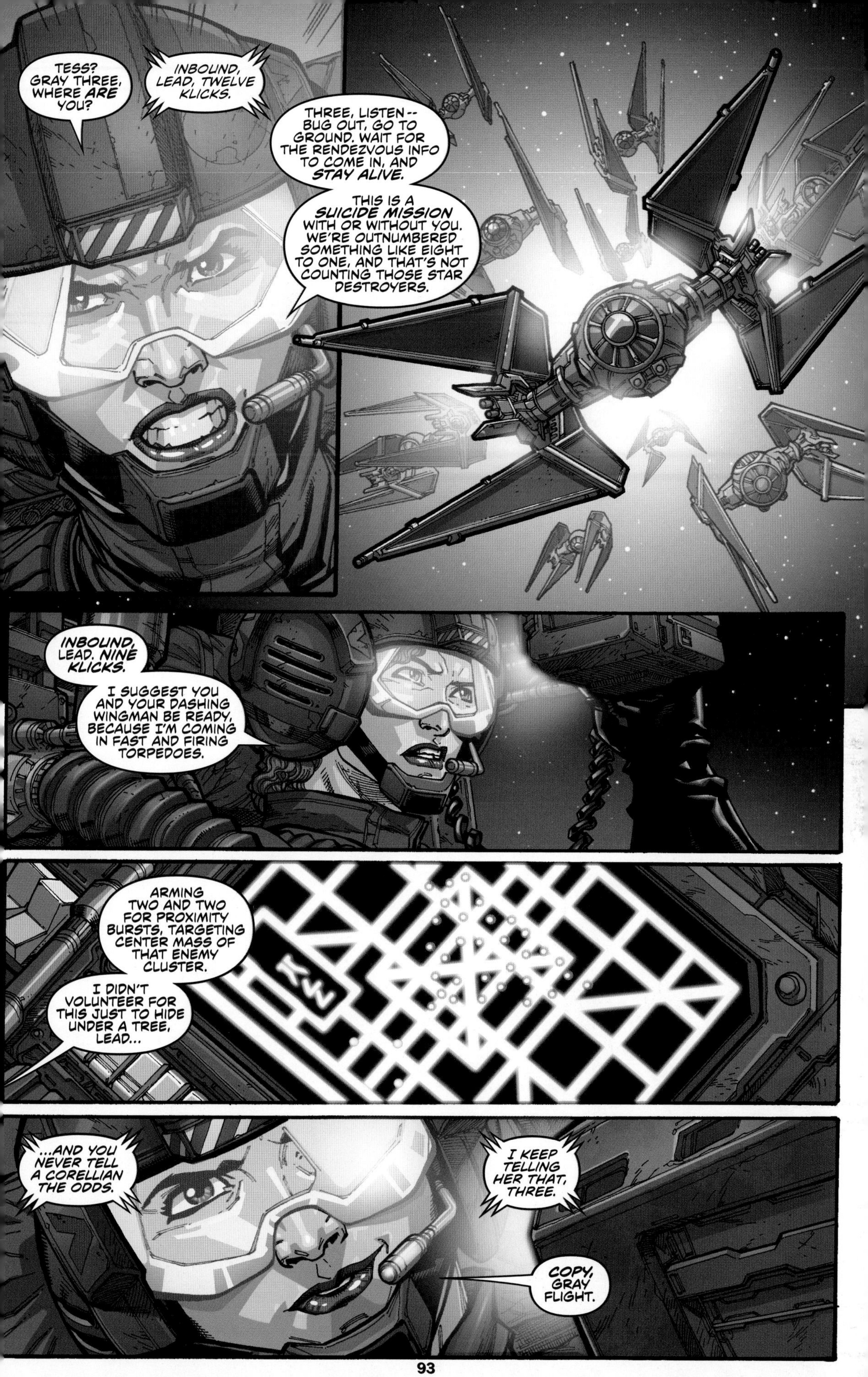
TESS? GRAY THREE, WHERE ARE YOU?
INBOUND, LEAD, TWELVE KLICKS.
THREE, LISTEN -- BUG OUT, GO TO GROUND. WAIT FOR THE RENDEZVOUS INFO TO COME IN, AND STAY ALIVE.
THIS IS A SUICIDE MISSION WITH OR WITHOUT YOU. WE'RE OUTNUMBERED SOMETHING LIKE EIGHT TO ONE, AND THAT'S NOT COUNTING THOSE STAR DESTROYERS.
INBOUND, LEAD. NINE KLICKS.
I SUGGEST YOU AND YOUR DASHING WINGMAN BE READY, BECAUSE I'M COMING IN FAST AND FIRING TORPEDOES.
ARMING TWO AND TWO FOR PROXIMITY BURSTS, TARGETING CENTER MASS OF THAT ENEMY CLUSTER.
I DIDN'T VOLUNTEER FOR THIS JUST TO HIDE UNDER A TREE, LEAD...
...AND YOU NEVER TELL A CORELLIAN THE ODDS.
I KEEP TELLING HER THAT, THREE.
COPY, GRAY FLIGHT.

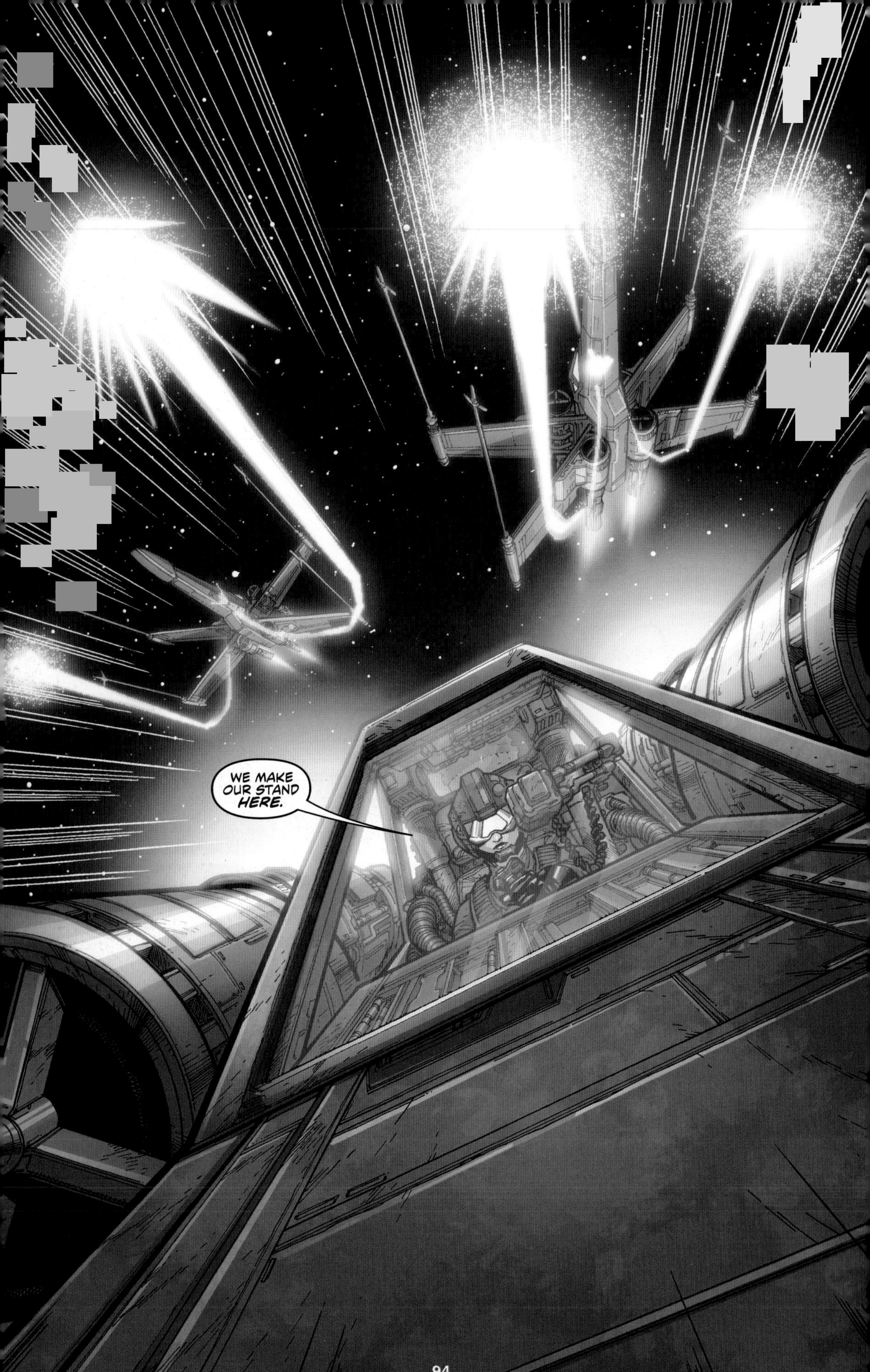
WE MAKE OUR STAND HERE.

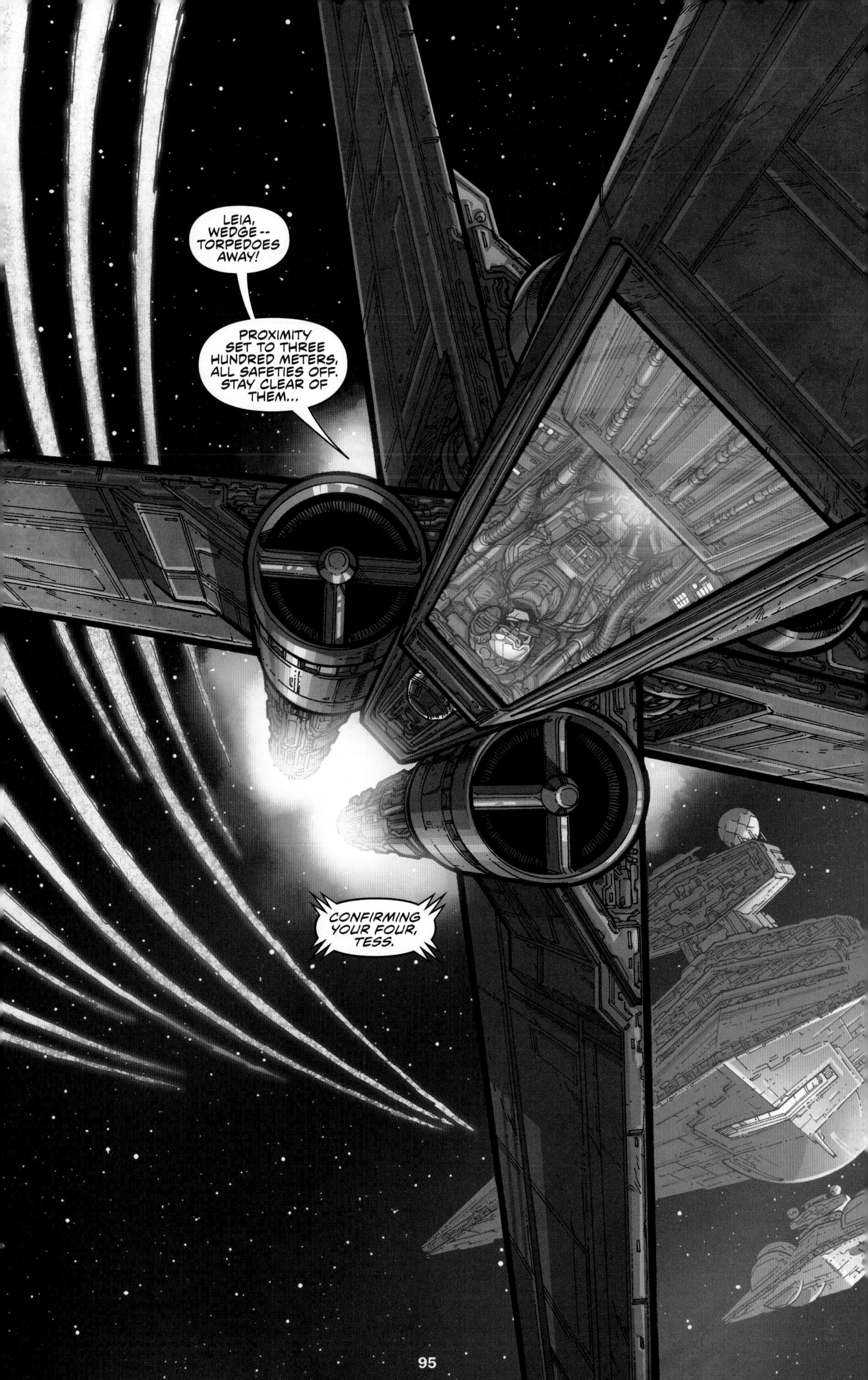
LEIA, WEDGE -- TORPEDOES AWAY!
PROXIMITY SET TO THREE HUNDRED METERS, ALL SAFETIES OFF. STAY CLEAR OF THEM...
CONFIRMING YOUR FOUR, TESS.

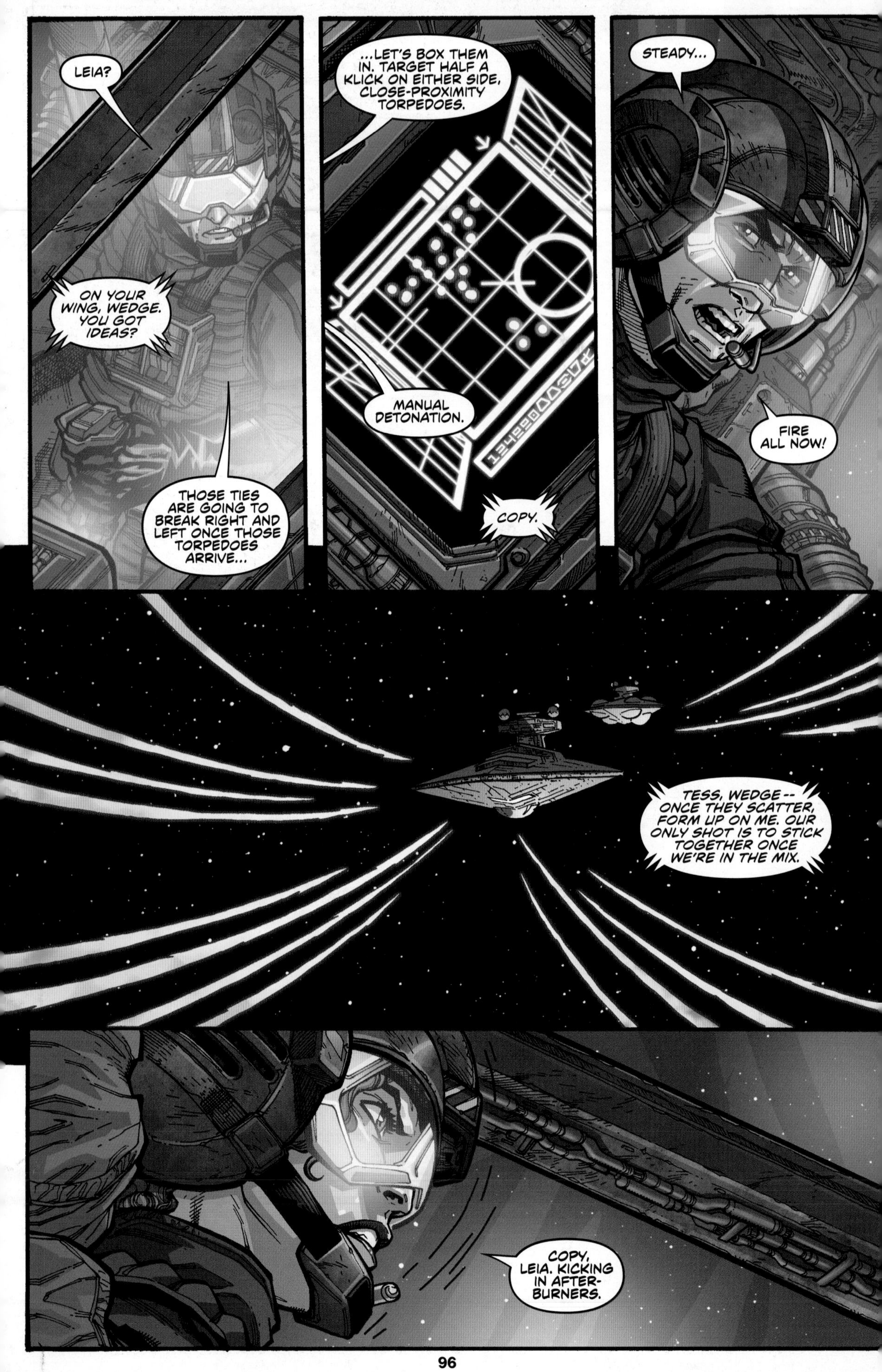
LEIA?
ON YOUR WING, WEDGE. YOU GOT IDEAS?
THOSE TIES ARE GOING TO BREAK RIGHT AND LEFT ONCE THOSE TORPEDOES ARRIVE...
...LET'S BOX THEM IN. TARGET HALF A KLICK ON EITHER SIDE, CLOSE-PROXIMITY TORPEDOES.
MANUAL DETONATION.
COPY.
STEADY...
FIRE ALL NOW!
TESS, WEDGE -- ONCE THEY SCATTER, FORM UP ON ME. OUR ONLY SHOT IS TO STICK TOGETHER ONCE WE'RE IN THE MIX.
COPY, LEIA. KICKING IN AFTER-BURNERS.

MEN, THIS IS BIRCHER. ACCELERATE TO MAXIMUM SPEED. WE'LL CLOSE THE GAP BEFORE THOSE MISSILES GO ACTIVE.

LET'S SHOW THESE REBELS THEY'RE NOT THE ONLY ONES WITH ADVANCE PROTOTYPE FIGHTERS AND HOTSHOT PILOTS.

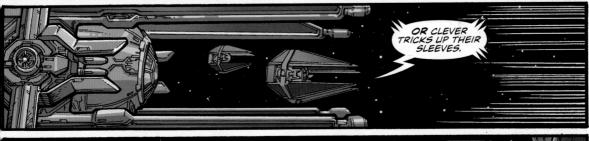

OR CLEVER TRICKS UP THEIR SLEEVES.

HOLD FAST.

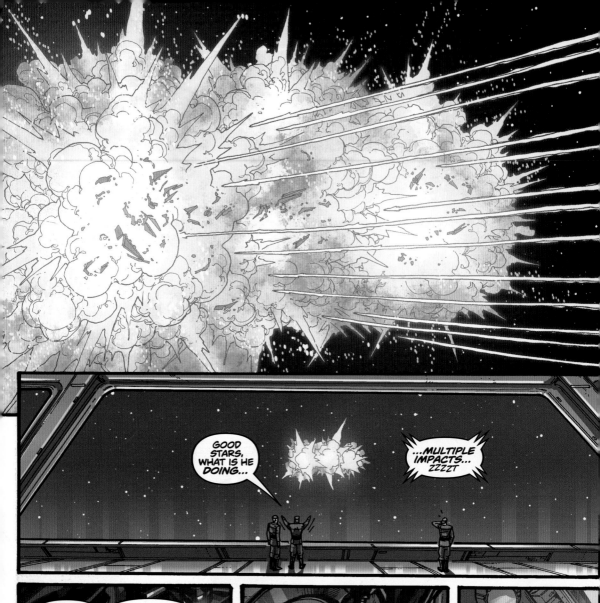

GOOD STARS, WHAT IS HE DOING...

...MULTIPLE IMPACTS... ZZZZT

BLASTED REBELS!

SQUADRON, EVADE PATTERN DELTA DELTA VICTOR. YOU ARE FREE TO ENGAGE, PICK YOUR TARGETS AT WILL.

COMMAND, WE ARE ELEVEN DOWN...

KKZZZTTT ADVISE RETURN TO HANGAR BAY ZZZZKKT

NEGATIVE.

THIS IS OUR MOMENT OF TRIUMPH!

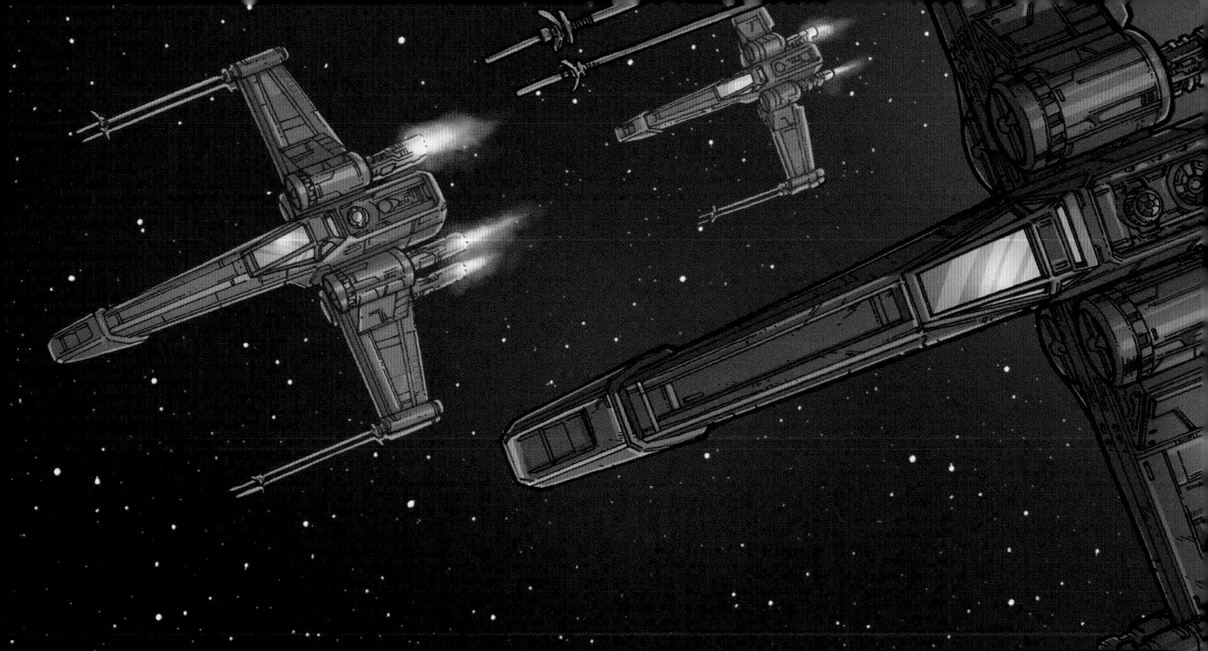

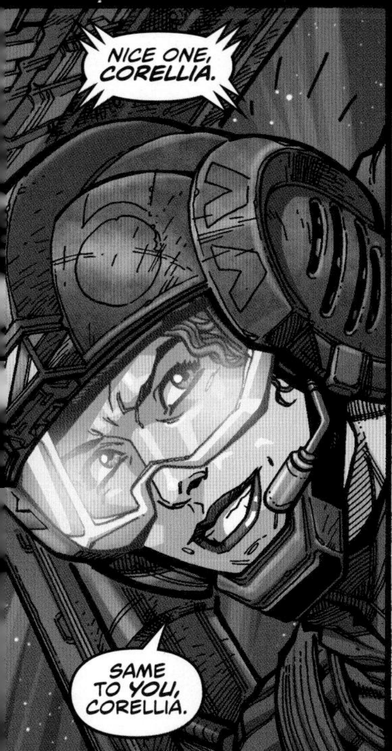
NICE ONE, CORELLIA.
SAME TO YOU, CORELLIA.

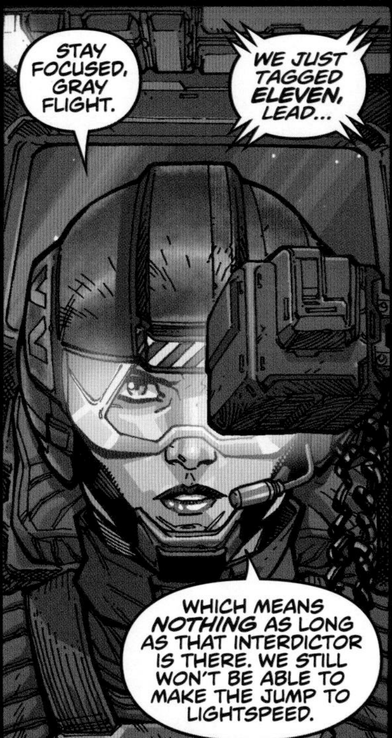
STAY FOCUSED, GRAY FLIGHT.
WE JUST TAGGED ELEVEN, LEAD...
WHICH MEANS NOTHING AS LONG AS THAT INTERDICTOR IS THERE. WE STILL WON'T BE ABLE TO MAKE THE JUMP TO LIGHTSPEED.

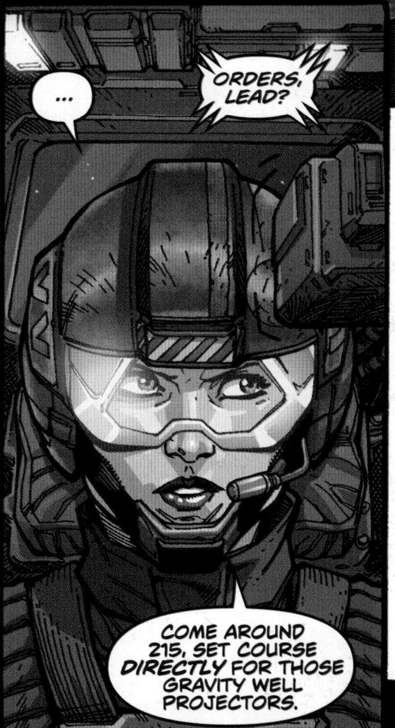
...
ORDERS, LEAD?
COME AROUND 215, SET COURSE DIRECTLY FOR THOSE GRAVITY WELL PROJECTORS.

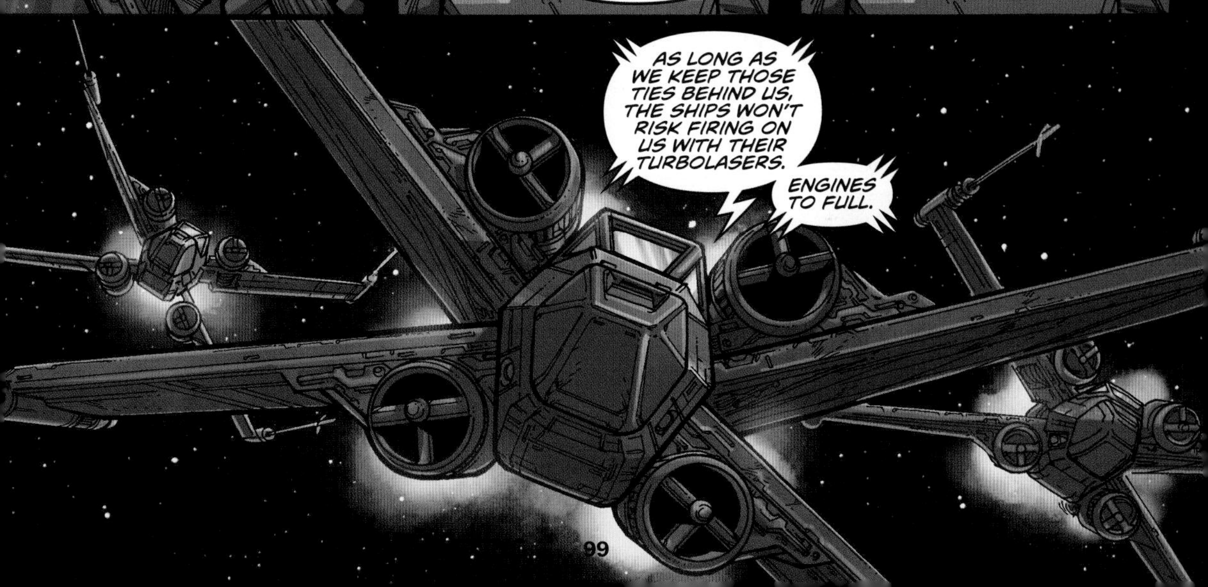
AS LONG AS WE KEEP THOSE TIES BEHIND US, THE SHIPS WON'T RISK FIRING ON US WITH THEIR TURBOLASERS.
ENGINES TO FULL.

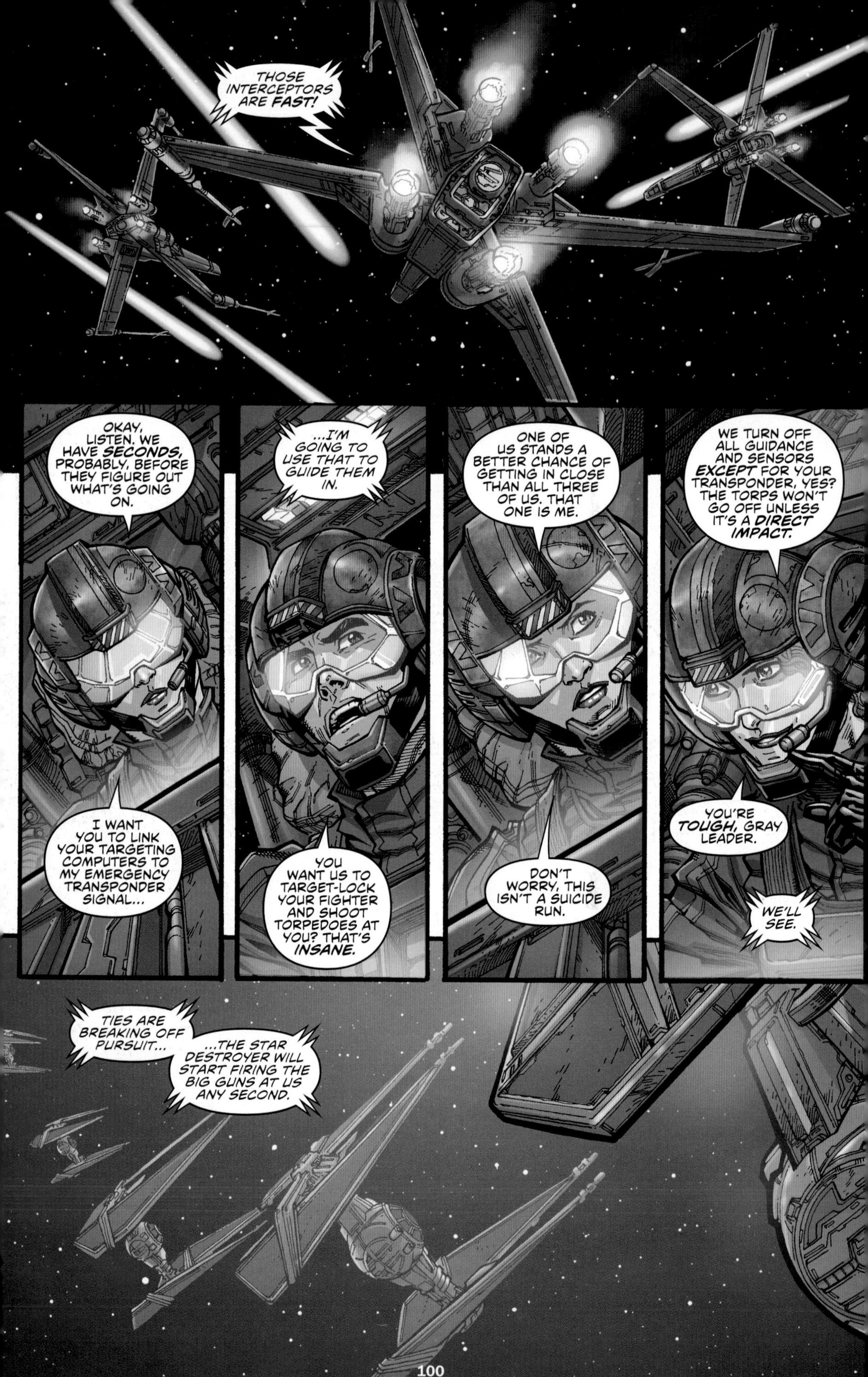
THOSE INTERCEPTORS ARE FAST!
OKAY, LISTEN. WE HAVE SECONDS, PROBABLY, BEFORE THEY FIGURE OUT WHAT'S GOING ON.
I WANT YOU TO LINK YOUR TARGETING COMPUTERS TO MY EMERGENCY TRANSPONDER SIGNAL...
...I'M GOING TO USE THAT TO GUIDE THEM IN.
YOU WANT US TO TARGET-LOCK YOUR FIGHTER AND SHOOT TORPEDOES AT YOU? THAT'S INSANE.
ONE OF US STANDS A BETTER CHANCE OF GETTING IN CLOSE THAN ALL THREE OF US. THAT ONE IS ME.
DON'T WORRY, THIS ISN'T A SUICIDE RUN.
WE TURN OFF ALL GUIDANCE AND SENSORS EXCEPT FOR YOUR TRANSPONDER, YES? THE TORPS WON'T GO OFF UNLESS IT'S A DIRECT IMPACT.
YOU'RE TOUGH, GRAY LEADER.
WE'LL SEE.
TIES ARE BREAKING OFF PURSUIT...
...THE STAR DESTROYER WILL START FIRING THE BIG GUNS AT US ANY SECOND.

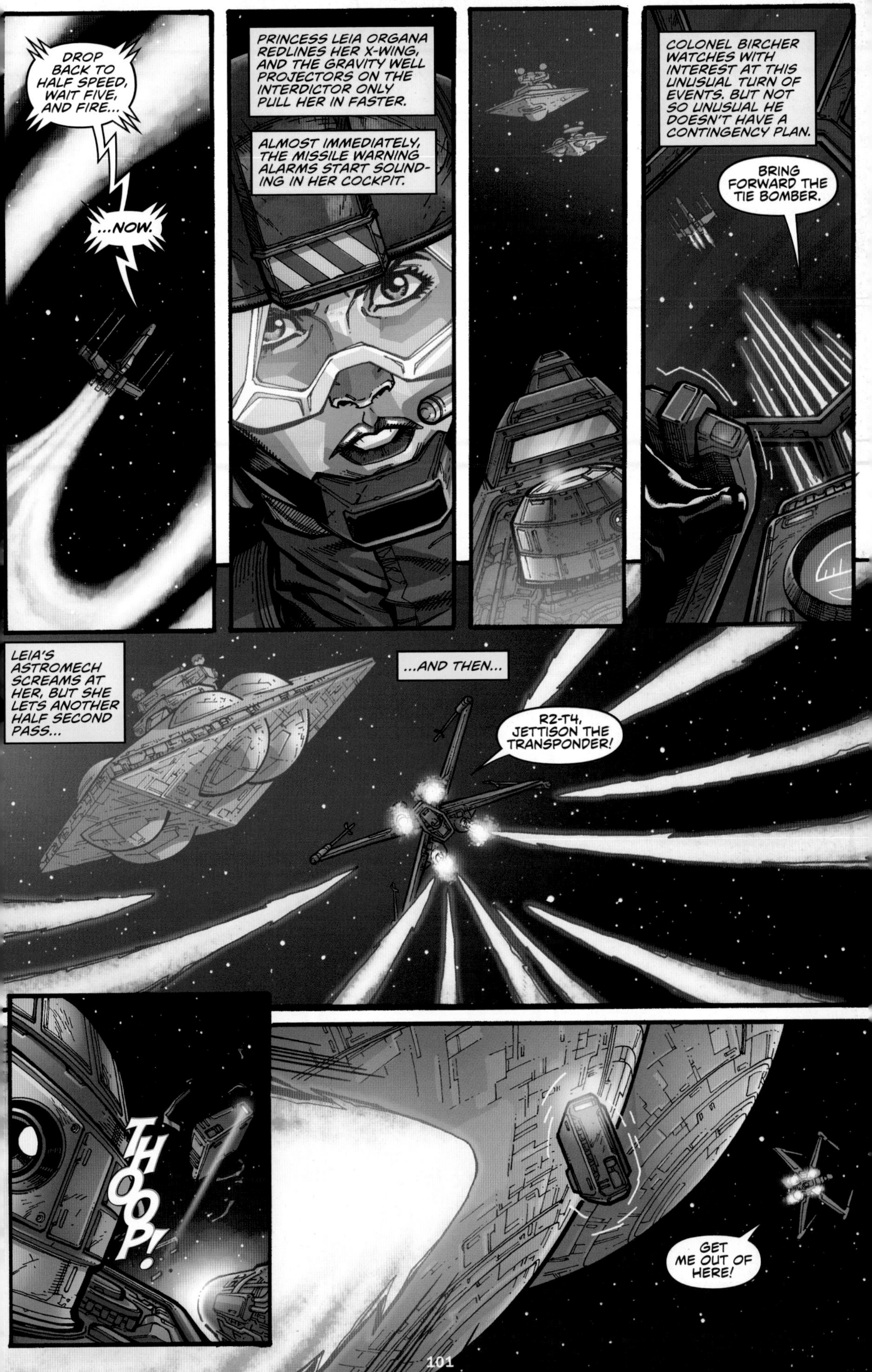
DROP BACK TO HALF SPEED, WAIT FIVE, AND FIRE...
...NOW.
PRINCESS LEIA ORGANA REDLINES HER X-WING, AND THE GRAVITY WELL PROJECTORS ON THE INTERDICTOR ONLY PULL HER IN FASTER.
ALMOST IMMEDIATELY, THE MISSILE WARNING ALARMS START SOUNDING IN HER COCKPIT.
COLONEL BIRCHER WATCHES WITH INTEREST AT THIS UNUSUAL TURN OF EVENTS. BUT NOT SO UNUSUAL HE DOESN'T HAVE A CONTINGENCY PLAN.
BRING FORWARD THE TIE BOMBER.
LEIA'S ASTROMECH SCREAMS AT HER, BUT SHE LETS ANOTHER HALF SECOND PASS...
...AND THEN...
R2-T4, JETTISON THE TRANSPONDER!
THOOP!
GET ME OUT OF HERE!

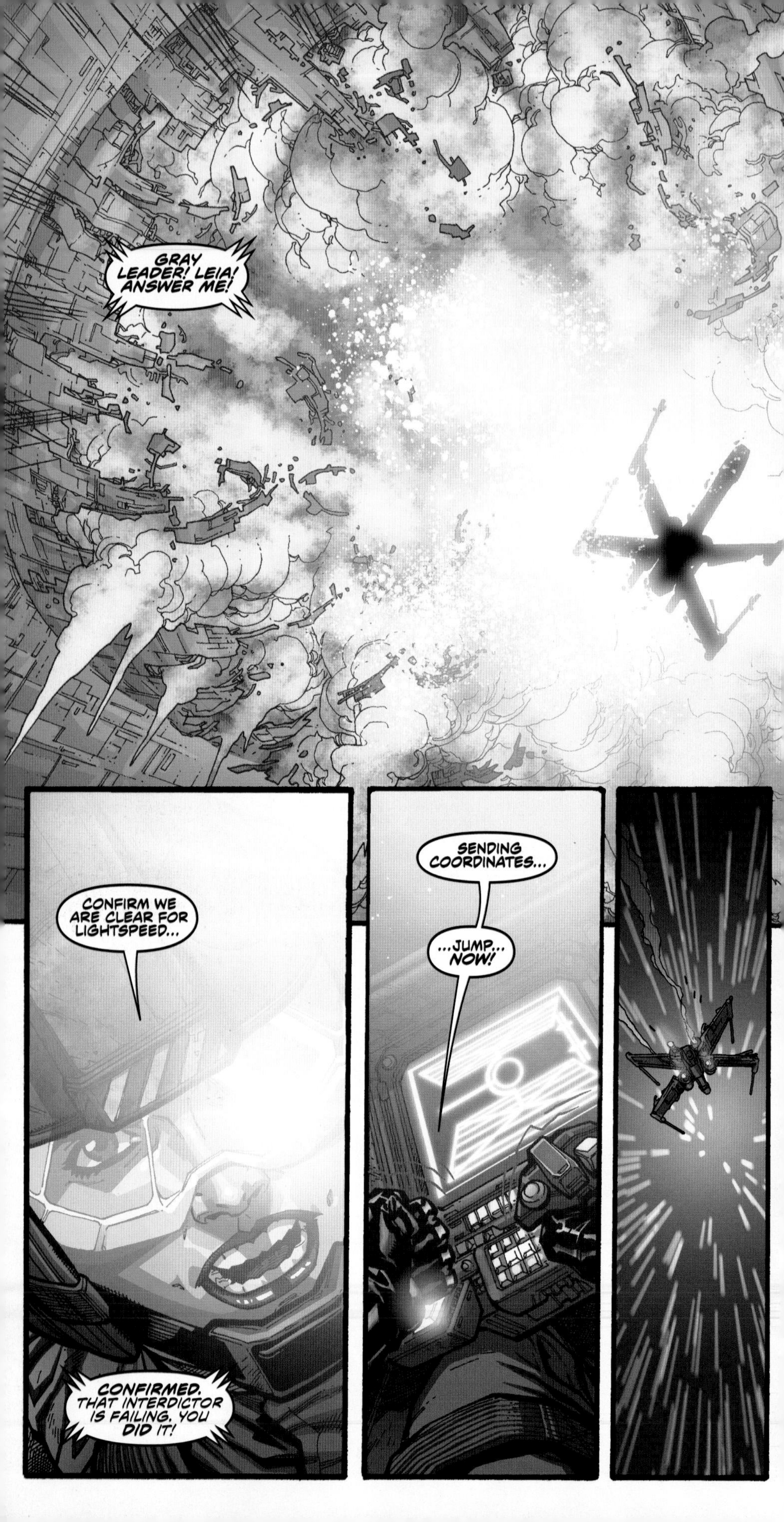
GRAY LEADER! LEIA! ANSWER ME!
CONFIRM WE ARE CLEAR FOR LIGHTSPEED...
CONFIRMED. THAT INTERDICTOR IS FAILING. YOU DID IT!
SENDING COORDINATES...
...JUMP... NOW!

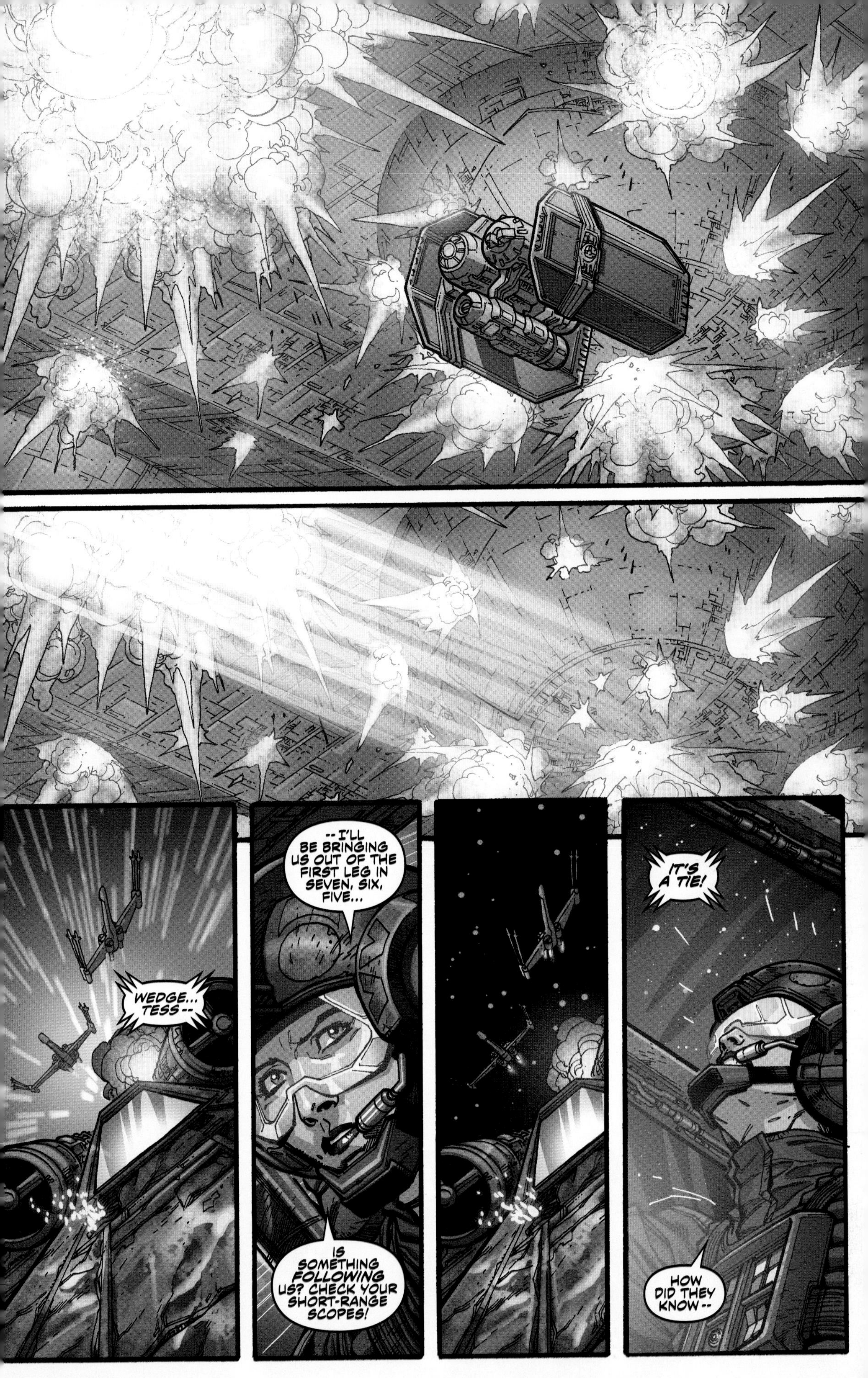
WEDGE... TESS --
-- I'LL BE BRINGING US OUT OF THE FIRST LEG IN SEVEN, SIX, FIVE...
IS SOMETHING FOLLOWING US? CHECK YOUR SHORT-RANGE SCOPES!
IT'S A TIE!
HOW DID THEY KNOW --

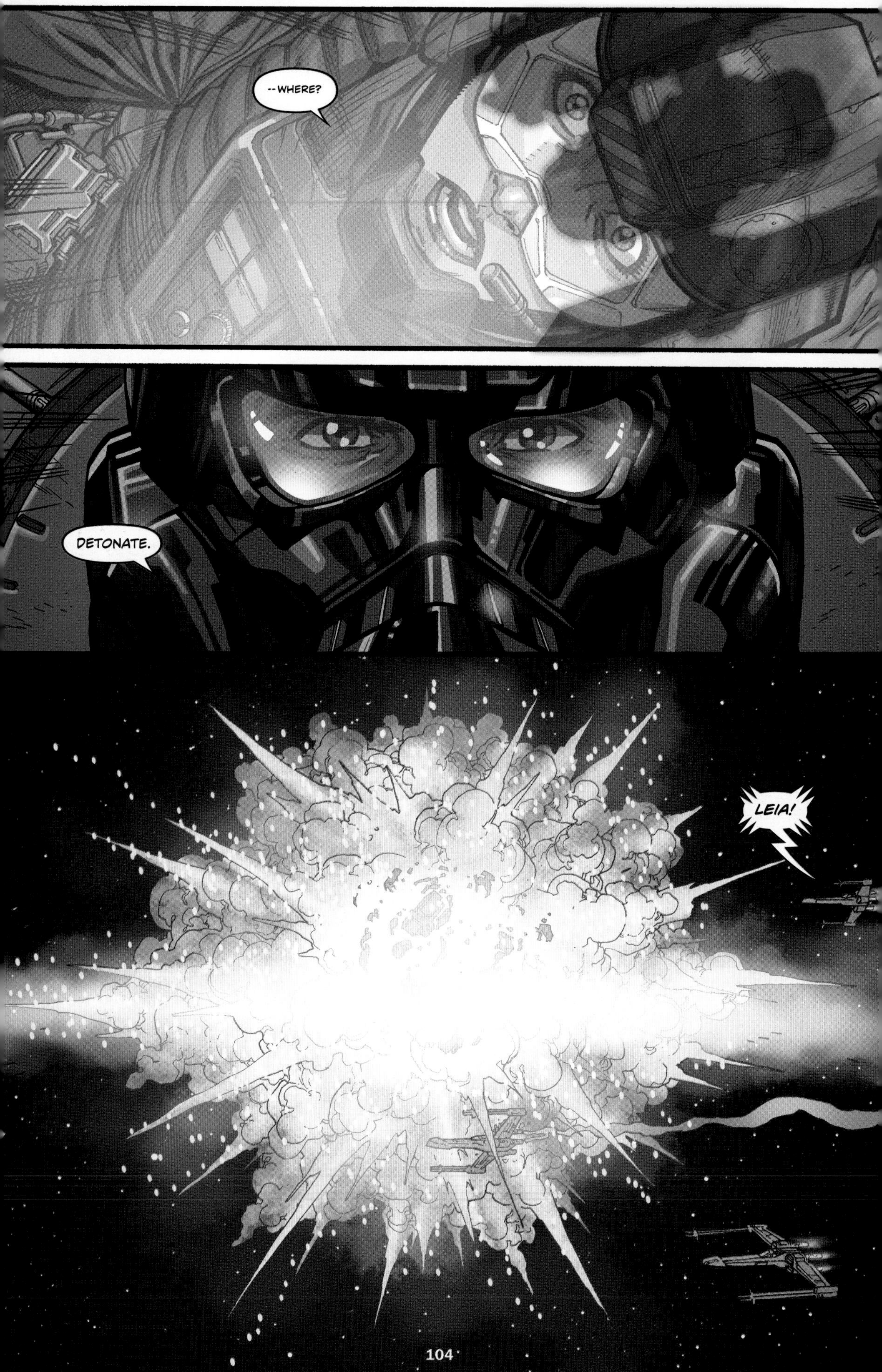
--WHERE?
DETONATE.
LEIA!

IMPERIAL CENTER.

THE CORUSCANT UNDERWORLD.

ALL I'M *SAYING*, CHEWIE, IS I DON'T *TRUST* THAT GUY.

I'VE DOCKED THE *FALCON* IN SOME ROUGH SPOTS IN THE PAST, BUT YOU COULD PRACTICALLY SEE HIM DISMANTLING HER WITH HIS EYES.

WE BETTER HAVE A PLAN SOON, OR WE'RE GONNA BECOME *PERMANENT RESIDENTS* OF THIS PLACE.

RWUFF WUFF

YOU CAN SAY *THAT* AGAIN.

LOOK, I NEED TO GET OUT OF SIGHT. THINK YOU CAN HANDLE INQUIRIES ON YOUR OWN?

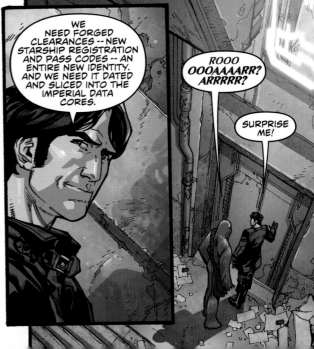

WE NEED FORGED CLEARANCES -- NEW STARSHIP REGISTRATION AND PASS CODES -- AN ENTIRE NEW IDENTITY, AND WE NEED IT DATED AND SLICED INTO THE IMPERIAL DATA CORES.

ROOO OOOAAAARR? ARRRRR?

SURPRISE ME!

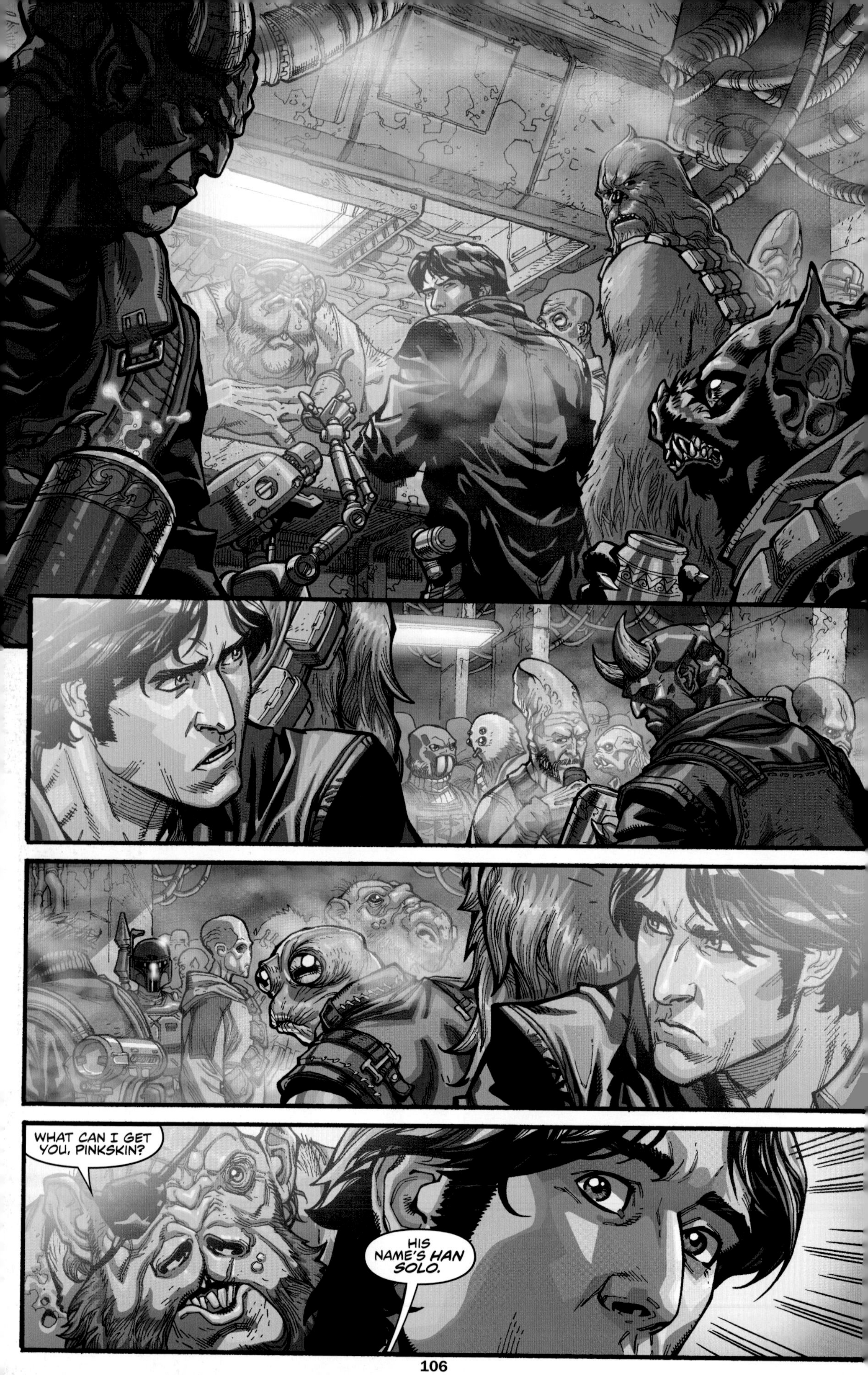
WHAT CAN I GET YOU, PINKSKIN?
HIS NAME'S HAN SOLO.

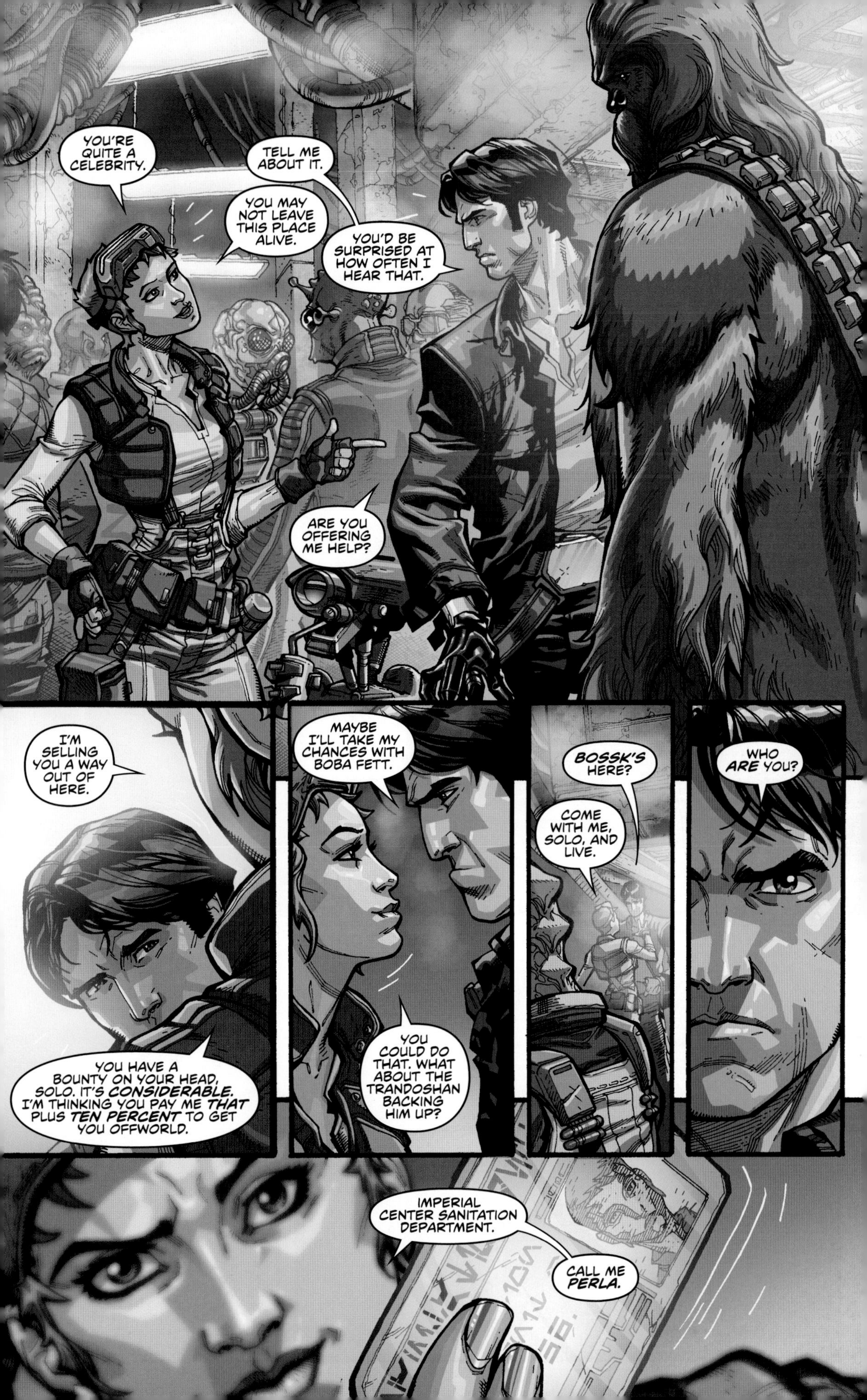
YOU'RE QUITE A CELEBRITY.
TELL ME ABOUT IT.
YOU MAY NOT LEAVE THIS PLACE ALIVE.
YOU'D BE SURPRISED AT HOW OFTEN I HEAR THAT.
ARE YOU OFFERING ME HELP?
I'M SELLING YOU A WAY OUT OF HERE.
YOU HAVE A BOUNTY ON YOUR HEAD, SOLO. IT'S *CONSIDERABLE*. I'M THINKING YOU PAY ME *THAT* PLUS *TEN PERCENT* TO GET YOU OFFWORLD.
MAYBE I'LL TAKE MY CHANCES WITH BOBA FETT.
YOU COULD DO THAT. WHAT ABOUT THE TRANDOSHAN BACKING HIM UP?
BOSSK'S HERE?
COME WITH ME, SOLO, AND LIVE.
WHO *ARE* YOU?
IMPERIAL CENTER SANITATION DEPARTMENT.
CALL ME *PERLA*.

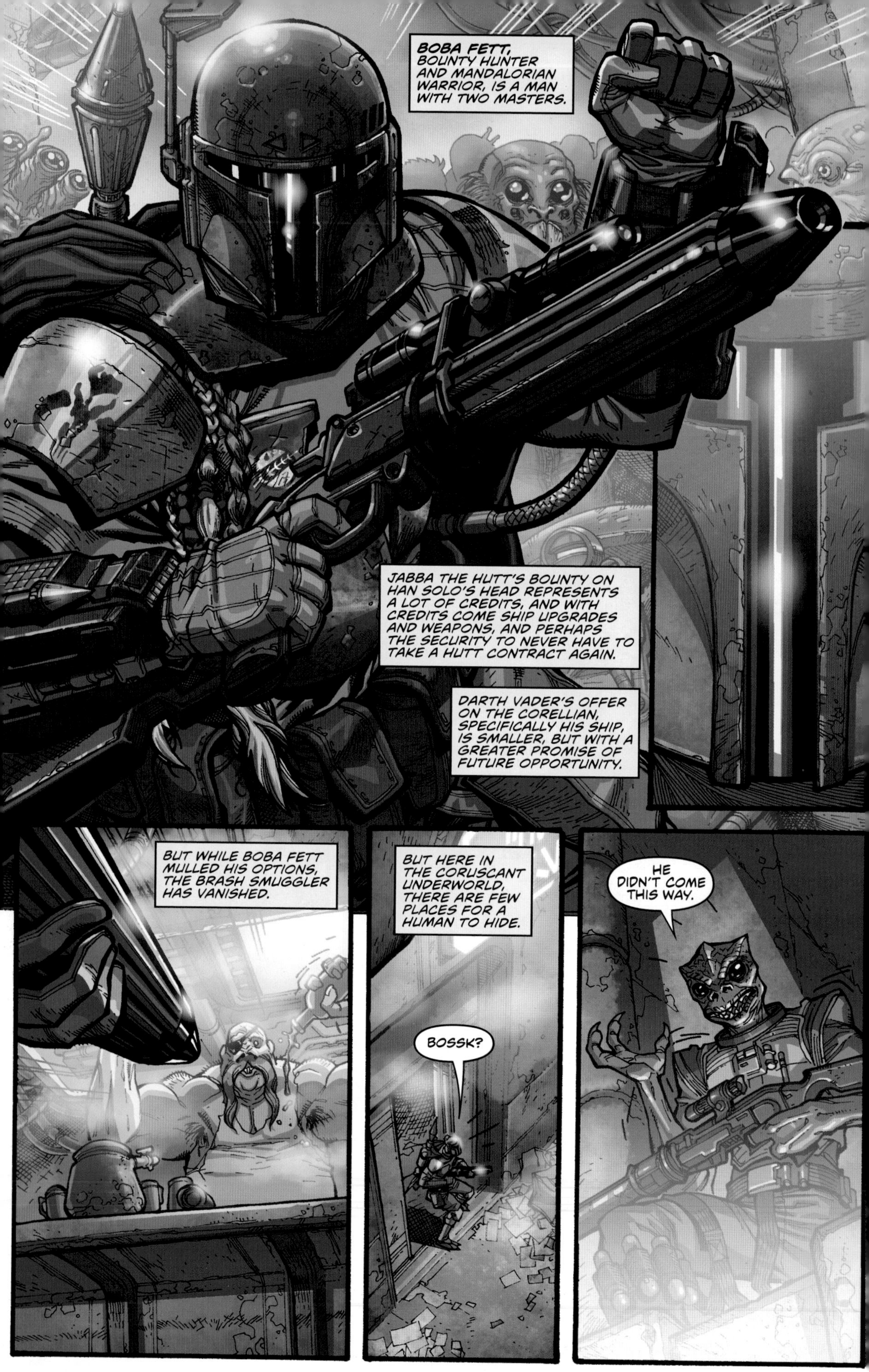
BOBA FETT, BOUNTY HUNTER AND MANDALORIAN WARRIOR, IS A MAN WITH TWO MASTERS.
JABBA THE HUTT'S BOUNTY ON HAN SOLO'S HEAD REPRESENTS A LOT OF CREDITS, AND WITH CREDITS COME SHIP UPGRADES AND WEAPONS, AND PERHAPS THE SECURITY TO NEVER HAVE TO TAKE A HUTT CONTRACT AGAIN.
DARTH VADER'S OFFER ON THE CORELLIAN, SPECIFICALLY HIS SHIP, IS SMALLER, BUT WITH A GREATER PROMISE OF FUTURE OPPORTUNITY.
BUT WHILE BOBA FETT MULLED HIS OPTIONS, THE BRASH SMUGGLER HAS VANISHED.
BUT HERE IN THE CORUSCANT UNDERWORLD, THERE ARE FEW PLACES FOR A HUMAN TO HIDE.
BOSSK?
HE DIDN'T COME THIS WAY.

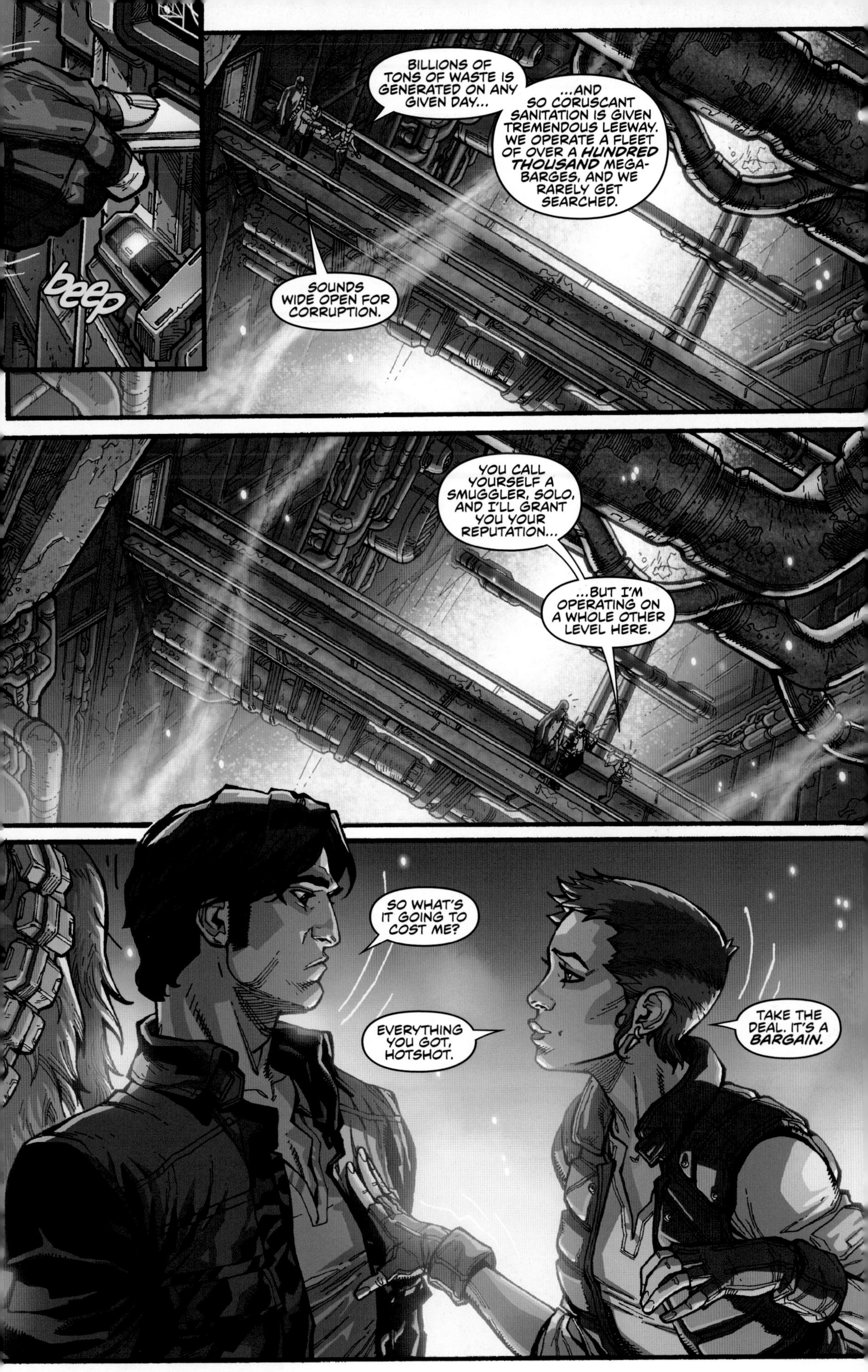
BILLIONS OF TONS OF WASTE IS GENERATED ON ANY GIVEN DAY...
...AND SO CORUSCANT SANITATION IS GIVEN TREMENDOUS LEEWAY. WE OPERATE A FLEET OF OVER A ***HUNDRED THOUSAND*** MEGA-BARGES, AND WE RARELY GET SEARCHED.
beep
SOUNDS WIDE OPEN FOR CORRUPTION.
YOU CALL YOURSELF A SMUGGLER, SOLO, AND I'LL GRANT YOU YOUR REPUTATION...
...BUT I'M OPERATING ON A WHOLE OTHER LEVEL HERE.
SO WHAT'S IT GOING TO COST ME?
EVERYTHING YOU GOT, HOTSHOT.
TAKE THE DEAL. IT'S A ***BARGAIN.***

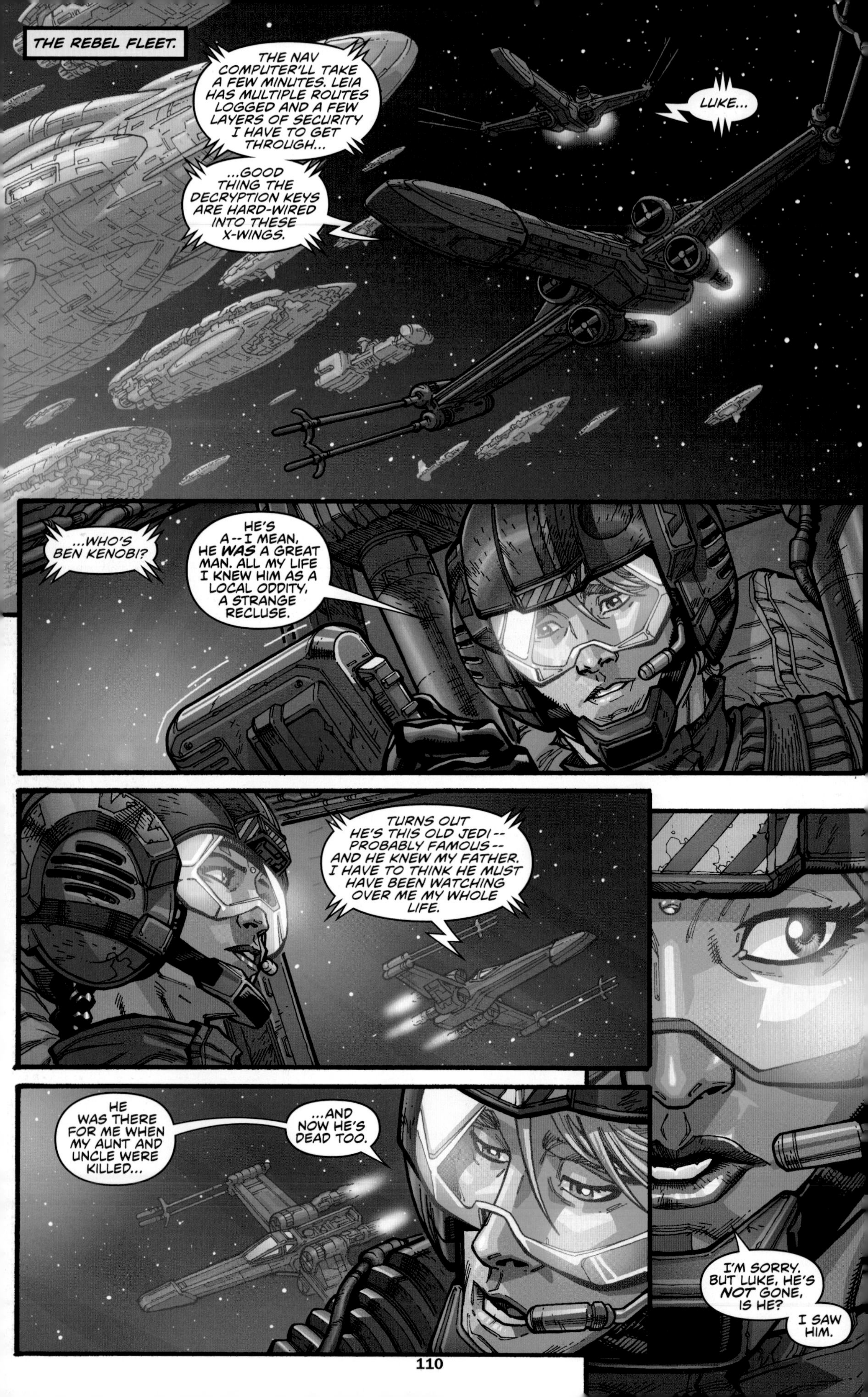
THE REBEL FLEET.
THE NAV COMPUTER'LL TAKE A FEW MINUTES. LEIA HAS MULTIPLE ROUTES LOGGED AND A FEW LAYERS OF SECURITY I HAVE TO GET THROUGH...
...GOOD THING THE DECRYPTION KEYS ARE HARD-WIRED INTO THESE X-WINGS.
LUKE...
...WHO'S BEN KENOBI?
HE'S A-- I MEAN, HE WAS A GREAT MAN. ALL MY LIFE I KNEW HIM AS A LOCAL ODDITY, A STRANGE RECLUSE.
TURNS OUT HE'S THIS OLD JEDI -- PROBABLY FAMOUS -- AND HE KNEW MY FATHER. I HAVE TO THINK HE MUST HAVE BEEN WATCHING OVER ME MY WHOLE LIFE.
HE WAS THERE FOR ME WHEN MY AUNT AND UNCLE WERE KILLED...
...AND NOW HE'S DEAD TOO.
I'M SORRY. BUT LUKE, HE'S NOT GONE, IS HE?
I SAW HIM.

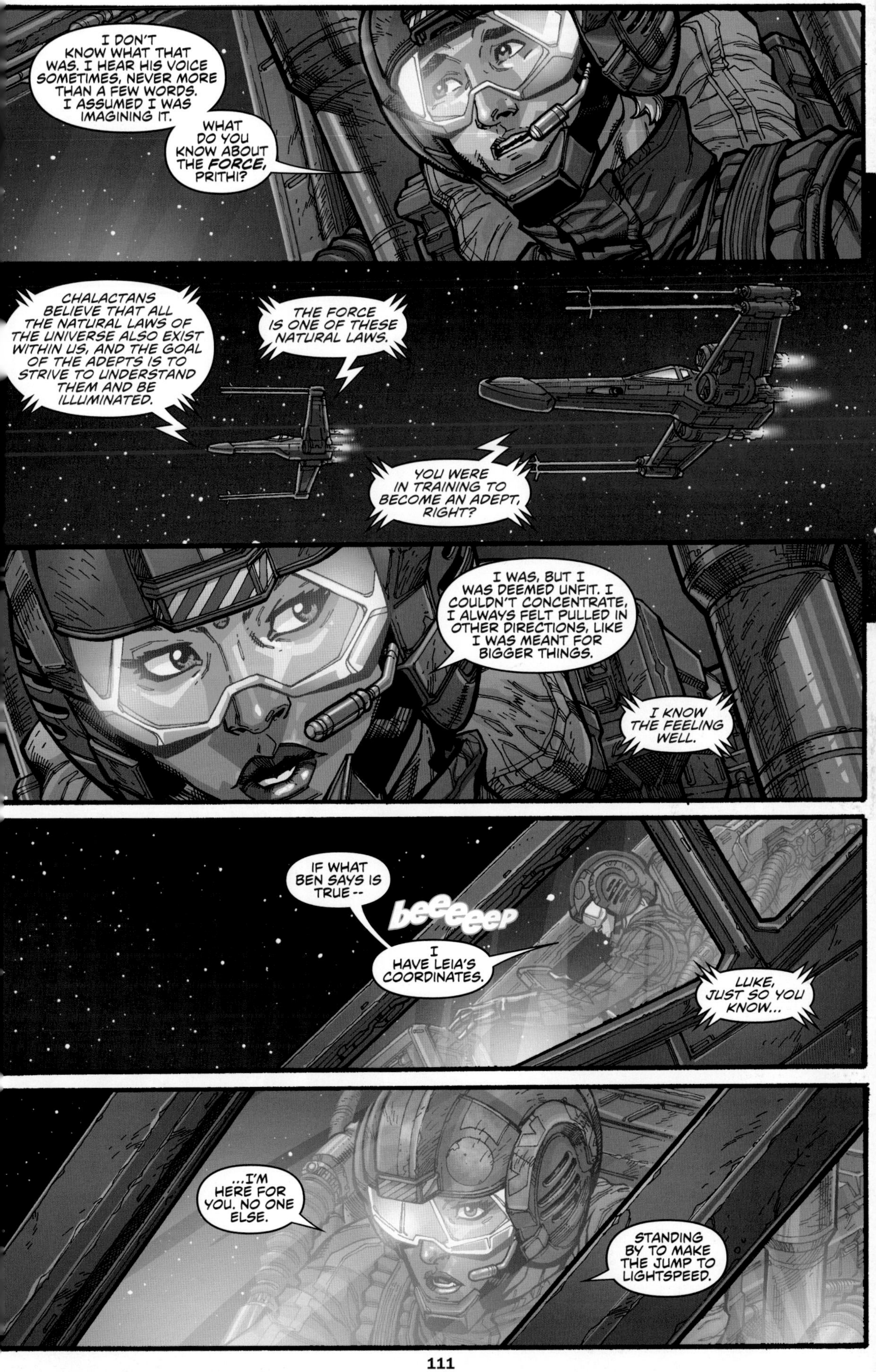
I DON'T KNOW WHAT THAT WAS. I HEAR HIS VOICE SOMETIMES, NEVER MORE THAN A FEW WORDS. I ASSUMED I WAS IMAGINING IT.
WHAT DO YOU KNOW ABOUT THE FORCE, PRITHI?
CHALACTANS BELIEVE THAT ALL THE NATURAL LAWS OF THE UNIVERSE ALSO EXIST WITHIN US, AND THE GOAL OF THE ADEPTS IS TO STRIVE TO UNDERSTAND THEM AND BE ILLUMINATED.
THE FORCE IS ONE OF THESE NATURAL LAWS.
YOU WERE IN TRAINING TO BECOME AN ADEPT, RIGHT?
I WAS, BUT I WAS DEEMED UNFIT. I COULDN'T CONCENTRATE, I ALWAYS FELT PULLED IN OTHER DIRECTIONS, LIKE I WAS MEANT FOR BIGGER THINGS.
I KNOW THE FEELING WELL.
IF WHAT BEN SAYS IS TRUE --
beeeeeep
I HAVE LEIA'S COORDINATES.
LUKE, JUST SO YOU KNOW...
...I'M HERE FOR YOU. NO ONE ELSE.
STANDING BY TO MAKE THE JUMP TO LIGHTSPEED.

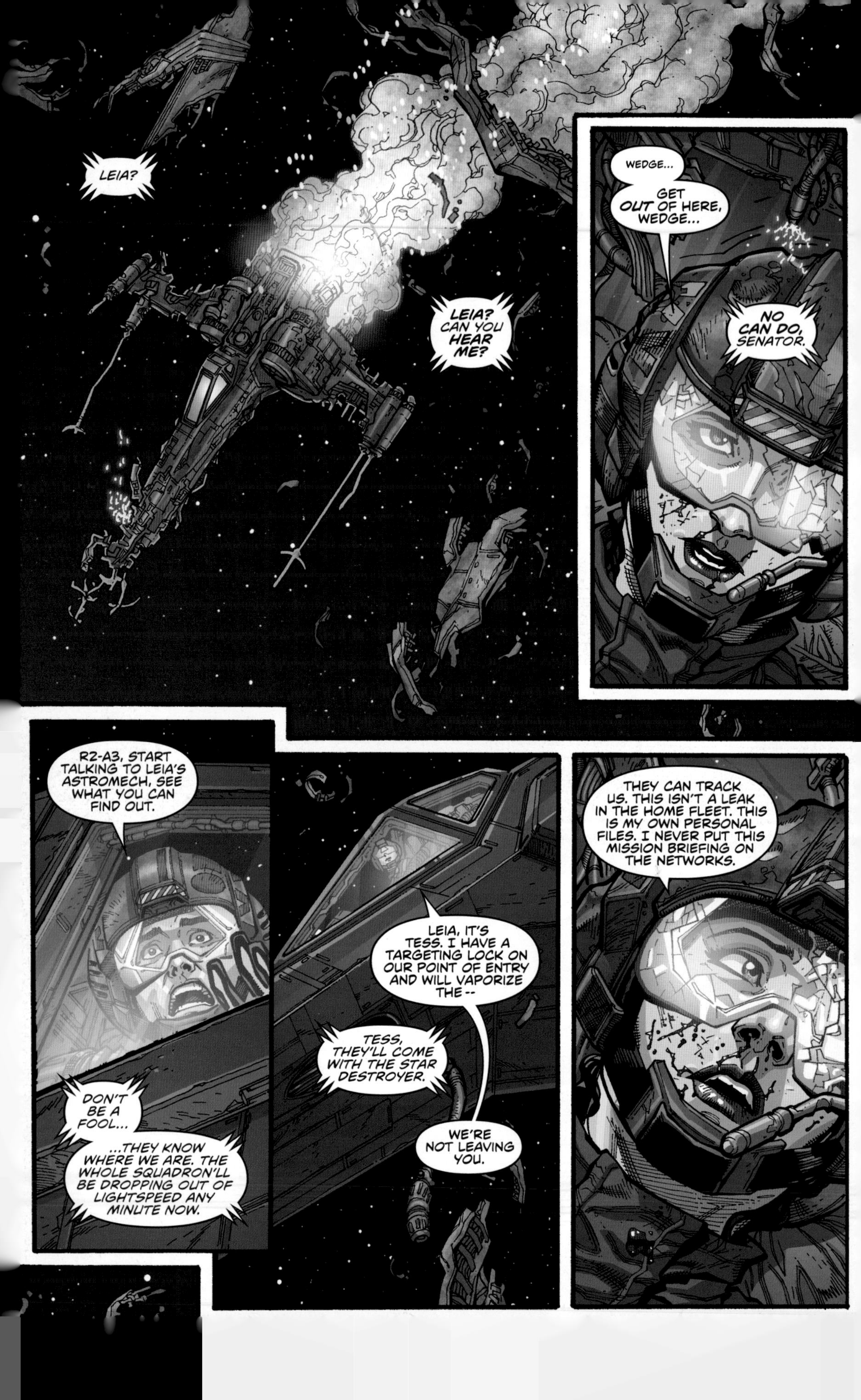
LEIA?
LEIA? CAN YOU HEAR ME?
WEDGE...
GET OUT OF HERE, WEDGE...
NO CAN DO, SENATOR.
R2-A3, START TALKING TO LEIA'S ASTROMECH, SEE WHAT YOU CAN FIND OUT.
DON'T BE A FOOL...
...THEY KNOW WHERE WE ARE. THE WHOLE SQUADRON'LL BE DROPPING OUT OF LIGHTSPEED ANY MINUTE NOW.
LEIA, IT'S TESS. I HAVE A TARGETING LOCK ON OUR POINT OF ENTRY AND WILL VAPORIZE THE --
TESS, THEY'LL COME WITH THE STAR DESTROYER.
WE'RE NOT LEAVING YOU.
THEY CAN TRACK US. THIS ISN'T A LEAK IN THE HOME FLEET. THIS IS MY OWN PERSONAL FILES. I NEVER PUT THIS MISSION BRIEFING ON THE NETWORKS.

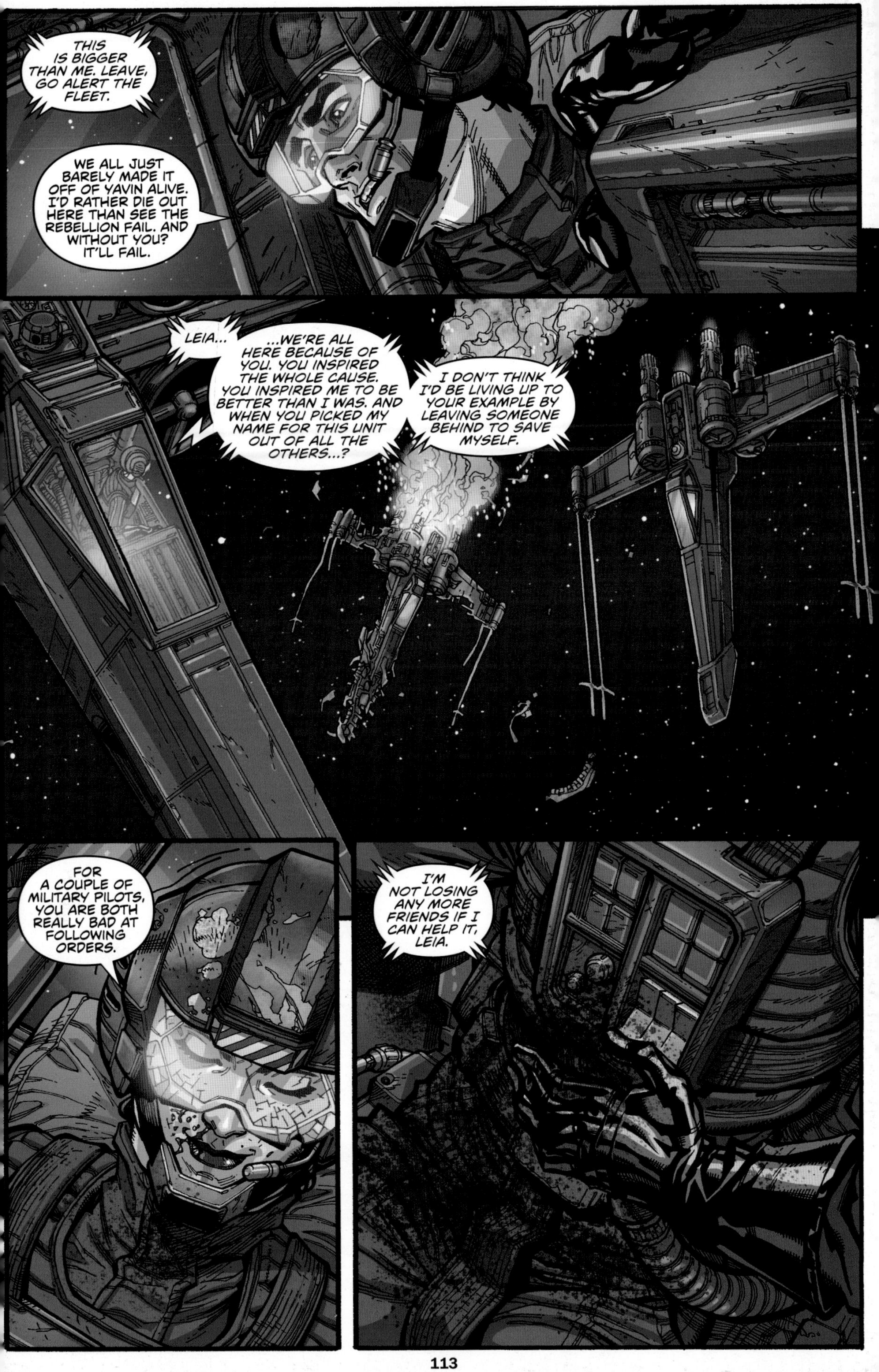
THIS IS BIGGER THAN ME. LEAVE, GO ALERT THE FLEET.
WE ALL JUST BARELY MADE IT OFF OF YAVIN ALIVE. I'D RATHER DIE OUT HERE THAN SEE THE REBELLION FAIL. AND WITHOUT YOU? IT'LL FAIL.
LEIA...
...WE'RE ALL HERE BECAUSE OF YOU. YOU INSPIRED THE WHOLE CAUSE. YOU INSPIRED ME TO BE BETTER THAN I WAS. AND WHEN YOU PICKED MY NAME FOR THIS UNIT OUT OF ALL THE OTHERS...?
I DON'T THINK I'D BE LIVING UP TO YOUR EXAMPLE BY LEAVING SOMEONE BEHIND TO SAVE MYSELF.
FOR A COUPLE OF MILITARY PILOTS, YOU ARE BOTH REALLY BAD AT FOLLOWING ORDERS.
I'M NOT LOSING ANY MORE FRIENDS IF I CAN HELP IT, LEIA.

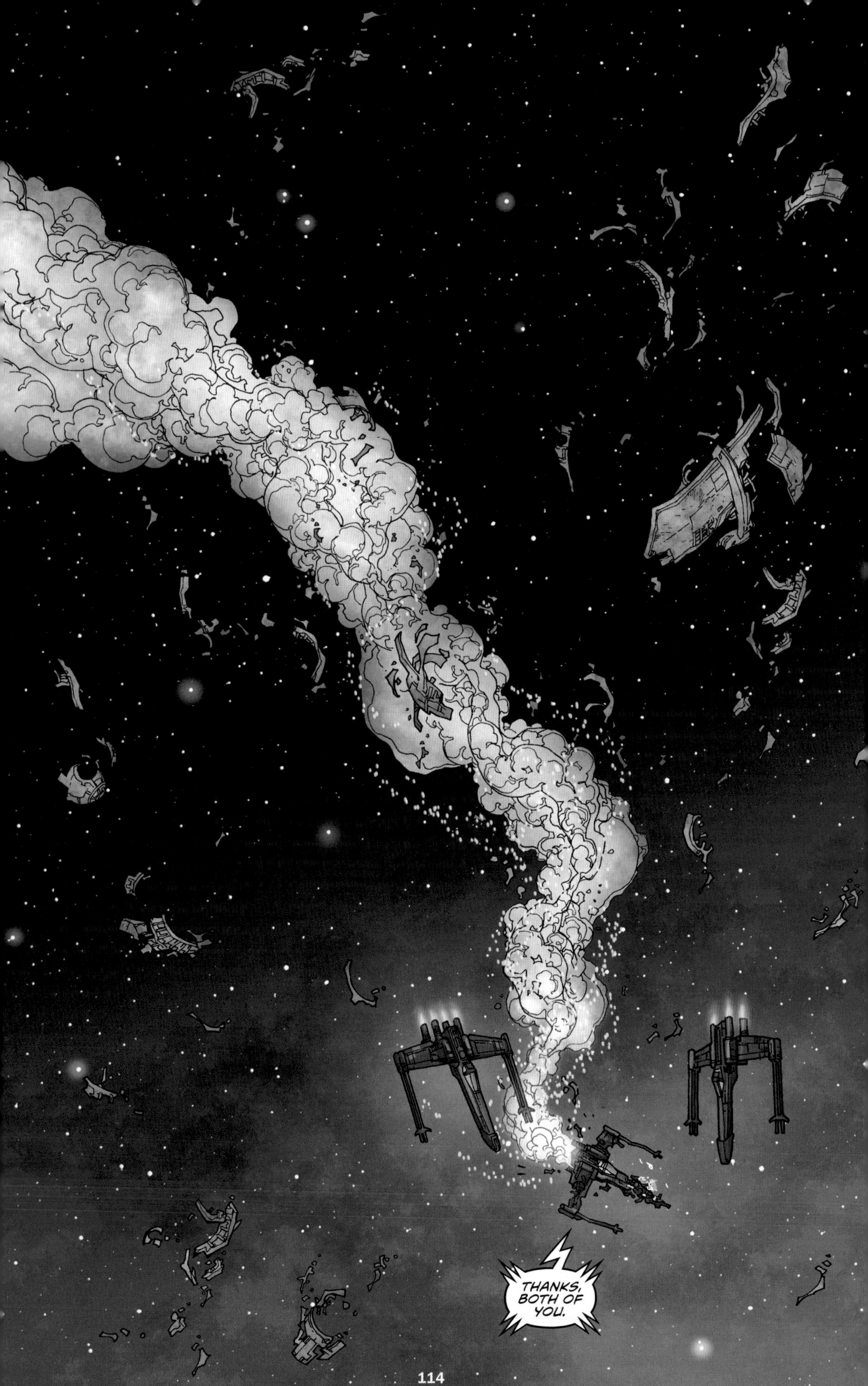
THANKS, BOTH OF YOU.

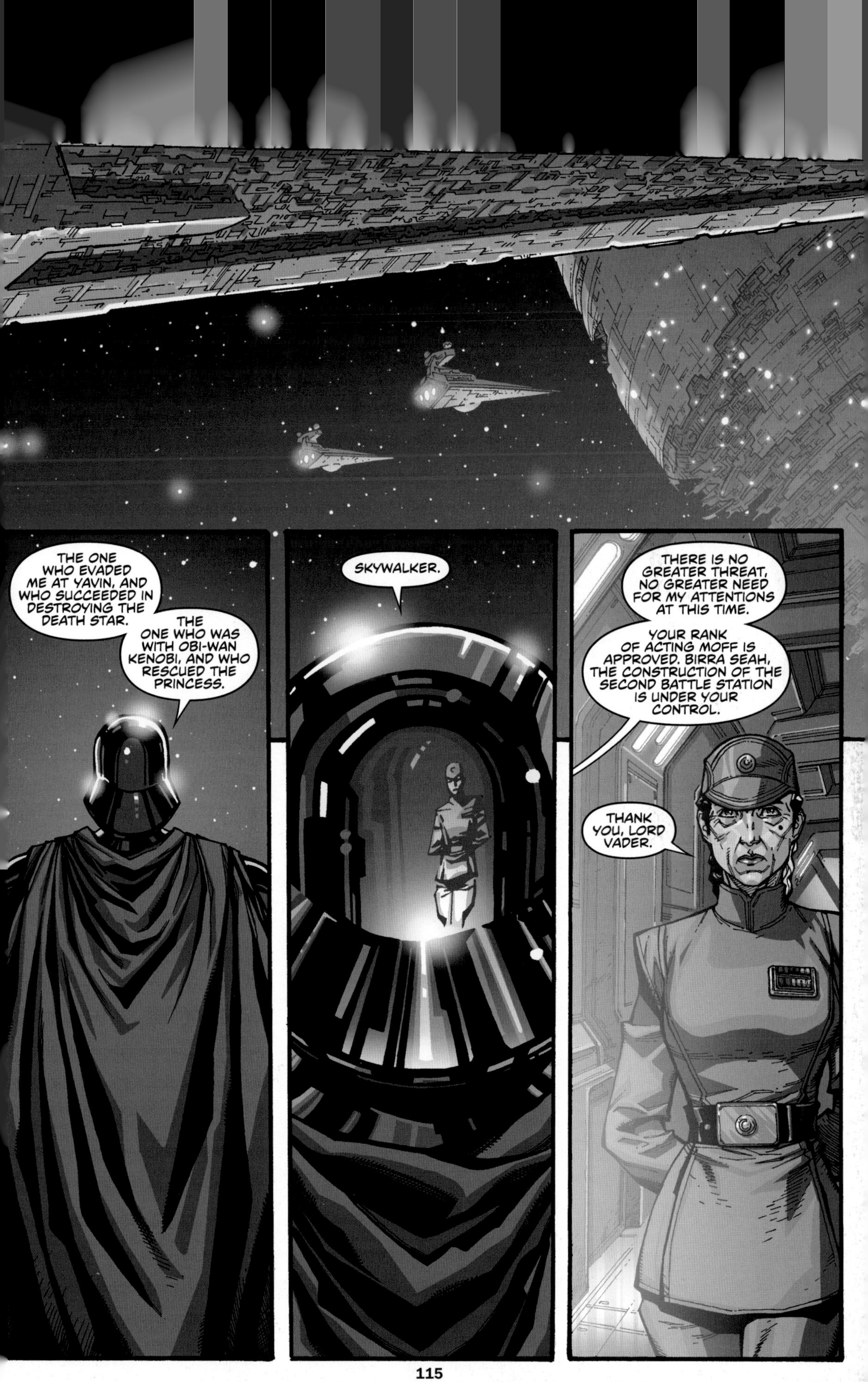

THE ONE WHO EVADED ME AT YAVIN, AND WHO SUCCEEDED IN DESTROYING THE DEATH STAR.
THE ONE WHO WAS WITH OBI-WAN KENOBI, AND WHO RESCUED THE PRINCESS.
SKYWALKER.
THERE IS NO GREATER THREAT, NO GREATER NEED FOR MY ATTENTIONS AT THIS TIME.
YOUR RANK OF ACTING MOFF IS APPROVED. BIRRA SEAH, THE CONSTRUCTION OF THE SECOND BATTLE STATION IS UNDER YOUR CONTROL.
THANK YOU, LORD VADER.

AND UPON THE EMPEROR'S ARRIVAL, YOU WILL BRIEF HIM ON YOUR PROGRESS.
PRAY IT IS TO HIS SATISFACTION. FAILURE AT THIS POINT WILL MEAN A FATE FROM WHICH NEITHER I, NOR THE FORCE, CAN PROTECT YOU.
Gabe

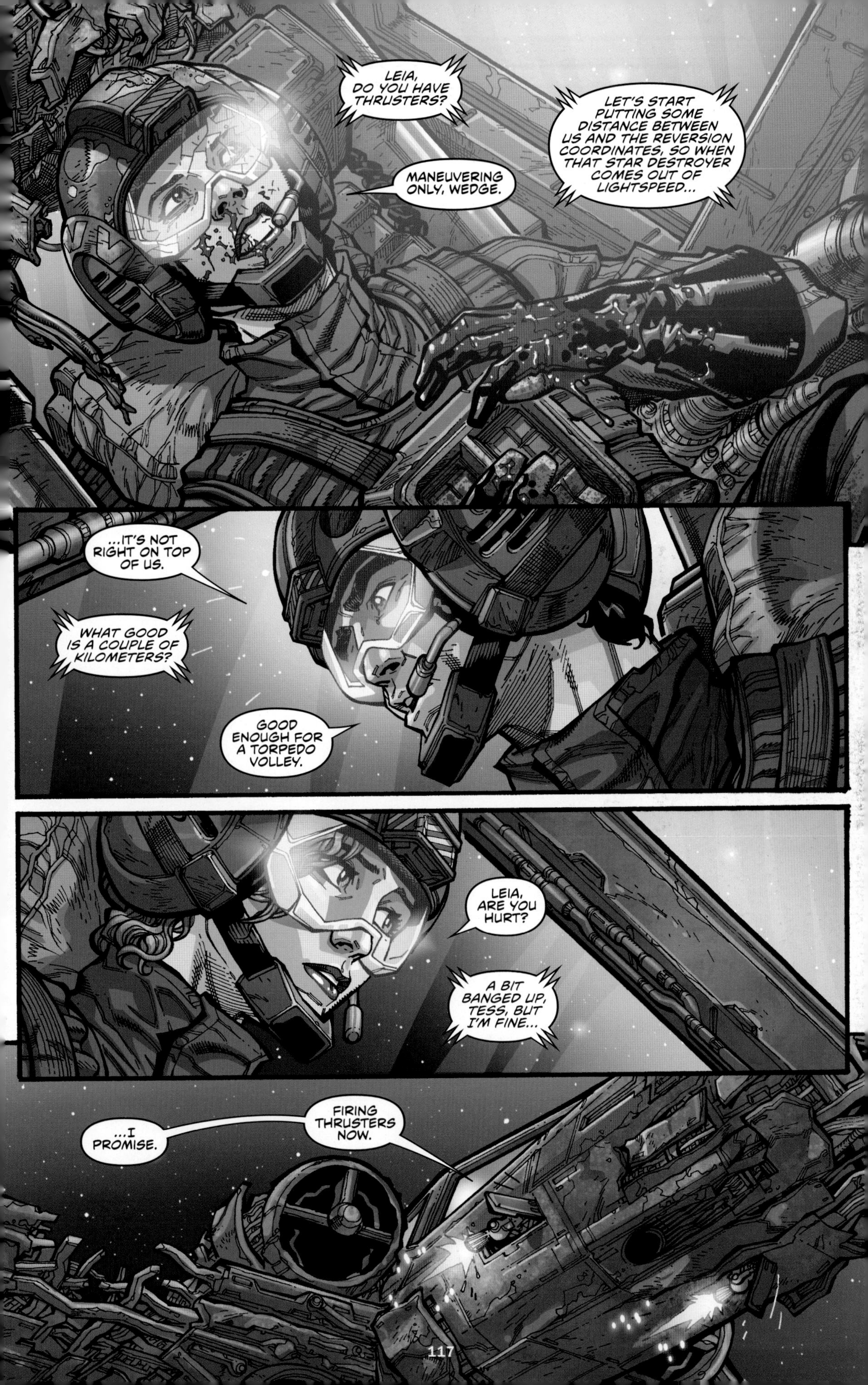
LEIA, DO YOU HAVE THRUSTERS?
MANEUVERING ONLY, WEDGE.
LET'S START PUTTING SOME DISTANCE BETWEEN US AND THE REVERSION COORDINATES, SO WHEN THAT STAR DESTROYER COMES OUT OF LIGHTSPEED...
...IT'S NOT RIGHT ON TOP OF US.
WHAT GOOD IS A COUPLE OF KILOMETERS?
GOOD ENOUGH FOR A TORPEDO VOLLEY.
LEIA, ARE YOU HURT?
A BIT BANGED UP, TESS, BUT I'M FINE...
...I PROMISE.
FIRING THRUSTERS NOW.

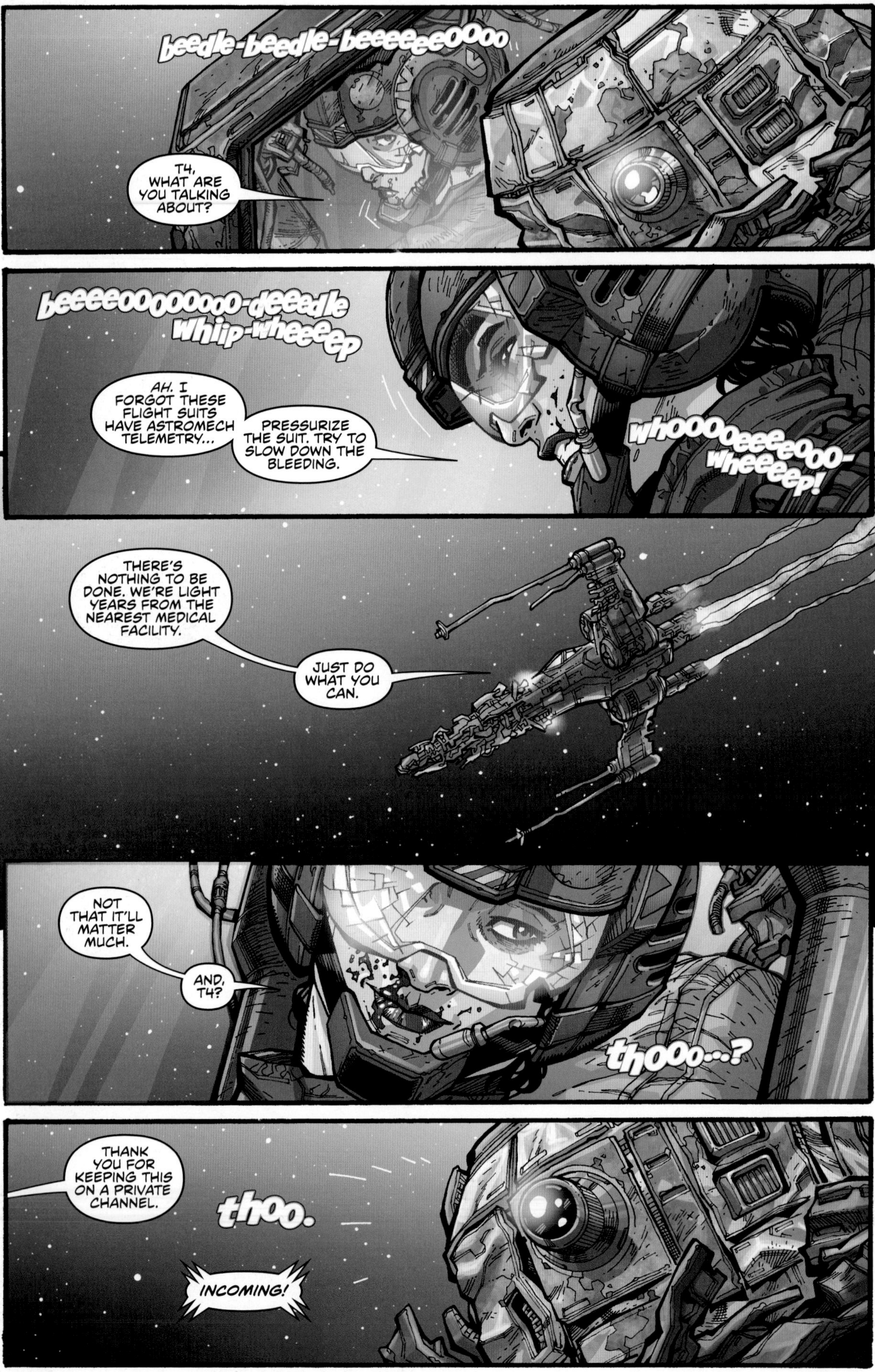
beedle-beedle-beeeeeeOOOo
T4, WHAT ARE YOU TALKING ABOUT?
beeeeOOOOOOOO-deeedle whiip-wheeeeep
AH. I FORGOT THESE FLIGHT SUITS HAVE ASTROMECH TELEMETRY...
PRESSURIZE THE SUIT. TRY TO SLOW DOWN THE BLEEDING.
whoooOeeeeOOO-wheeeep!
THERE'S NOTHING TO BE DONE. WE'RE LIGHT YEARS FROM THE NEAREST MEDICAL FACILITY.
JUST DO WHAT YOU CAN.
NOT THAT IT'LL MATTER MUCH.
AND, T4?
thOOo...?
THANK YOU FOR KEEPING THIS ON A PRIVATE CHANNEL.
thoo.
INCOMING!

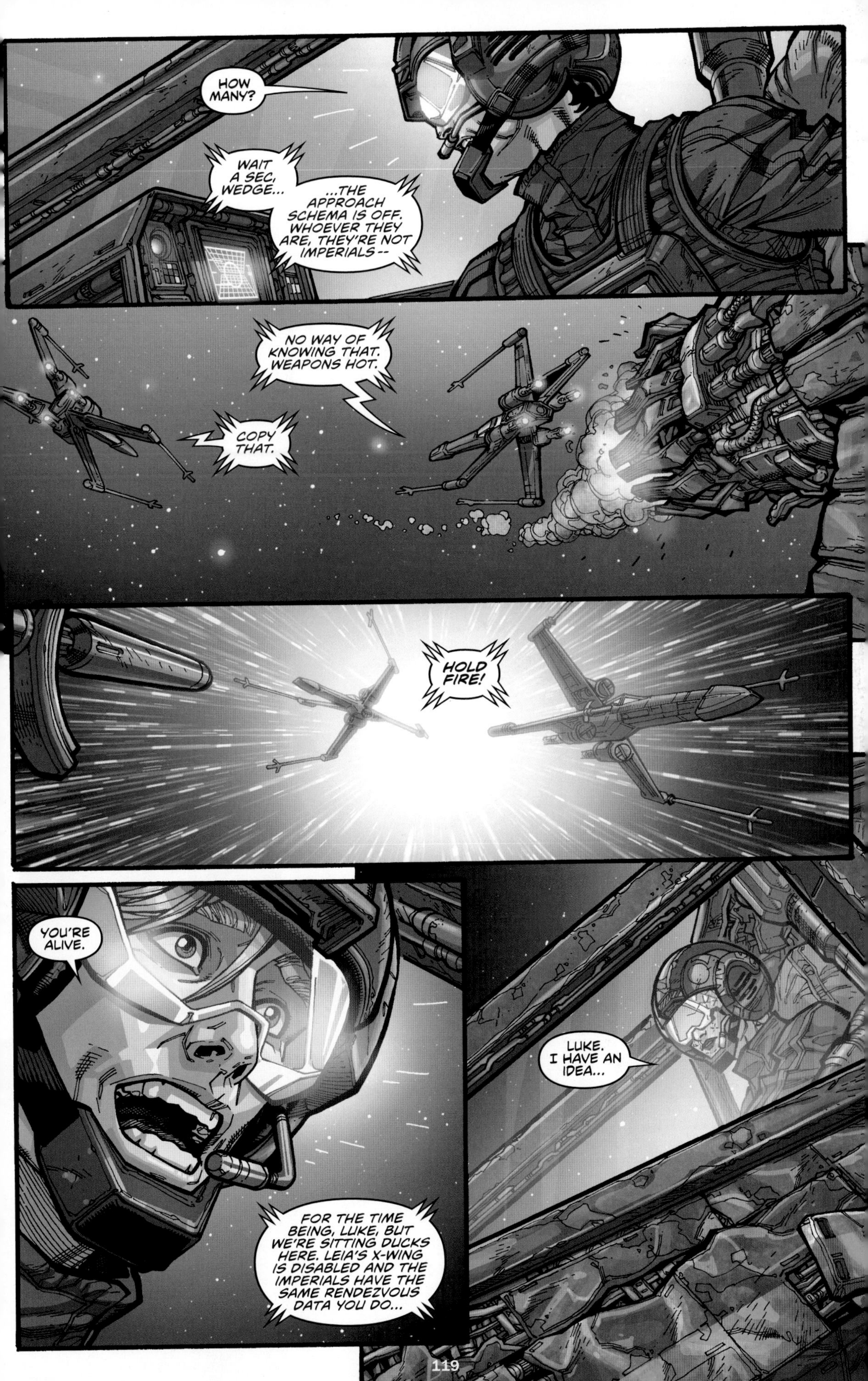
HOW MANY?
WAIT A SEC, WEDGE...
...THE APPROACH SCHEMA IS OFF. WHOEVER THEY ARE, THEY'RE NOT IMPERIALS--
NO WAY OF KNOWING THAT. WEAPONS HOT.
COPY THAT.
HOLD FIRE!
YOU'RE ALIVE.
FOR THE TIME BEING, LUKE, BUT WE'RE SITTING DUCKS HERE. LEIA'S X-WING IS DISABLED AND THE IMPERIALS HAVE THE SAME RENDEZVOUS DATA YOU DO...
LUKE. I HAVE AN IDEA...

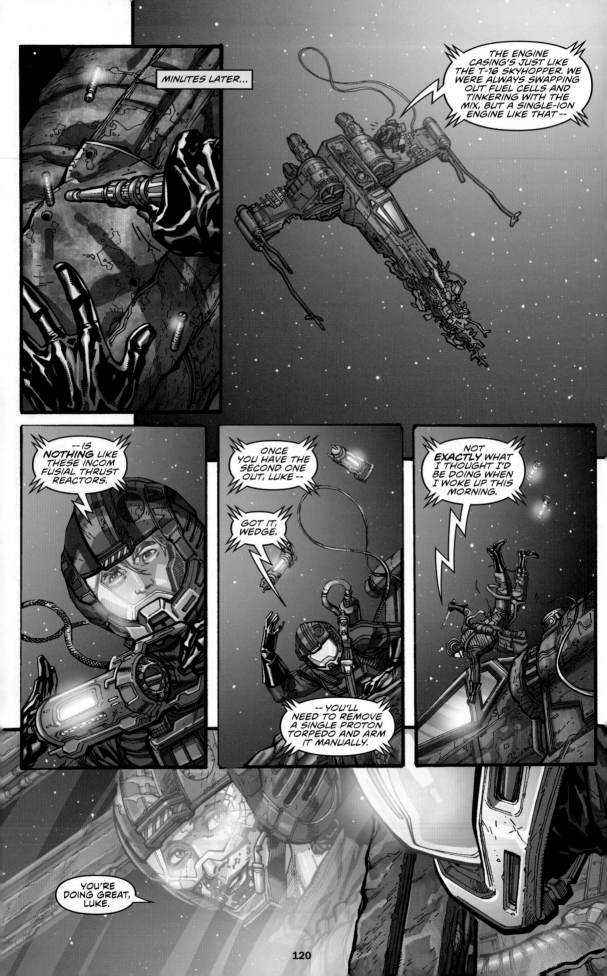

MINUTES LATER...

THE ENGINE CASING'S JUST LIKE THE T-16 SKYHOPPER. WE WERE ALWAYS SWAPPING OUT FUEL CELLS AND TINKERING WITH THE MIX, BUT A SINGLE-ION ENGINE LIKE THAT--

--IS **NOTHING** LIKE THESE INCOM FUSIAL THRUST REACTORS.

ONCE YOU HAVE THE SECOND ONE OUT, LUKE--

GOT IT, WEDGE.

--YOU'LL NEED TO REMOVE A SINGLE PROTON TORPEDO AND ARM IT MANUALLY.

NOT **EXACTLY** WHAT I THOUGHT I'D BE DOING WHEN I WOKE UP THIS MORNING.

YOU'RE DOING GREAT, LUKE.

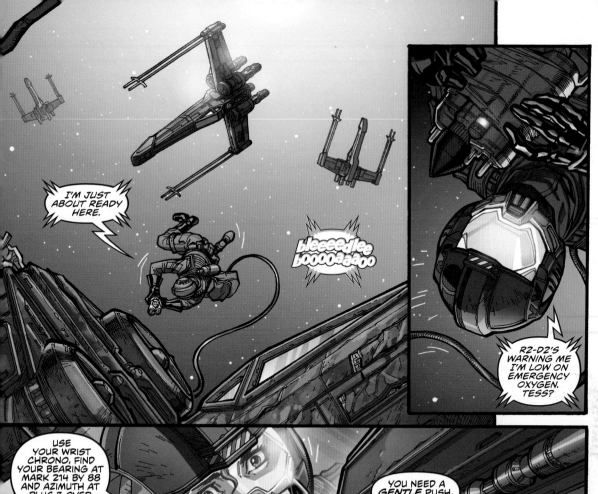

I'M JUST ABOUT READY HERE.

bleeeedlee booooaaaoo

R2-D2'S WARNING ME I'M LOW ON EMERGENCY OXYGEN. TESS?

USE YOUR WRIST CHRONO, FIND YOUR BEARING AT MARK 214 BY 88 AND AZIMUTH AT PLUS 7 OVER NULL.

GOT IT...

YOU NEED A GENTLE PUSH, LUKE --

-- LIKE BRUSHING LINT OFF YOUR SHIRT.

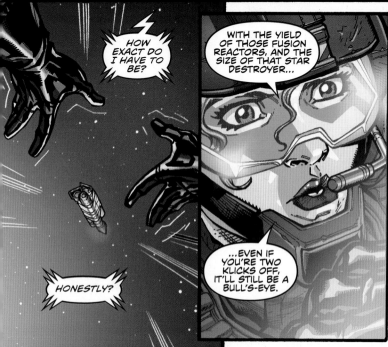

HOW EXACT DO I HAVE TO BE?

WITH THE YIELD OF THOSE FUSION REACTORS, AND THE SIZE OF THAT STAR DESTROYER...

...EVEN IF YOU'RE TWO KLICKS OFF, IT'LL STILL BE A BULL'S-EYE.

HONESTLY?

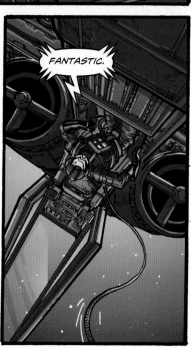

FANTASTIC.

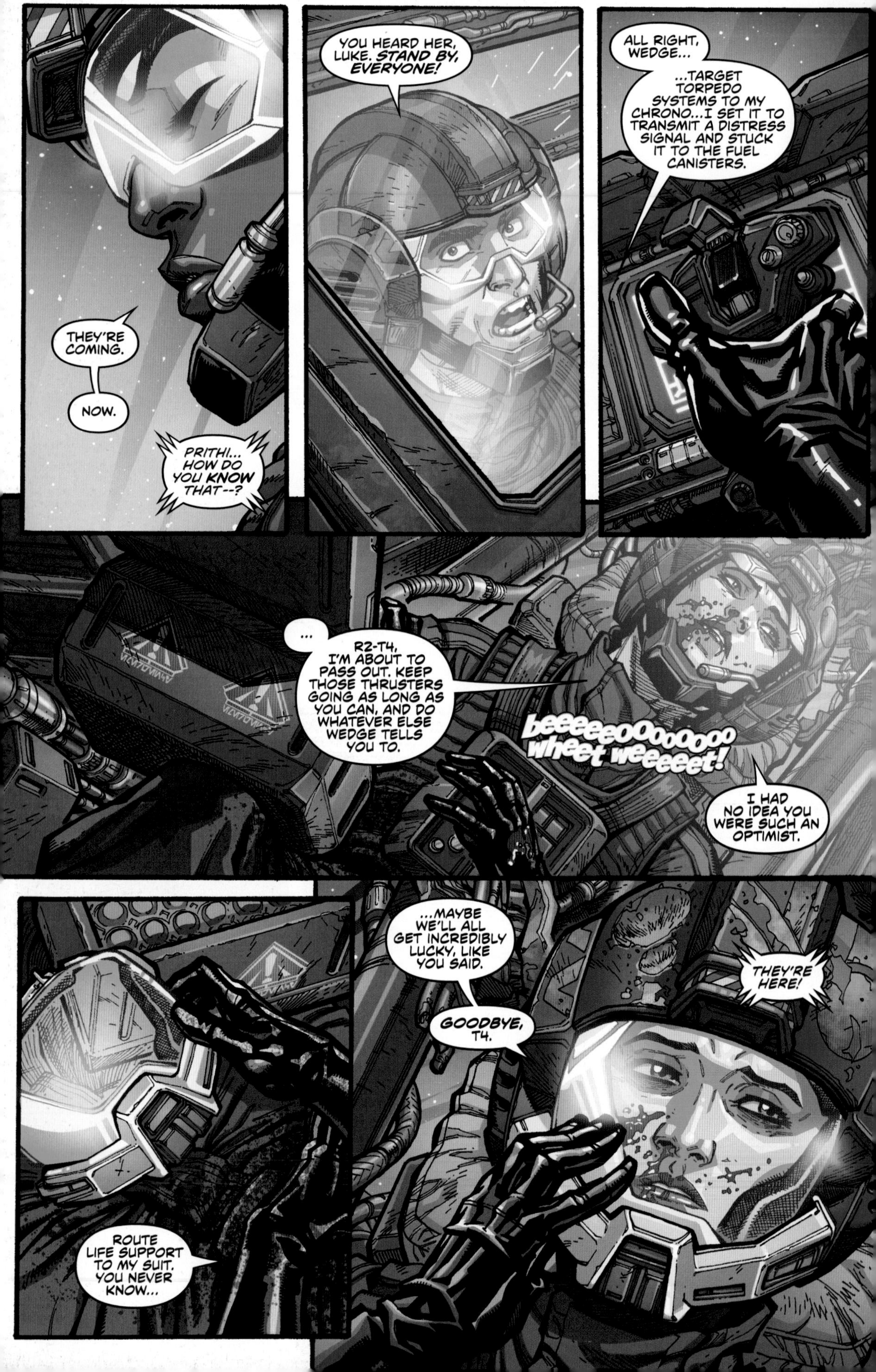
THEY'RE COMING.
NOW.
PRITHI... HOW DO YOU KNOW THAT--?
YOU HEARD HER, LUKE. STAND BY, EVERYONE!
ALL RIGHT, WEDGE...
...TARGET TORPEDO SYSTEMS TO MY CHRONO...I SET IT TO TRANSMIT A DISTRESS SIGNAL AND STUCK IT TO THE FUEL CANISTERS.
...
R2-T4, I'M ABOUT TO PASS OUT. KEEP THOSE THRUSTERS GOING AS LONG AS YOU CAN, AND DO WHATEVER ELSE WEDGE TELLS YOU TO.
beeeeeeoooooooo wheet weeeeeet!
I HAD NO IDEA YOU WERE SUCH AN OPTIMIST.
ROUTE LIFE SUPPORT TO MY SUIT. YOU NEVER KNOW...
...MAYBE WE'LL ALL GET INCREDIBLY LUCKY, LIKE YOU SAID.
GOODBYE, T4.
THEY'RE HERE!

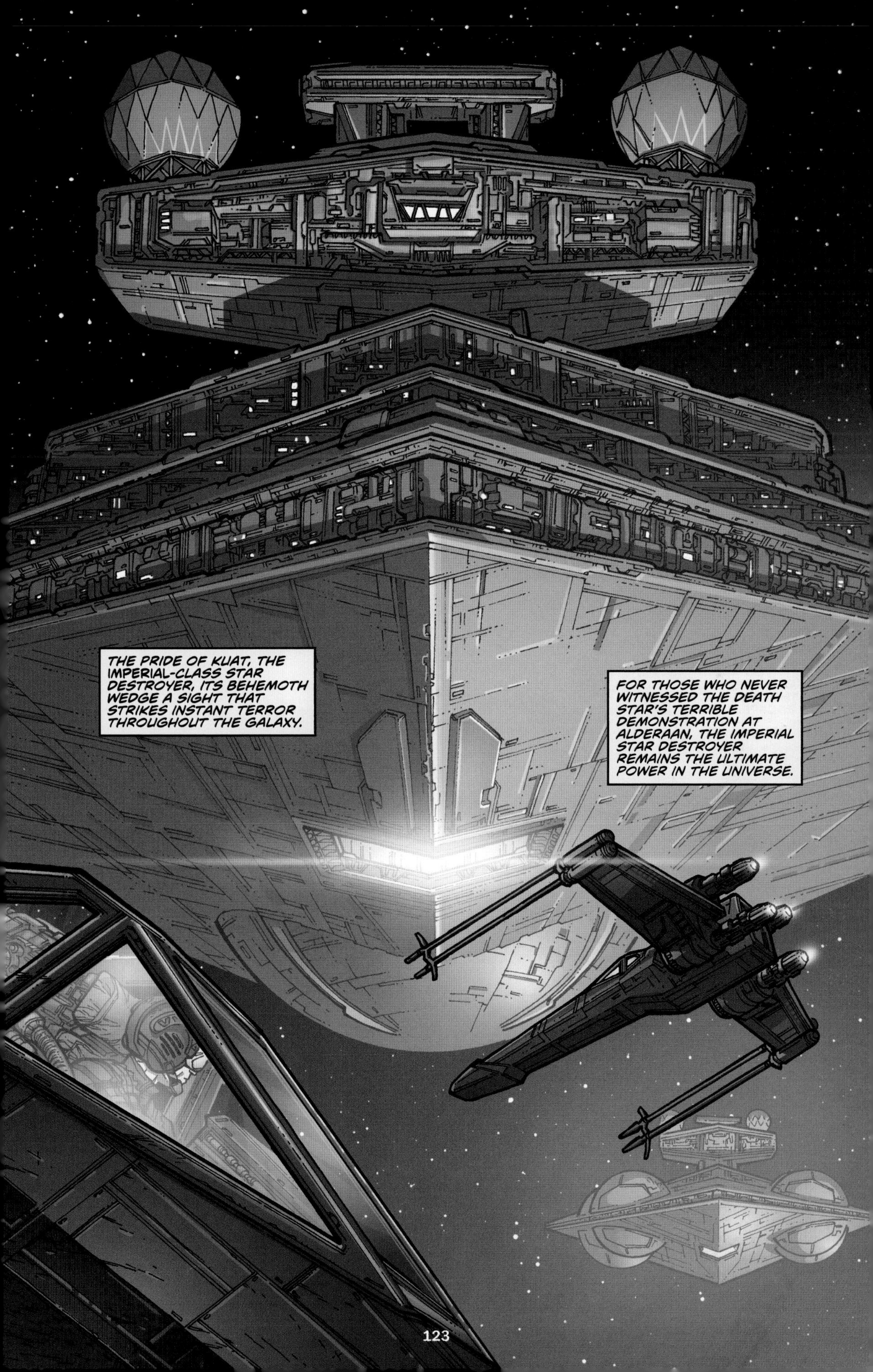
THE PRIDE OF KUAT, THE IMPERIAL-CLASS STAR DESTROYER, ITS BEHEMOTH WEDGE A SIGHT THAT STRIKES INSTANT TERROR THROUGHOUT THE GALAXY.
FOR THOSE WHO NEVER WITNESSED THE DEATH STAR'S TERRIBLE DEMONSTRATION AT ALDERAAN, THE IMPERIAL STAR DESTROYER REMAINS THE ULTIMATE POWER IN THE UNIVERSE.

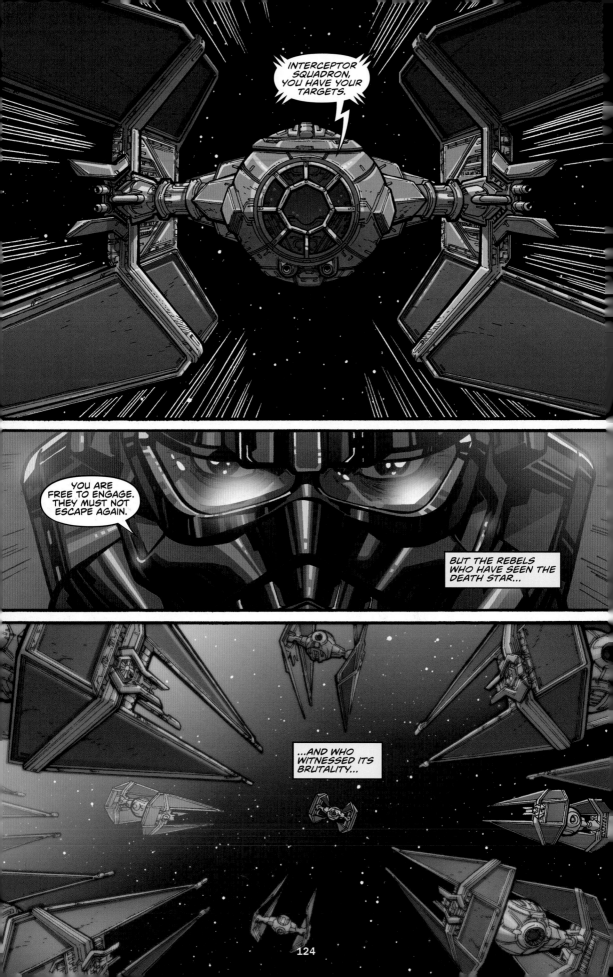

INTERCEPTOR SQUADRON, YOU HAVE YOUR TARGETS.

YOU ARE FREE TO ENGAGE. THEY MUST NOT ESCAPE AGAIN.

BUT THE REBELS WHO HAVE SEEN THE DEATH STAR...

...AND WHO WITNESSED ITS BRUTALITY...

...THEY KNOW NOTHING IS UNBEATABLE.

FIRE.

THEY'VE MISSED...

TIE COMMAND, THIS IS DEVASTATOR. WE ARE TRACKING INCOMING TORPEDOES FOUR POINTS TO STARBOARD. CONFIRM?

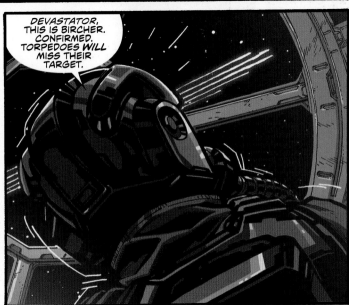

DEVASTATOR, THIS IS BIRCHER. CONFIRMED. TORPEDOES *WILL* MISS THEIR TARGET.

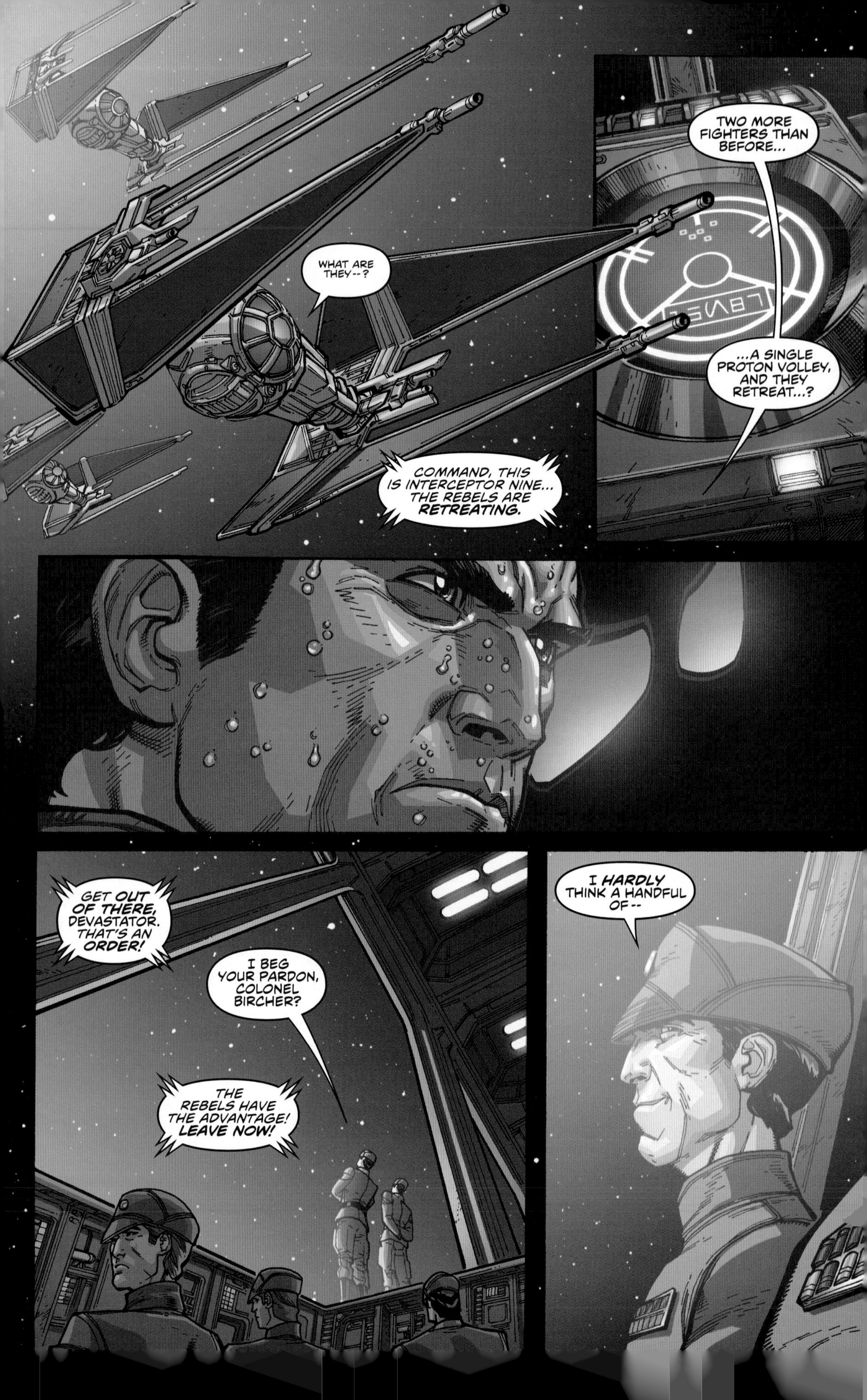
WHAT ARE THEY--?
COMMAND, THIS IS INTERCEPTOR NINE... THE REBELS ARE RETREATING.
TWO MORE FIGHTERS THAN BEFORE...
...A SINGLE PROTON VOLLEY, AND THEY RETREAT...?
GET OUT OF THERE, DEVASTATOR. THAT'S AN ORDER!
I BEG YOUR PARDON, COLONEL BIRCHER?
THE REBELS HAVE THE ADVANTAGE! LEAVE NOW!
I HARDLY THINK A HANDFUL OF --

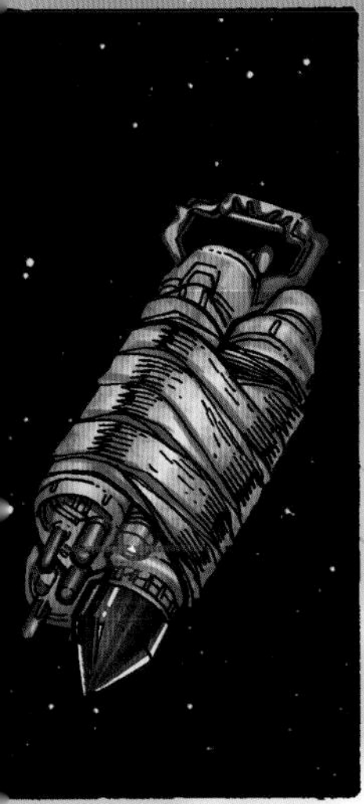

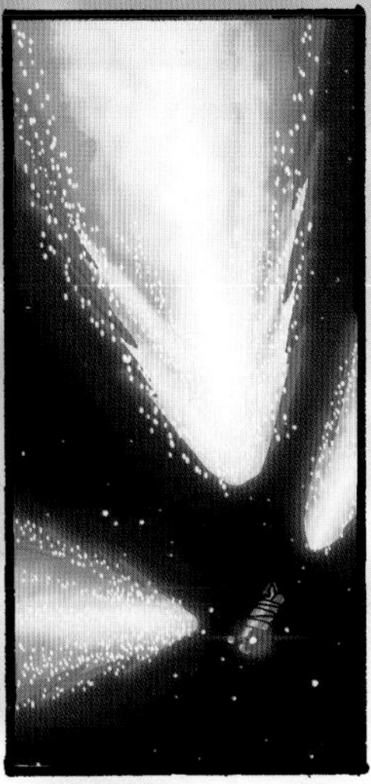

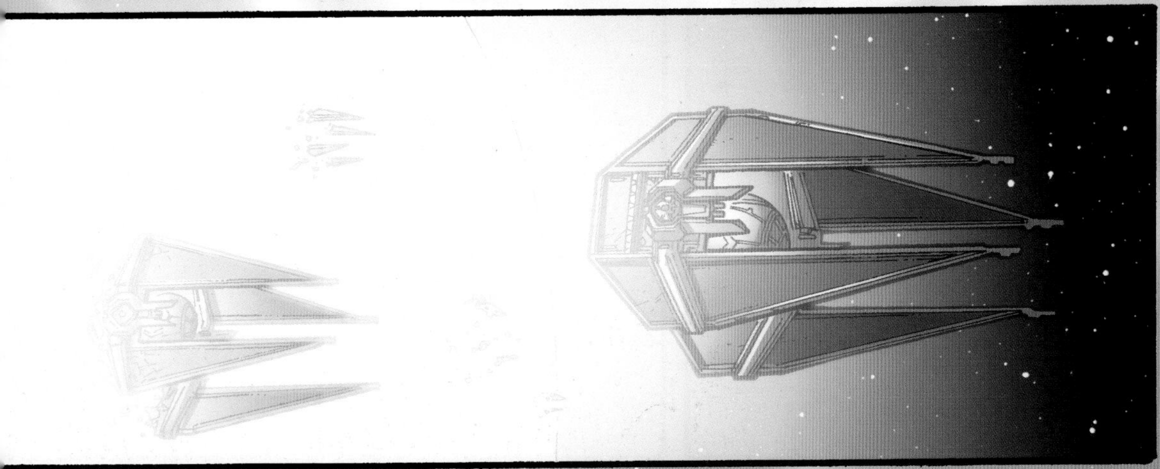

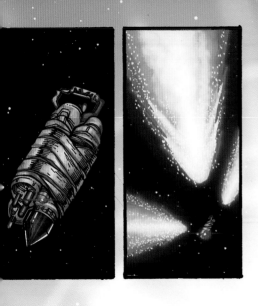

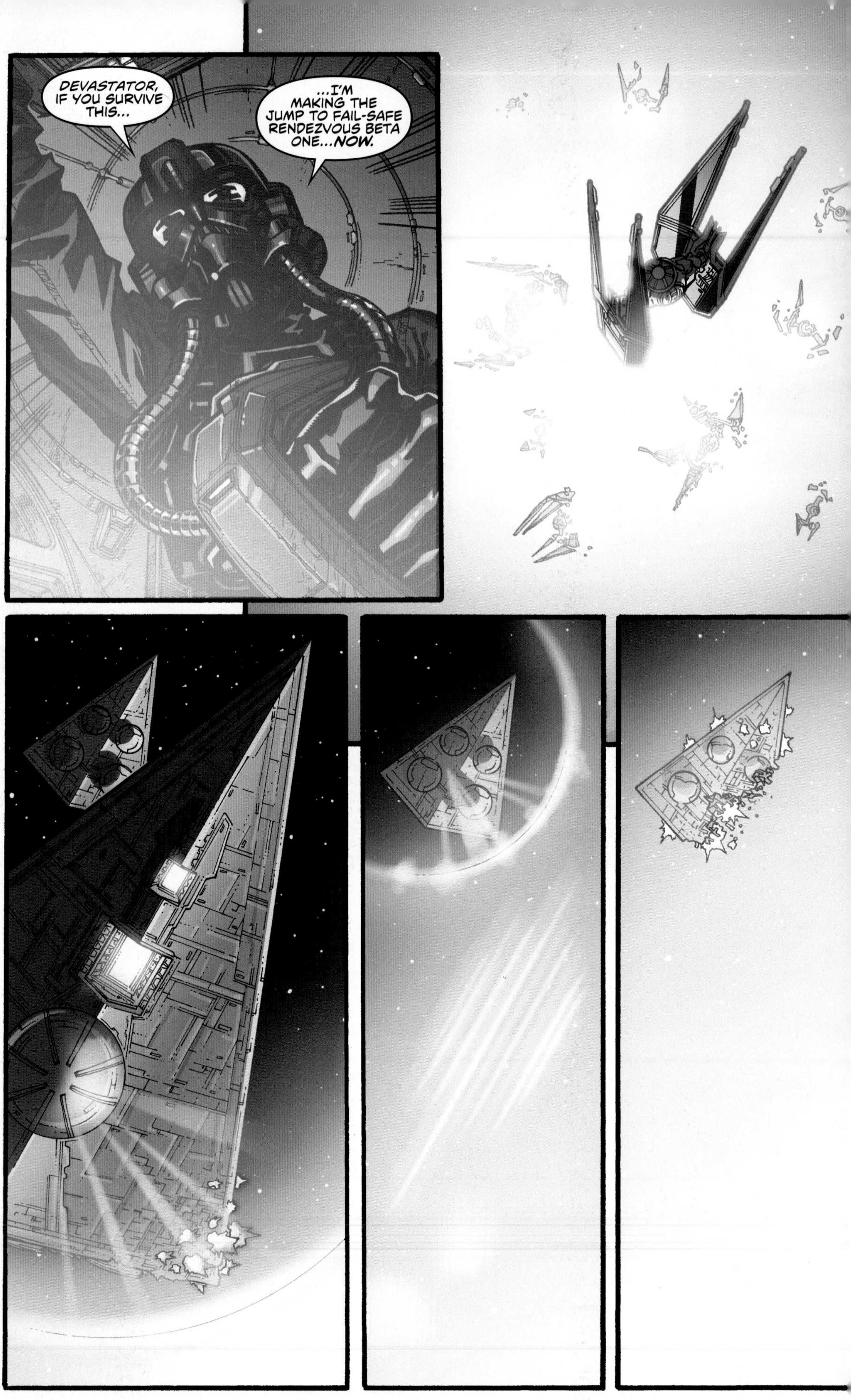
DEVASTATOR, IF YOU SURVIVE THIS...
...I'M MAKING THE JUMP TO FAIL-SAFE RENDEZVOUS BETA ONE...NOW.

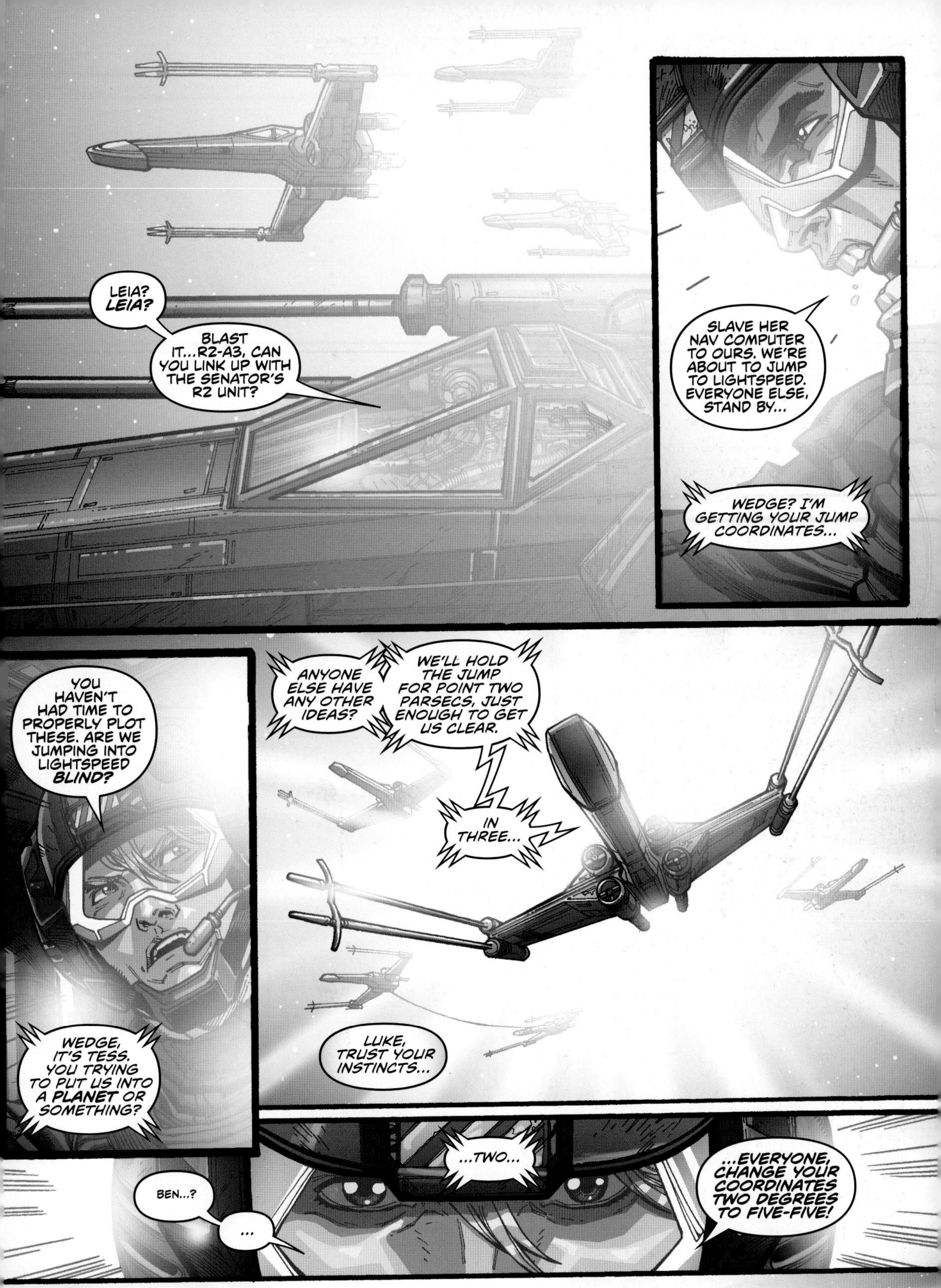

LEIA? LEIA?
BLAST IT...R2-A3, CAN YOU LINK UP WITH THE SENATOR'S R2 UNIT?
SLAVE HER NAV COMPUTER TO OURS. WE'RE ABOUT TO JUMP TO LIGHTSPEED. EVERYONE ELSE, STAND BY...
WEDGE? I'M GETTING YOUR JUMP COORDINATES...
YOU HAVEN'T HAD TIME TO PROPERLY PLOT THESE. ARE WE JUMPING INTO LIGHTSPEED BLIND?
WEDGE, IT'S TESS. YOU TRYING TO PUT US INTO A PLANET OR SOMETHING?
ANYONE ELSE HAVE ANY OTHER IDEAS?
WE'LL HOLD THE JUMP FOR POINT TWO PARSECS, JUST ENOUGH TO GET US CLEAR.
IN THREE...
LUKE, TRUST YOUR INSTINCTS...
BEN...?
...
...TWO...
...EVERYONE, CHANGE YOUR COORDINATES TWO DEGREES TO FIVE-FIVE!

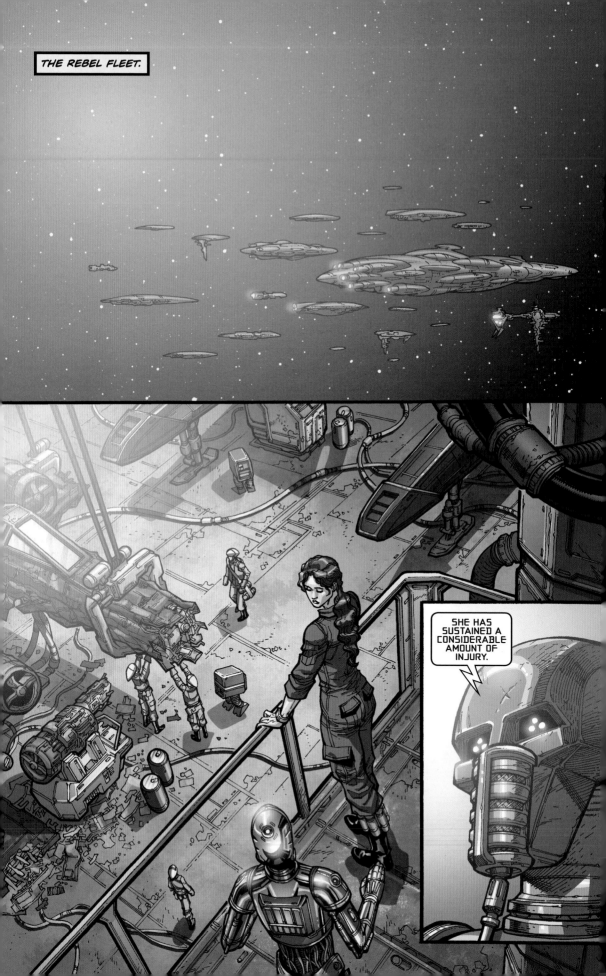

THE REBEL FLEET.

SHE HAS SUSTAINED A CONSIDERABLE AMOUNT OF INJURY.

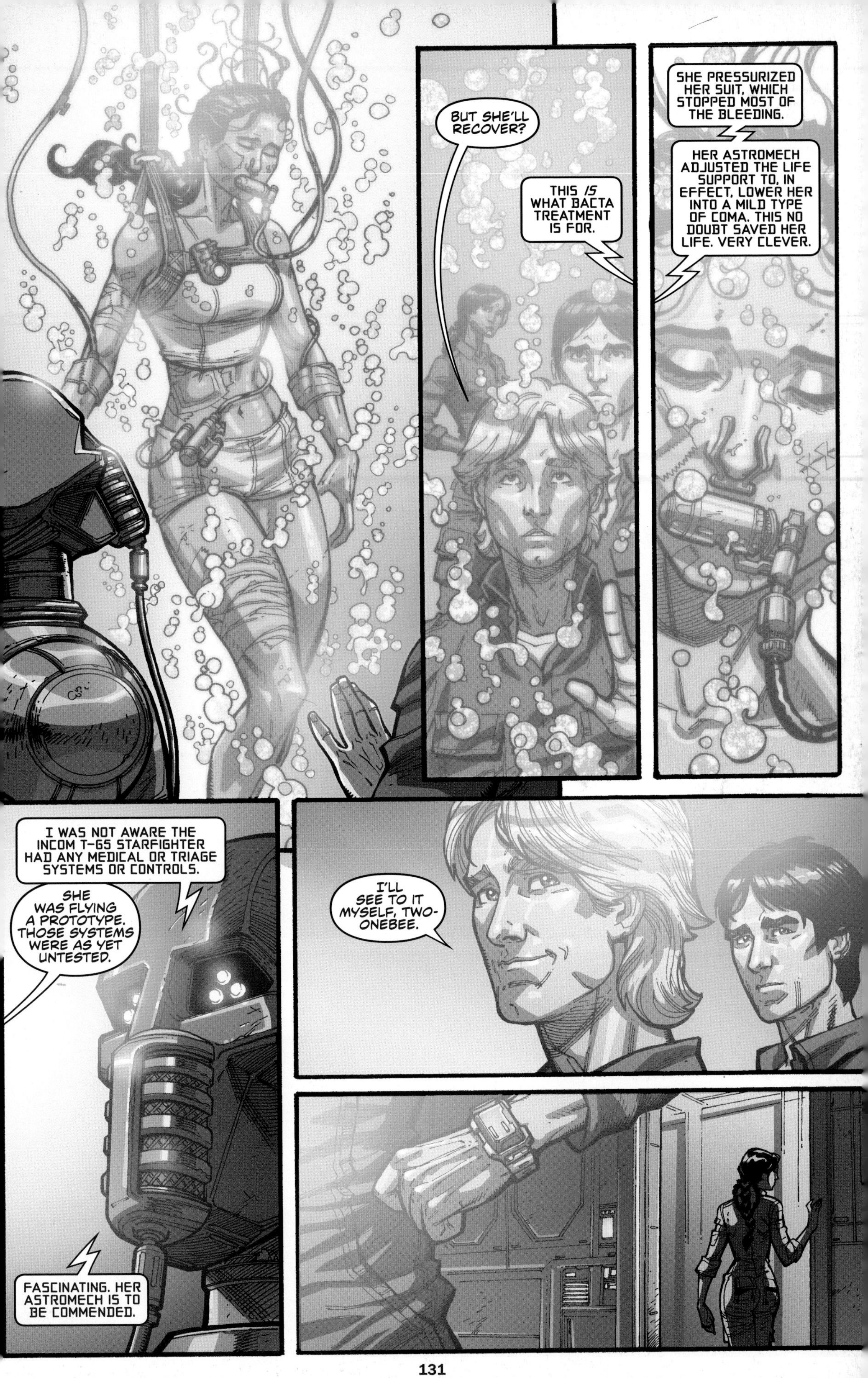
BUT SHE'LL RECOVER?
THIS IS WHAT BACTA TREATMENT IS FOR.
SHE PRESSURIZED HER SUIT, WHICH STOPPED MOST OF THE BLEEDING.
HER ASTROMECH ADJUSTED THE LIFE SUPPORT TO, IN EFFECT, LOWER HER INTO A MILD TYPE OF COMA. THIS NO DOUBT SAVED HER LIFE. VERY CLEVER.
I WAS NOT AWARE THE INCOM T-65 STARFIGHTER HAD ANY MEDICAL OR TRIAGE SYSTEMS OR CONTROLS.
SHE WAS FLYING A PROTOTYPE. THOSE SYSTEMS WERE AS YET UNTESTED.
FASCINATING. HER ASTROMECH IS TO BE COMMENDED.
I'LL SEE TO IT MYSELF, TWO-ONEBEE.

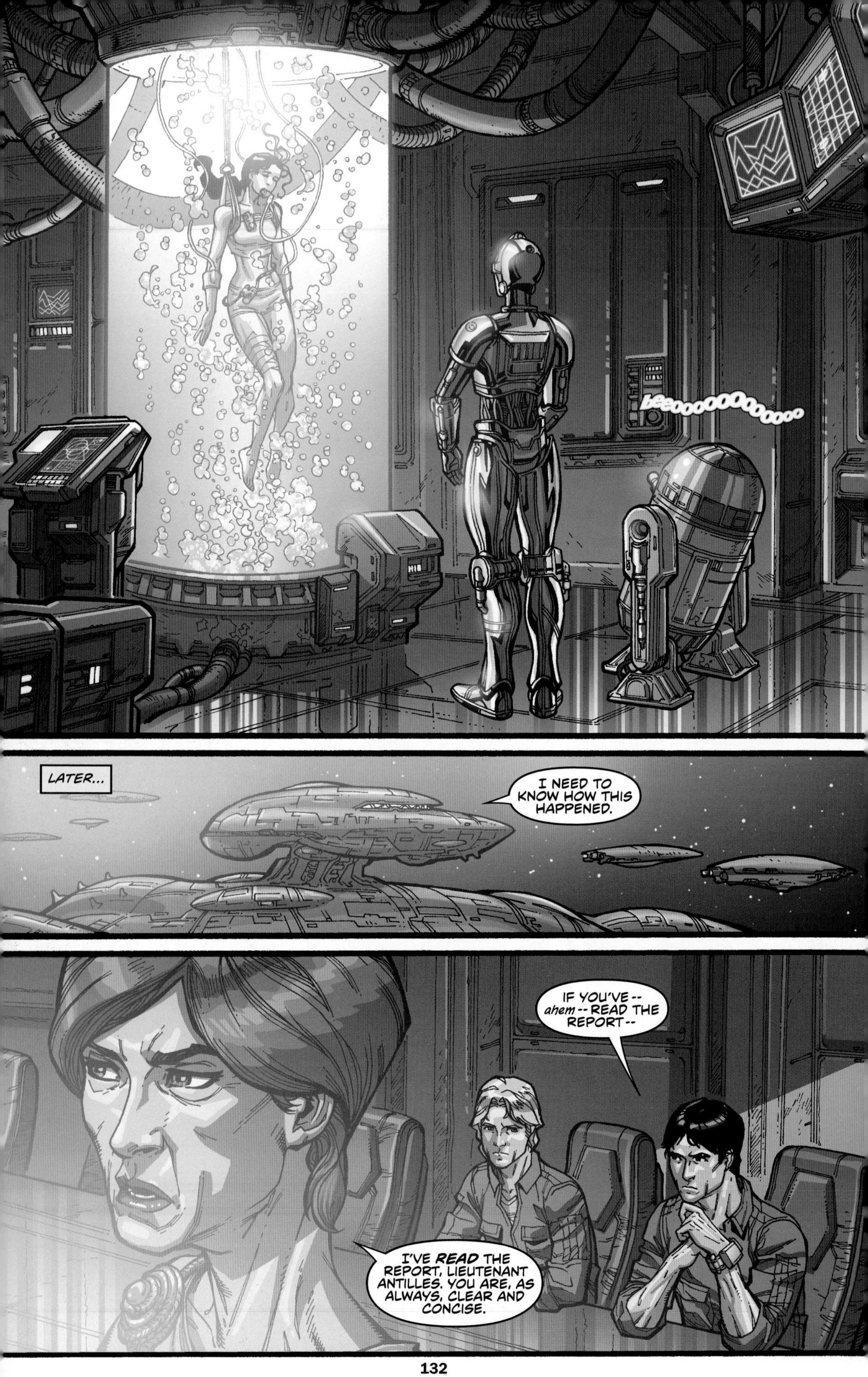
beeoooooOOOooooo
LATER...
I NEED TO KNOW HOW THIS HAPPENED.
IF YOU'VE -- *ahem* -- READ THE REPORT --
I'VE **READ** THE REPORT, LIEUTENANT ANTILLES. YOU ARE, AS ALWAYS, CLEAR AND CONCISE.

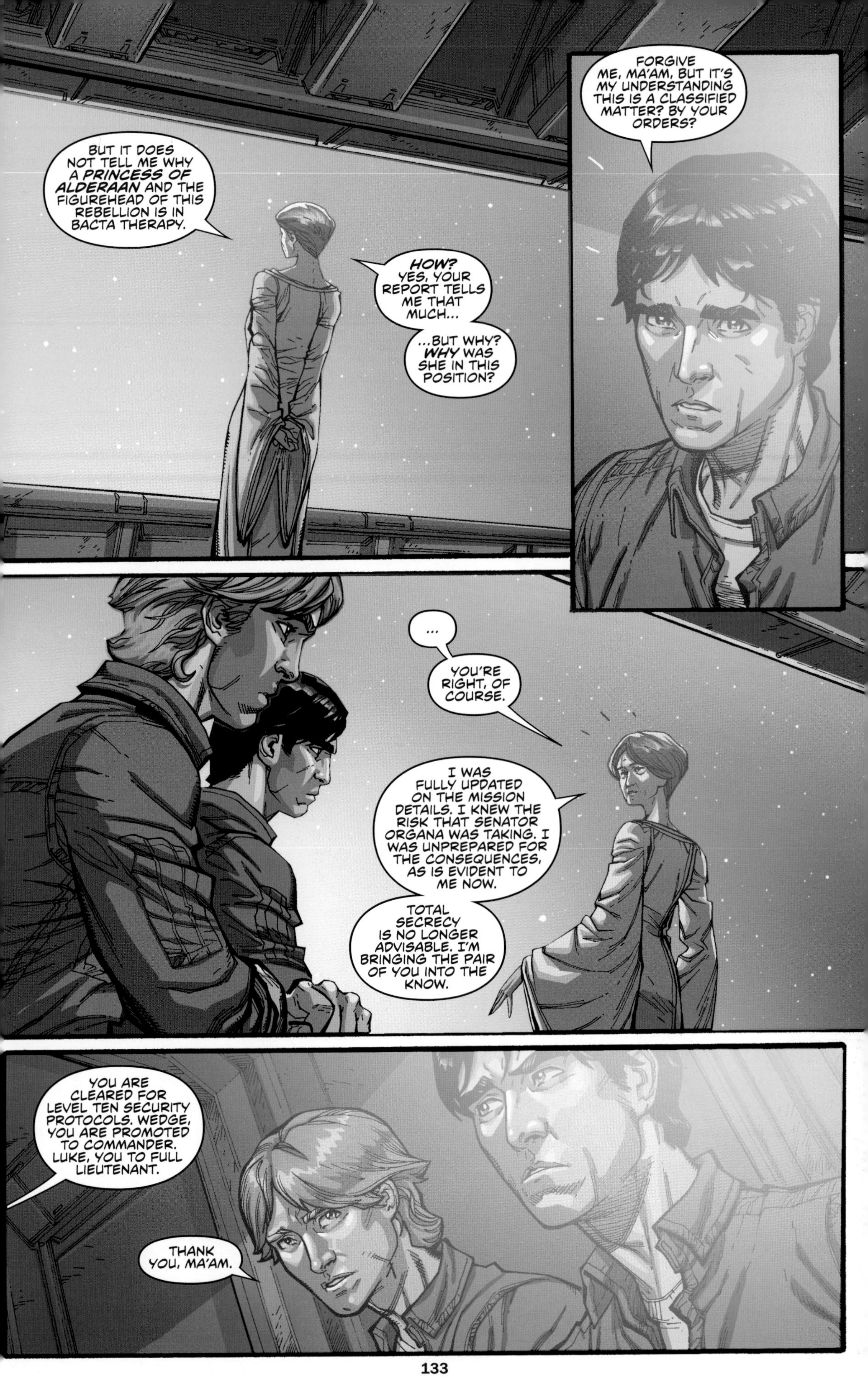
BUT IT DOES NOT TELL ME WHY A PRINCESS OF ALDERAAN AND THE FIGUREHEAD OF THIS REBELLION IS IN BACTA THERAPY.
HOW? YES, YOUR REPORT TELLS ME THAT MUCH...
...BUT WHY? WHY WAS SHE IN THIS POSITION?
FORGIVE ME, MA'AM, BUT IT'S MY UNDERSTANDING THIS IS A CLASSIFIED MATTER? BY YOUR ORDERS?
...
YOU'RE RIGHT, OF COURSE.
I WAS FULLY UPDATED ON THE MISSION DETAILS. I KNEW THE RISK THAT SENATOR ORGANA WAS TAKING. I WAS UNPREPARED FOR THE CONSEQUENCES, AS IS EVIDENT TO ME NOW.
TOTAL SECRECY IS NO LONGER ADVISABLE. I'M BRINGING THE PAIR OF YOU INTO THE KNOW.
YOU ARE CLEARED FOR LEVEL TEN SECURITY PROTOCOLS. WEDGE, YOU ARE PROMOTED TO COMMANDER. LUKE, YOU TO FULL LIEUTENANT.
THANK YOU, MA'AM.

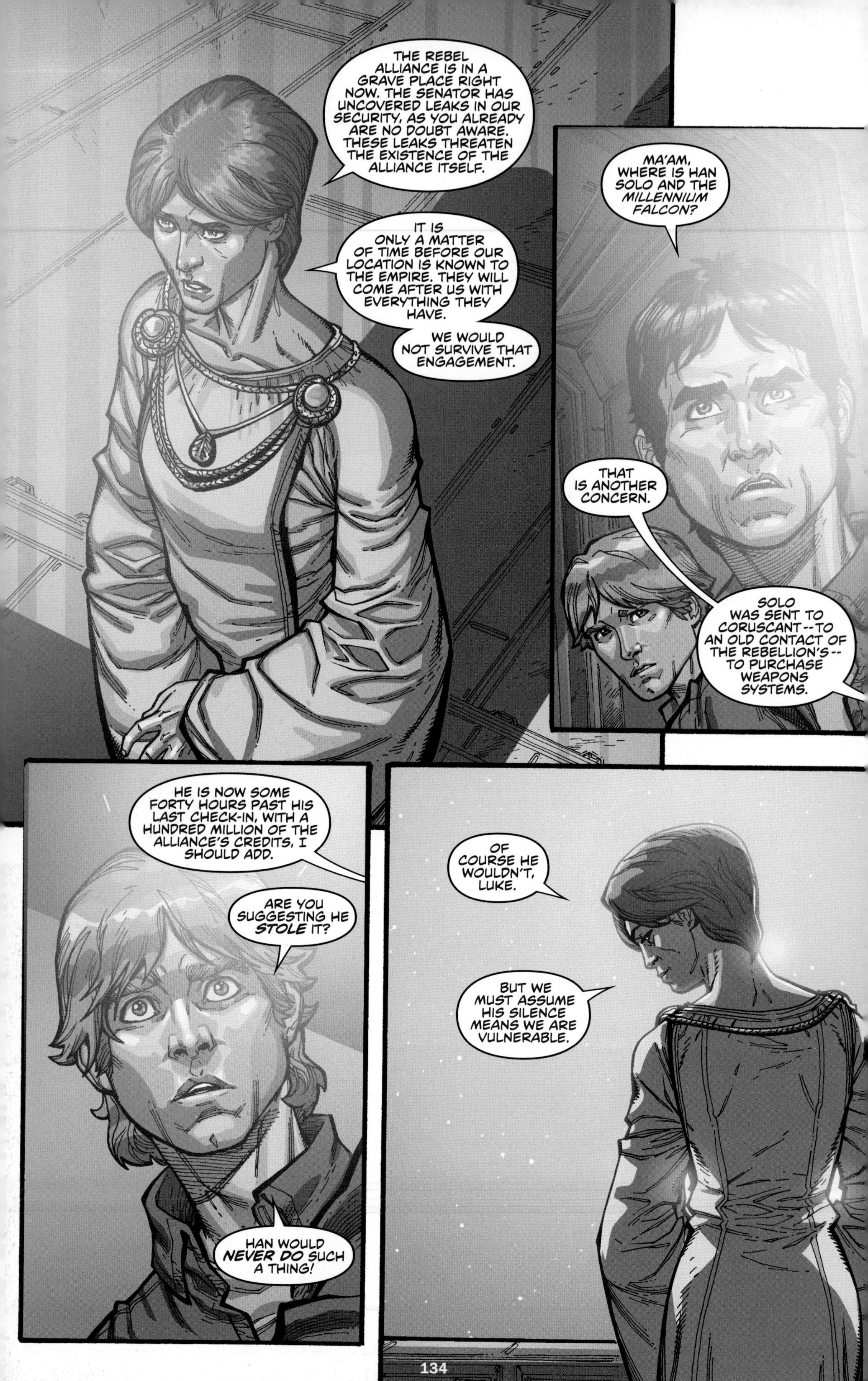

THE REBEL ALLIANCE IS IN A GRAVE PLACE RIGHT NOW. THE SENATOR HAS UNCOVERED LEAKS IN OUR SECURITY, AS YOU ALREADY ARE NO DOUBT AWARE. THESE LEAKS THREATEN THE EXISTENCE OF THE ALLIANCE ITSELF.
IT IS ONLY A MATTER OF TIME BEFORE OUR LOCATION IS KNOWN TO THE EMPIRE. THEY WILL COME AFTER US WITH EVERYTHING THEY HAVE.
WE WOULD NOT SURVIVE THAT ENGAGEMENT.
MA'AM, WHERE IS HAN SOLO AND THE *MILLENNIUM FALCON?*
THAT IS ANOTHER CONCERN.
SOLO WAS SENT TO CORUSCANT--TO AN OLD CONTACT OF THE REBELLION'S--TO PURCHASE WEAPONS SYSTEMS.
HE IS NOW SOME FORTY HOURS PAST HIS LAST CHECK-IN, WITH A HUNDRED MILLION OF THE ALLIANCE'S CREDITS, I SHOULD ADD.
ARE YOU SUGGESTING HE ***STOLE*** IT?
HAN WOULD ***NEVER DO*** SUCH A THING!
OF COURSE HE WOULDN'T, LUKE.
BUT WE MUST ASSUME HIS SILENCE MEANS WE ARE VULNERABLE.

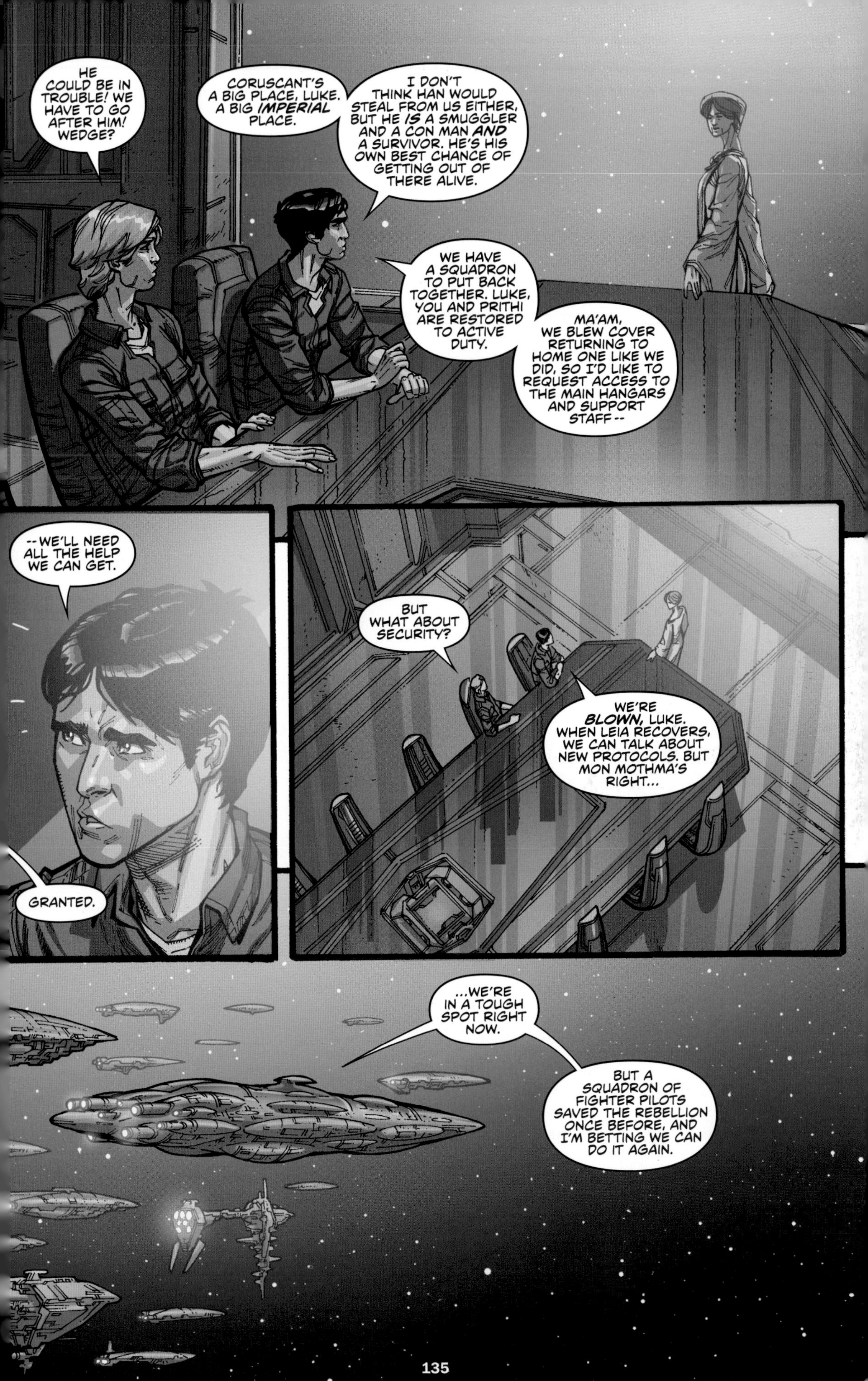
HE COULD BE IN TROUBLE! WE HAVE TO GO AFTER HIM! WEDGE?
CORUSCANT'S A BIG PLACE, LUKE. A BIG *IMPERIAL* PLACE.
I DON'T THINK HAN WOULD STEAL FROM US EITHER, BUT HE *IS* A SMUGGLER AND A CON MAN *AND* A SURVIVOR. HE'S HIS OWN BEST CHANCE OF GETTING OUT OF THERE ALIVE.
WE HAVE A SQUADRON TO PUT BACK TOGETHER. LUKE, YOU AND PRITHI ARE RESTORED TO ACTIVE DUTY.
MA'AM, WE BLEW COVER RETURNING TO HOME ONE LIKE WE DID, SO I'D LIKE TO REQUEST ACCESS TO THE MAIN HANGARS AND SUPPORT STAFF--
--WE'LL NEED ALL THE HELP WE CAN GET.
GRANTED.
BUT WHAT ABOUT SECURITY?
WE'RE *BLOWN,* LUKE. WHEN LEIA RECOVERS, WE CAN TALK ABOUT NEW PROTOCOLS. BUT MON MOTHMA'S RIGHT...
...WE'RE IN A TOUGH SPOT RIGHT NOW.
BUT A SQUADRON OF FIGHTER PILOTS SAVED THE REBELLION ONCE BEFORE, AND I'M BETTING WE CAN DO IT AGAIN.

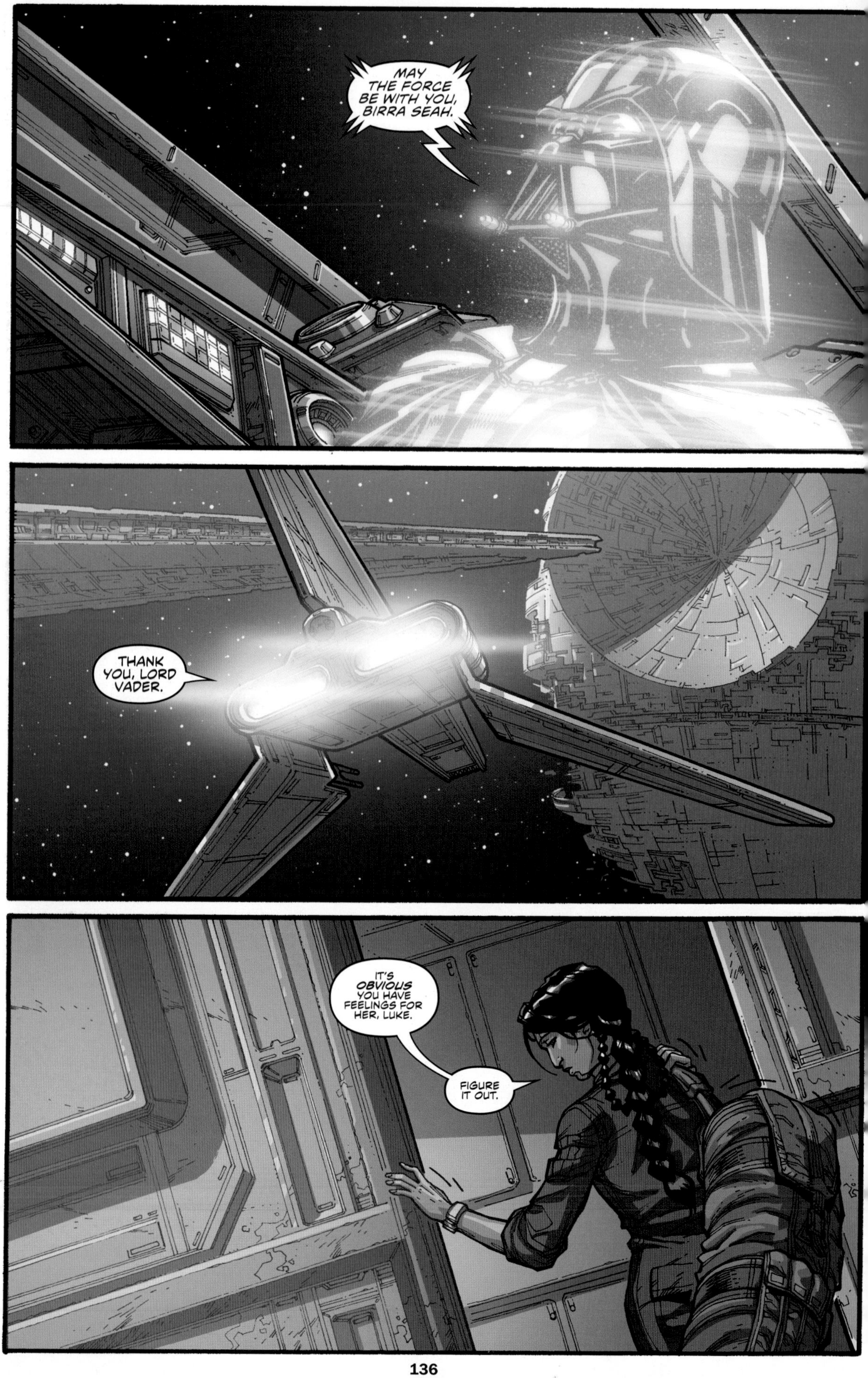
MAY THE FORCE BE WITH YOU, BIRRA SEAH.
THANK YOU, LORD VADER.
IT'S OBVIOUS YOU HAVE FEELINGS FOR HER, LUKE.
FIGURE IT OUT.

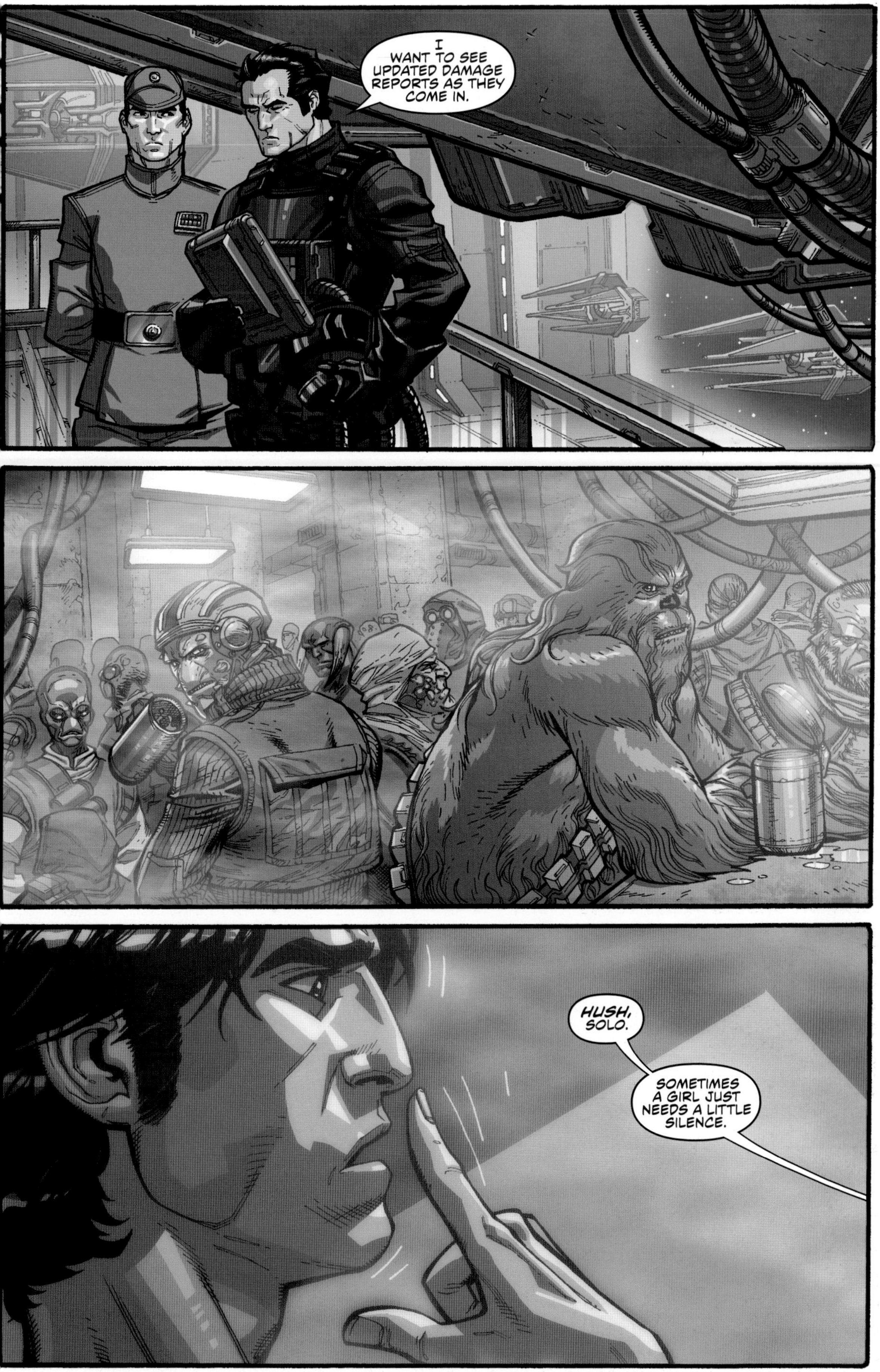
I WANT TO SEE UPDATED DAMAGE REPORTS AS THEY COME IN.
HUSH, SOLO.
SOMETIMES A GIRL JUST NEEDS A LITTLE SILENCE.

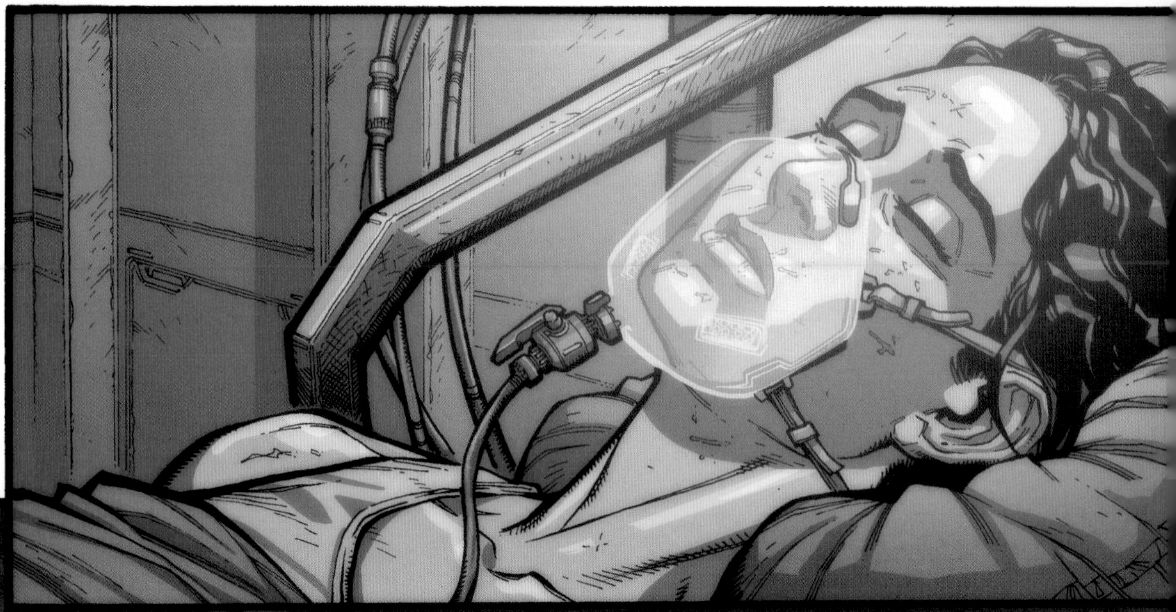

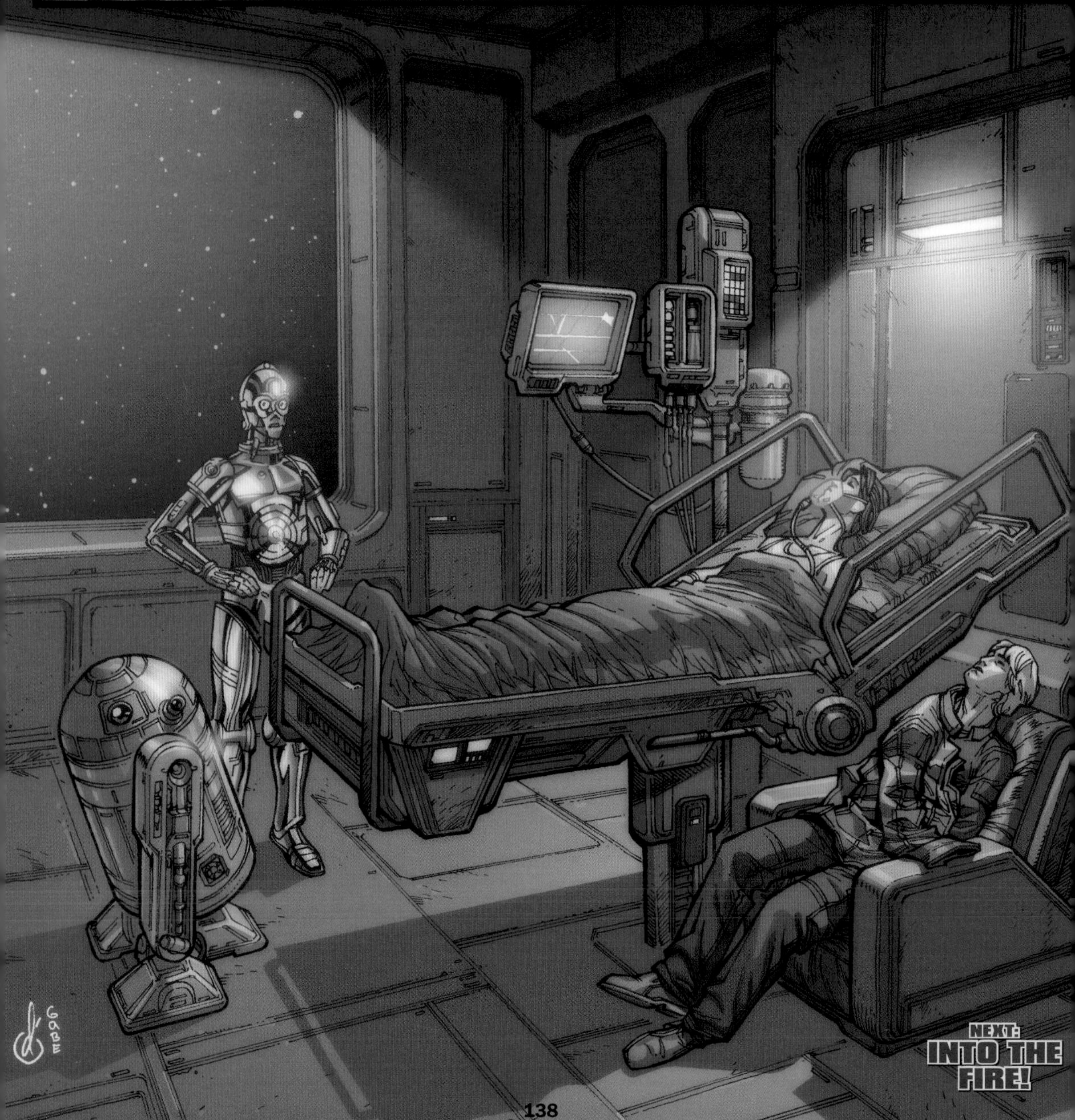
NEXT:
INTO THE FIRE!

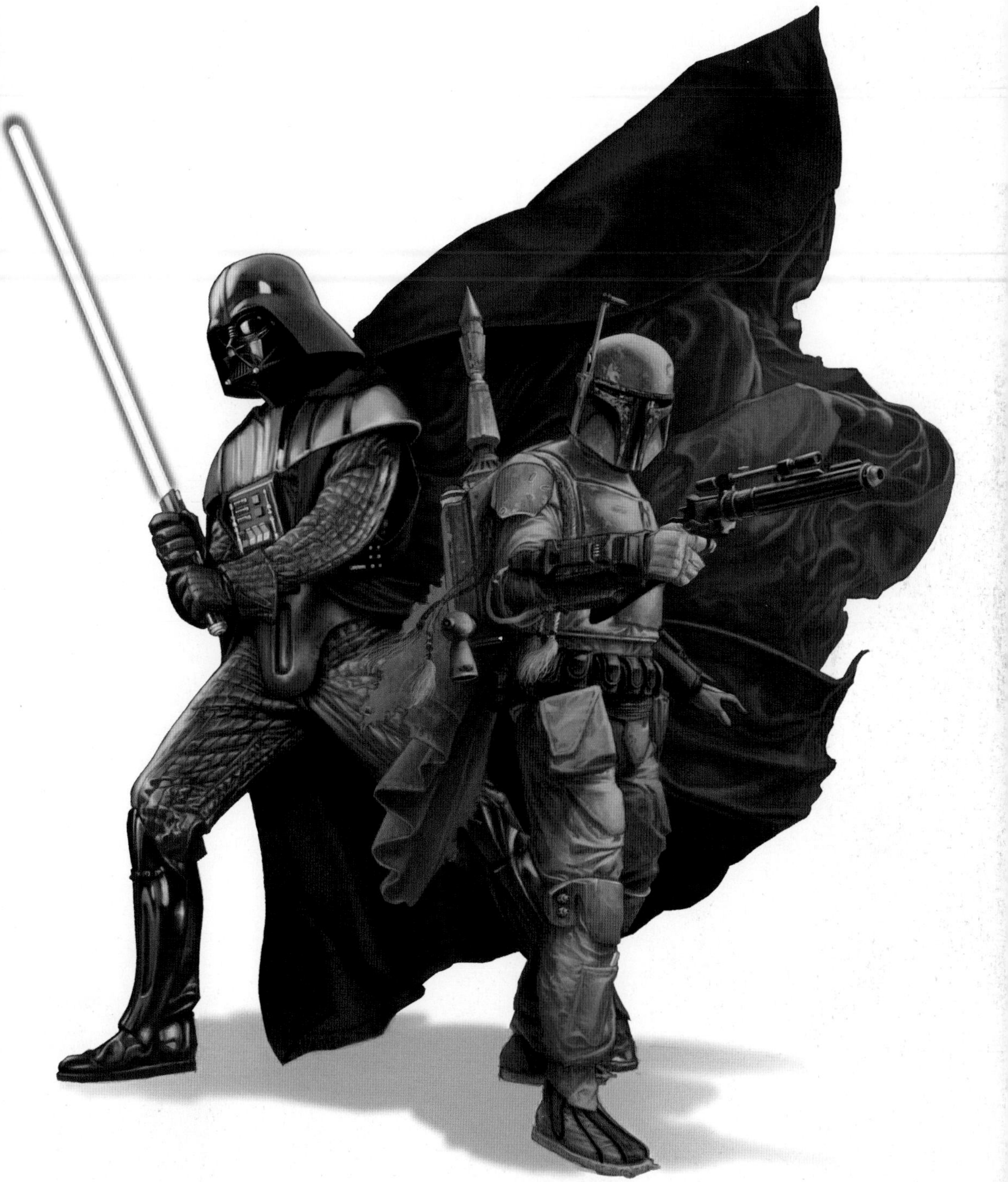
DOUGLAS
WHEATLEY
2012

Illustration by Doug Wheatley

THE ASSASSINATION OF LORD VADER

The events in this story take place shortly before the events in *Star Wars:* Episode IV—*A New Hope*.

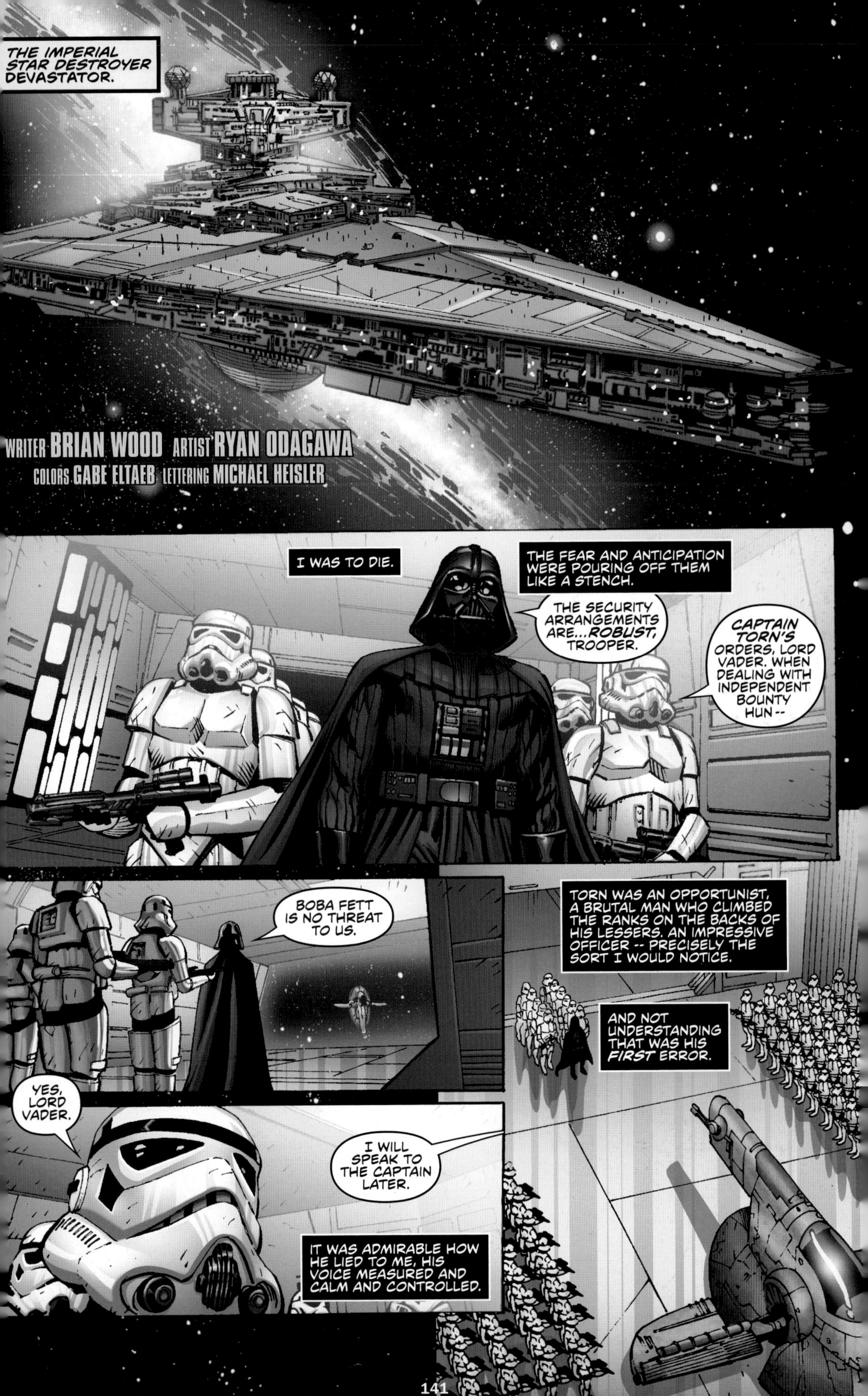
THE IMPERIAL STAR DESTROYER DEVASTATOR.
WRITER BRIAN WOOD ARTIST RYAN ODAGAWA
COLORS GABE ELTAEB LETTERING MICHAEL HEISLER
I WAS TO DIE.
THE FEAR AND ANTICIPATION WERE POURING OFF THEM LIKE A STENCH.
THE SECURITY ARRANGEMENTS ARE... ROBUST, TROOPER.
CAPTAIN TORN'S ORDERS, LORD VADER. WHEN DEALING WITH INDEPENDENT BOUNTY HUN--
BOBA FETT IS NO THREAT TO US.
YES, LORD VADER.
I WILL SPEAK TO THE CAPTAIN LATER.
IT WAS ADMIRABLE HOW HE LIED TO ME, HIS VOICE MEASURED AND CALM AND CONTROLLED.
TORN WAS AN OPPORTUNIST, A BRUTAL MAN WHO CLIMBED THE RANKS ON THE BACKS OF HIS LESSERS. AN IMPRESSIVE OFFICER -- PRECISELY THE SORT I WOULD NOTICE.
AND NOT UNDERSTANDING THAT WAS HIS FIRST ERROR.

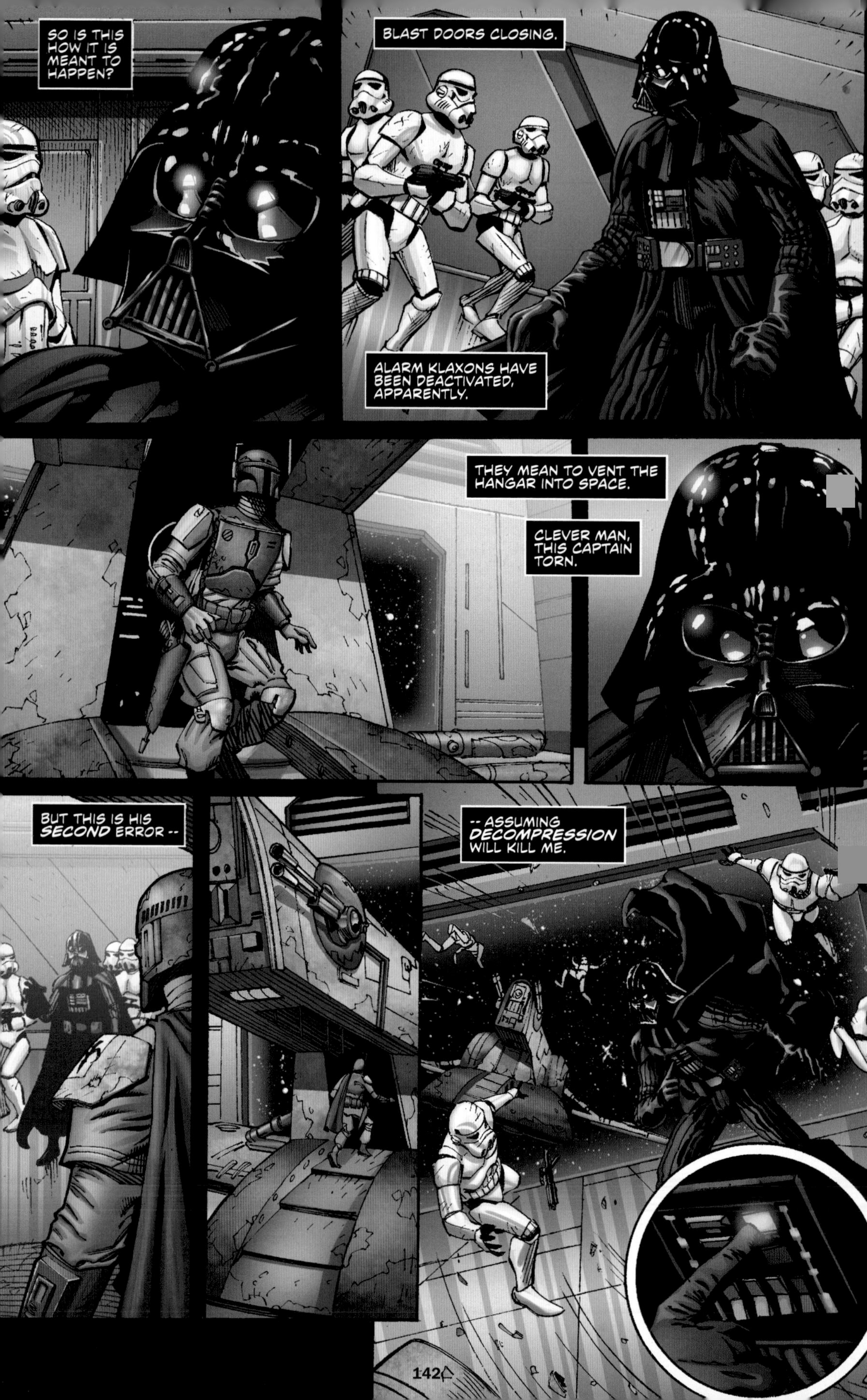
SO IS THIS HOW IT IS MEANT TO HAPPEN?
BLAST DOORS CLOSING.
ALARM KLAXONS HAVE BEEN DEACTIVATED, APPARENTLY.
THEY MEAN TO VENT THE HANGAR INTO SPACE.
CLEVER MAN, THIS CAPTAIN TORN.
BUT THIS IS HIS *SECOND* ERROR --
-- ASSUMING *DECOMPRESSION* WILL KILL ME.

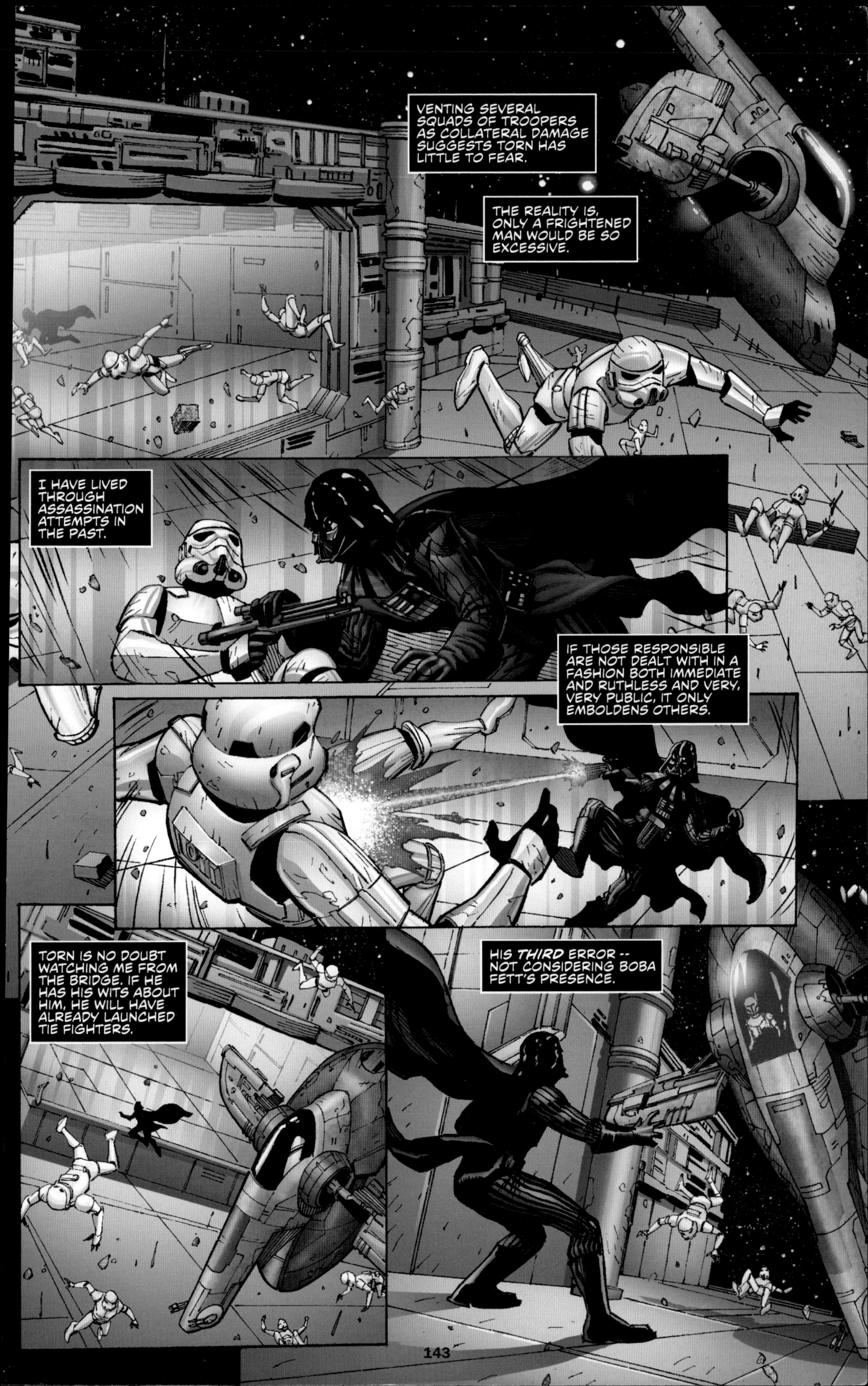
VENTING SEVERAL SQUADS OF TROOPERS AS COLLATERAL DAMAGE SUGGESTS TORN HAS LITTLE TO FEAR.
THE REALITY IS, ONLY A FRIGHTENED MAN WOULD BE SO EXCESSIVE.
I HAVE LIVED THROUGH ASSASSINATION ATTEMPTS IN THE PAST.
IF THOSE RESPONSIBLE ARE NOT DEALT WITH IN A FASHION BOTH IMMEDIATE AND RUTHLESS AND VERY, VERY PUBLIC, IT ONLY EMBOLDENS OTHERS.
TORN IS NO DOUBT WATCHING ME FROM THE BRIDGE. IF HE HAS HIS WITS ABOUT HIM, HE WILL HAVE ALREADY LAUNCHED TIE FIGHTERS.
HIS *THIRD* ERROR -- NOT CONSIDERING BOBA FETT'S PRESENCE.

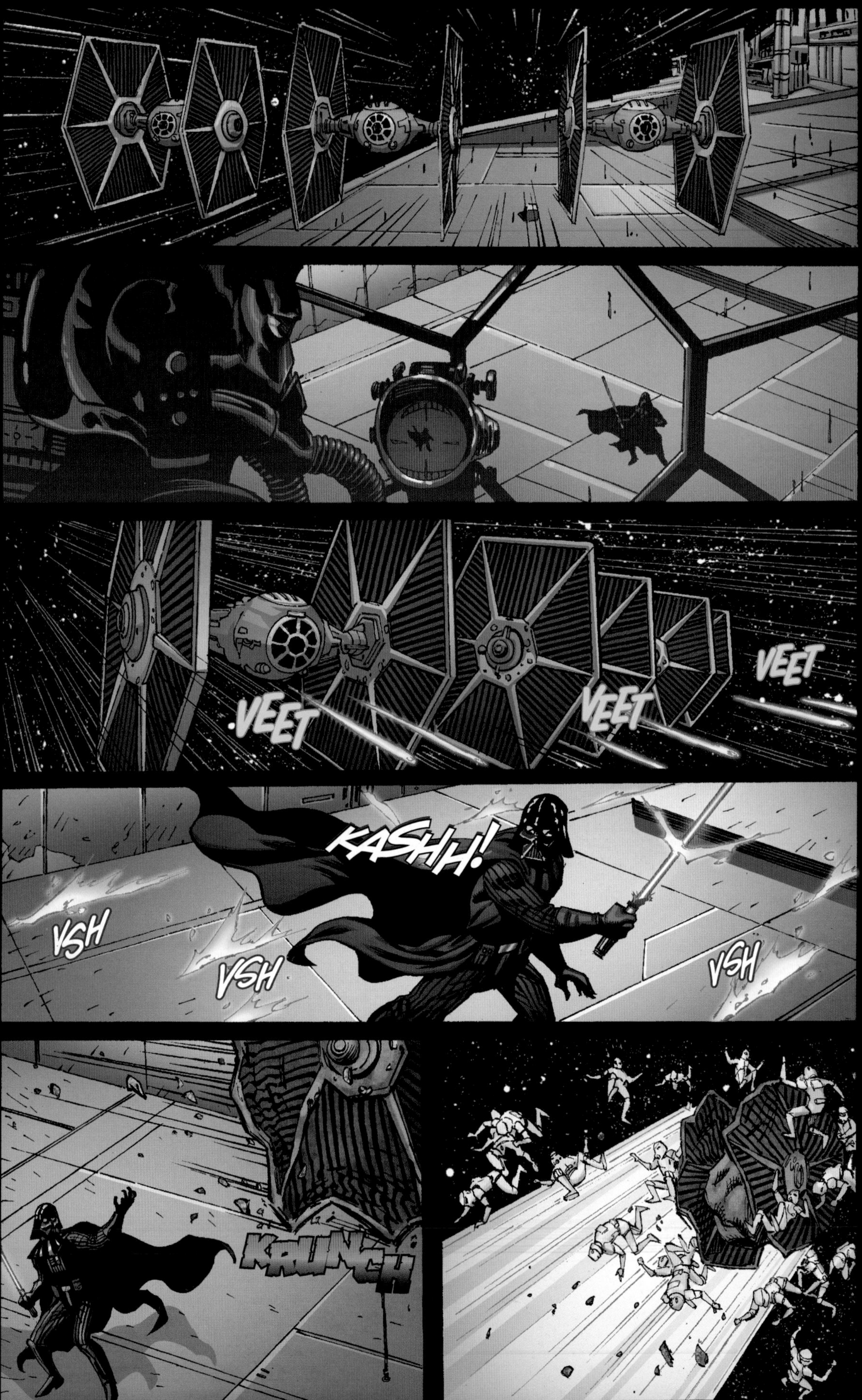
VEET
VEET
VEET
KASHH!
VSH
VSH
VSH
KRUNCH

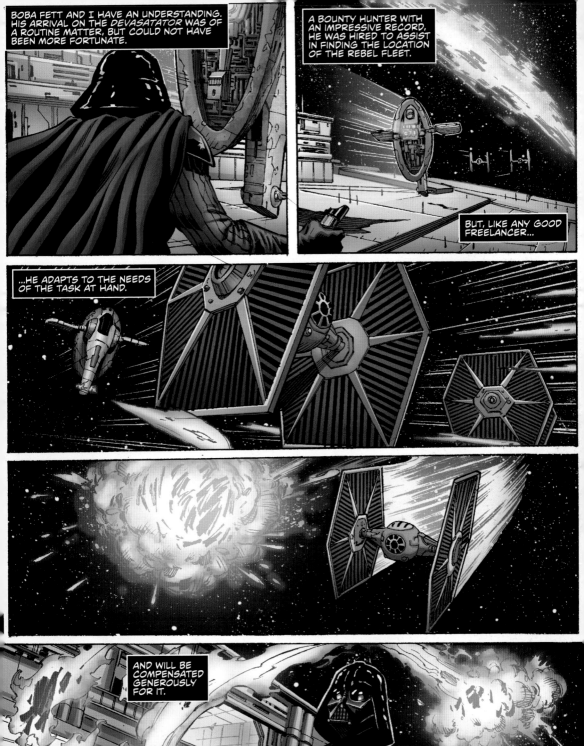

BOBA FETT AND I HAVE AN UNDERSTANDING. HIS ARRIVAL ON THE *DEVASATATOR* WAS OF A ROUTINE MATTER, BUT COULD NOT HAVE BEEN MORE FORTUNATE.

A BOUNTY HUNTER WITH AN IMPRESSIVE RECORD, HE WAS HIRED TO ASSIST IN FINDING THE LOCATION OF THE REBEL FLEET.

BUT, LIKE ANY GOOD FREELANCER...

...HE ADAPTS TO THE NEEDS OF THE TASK AT HAND.

AND WILL BE COMPENSATED GENEROUSLY FOR IT.

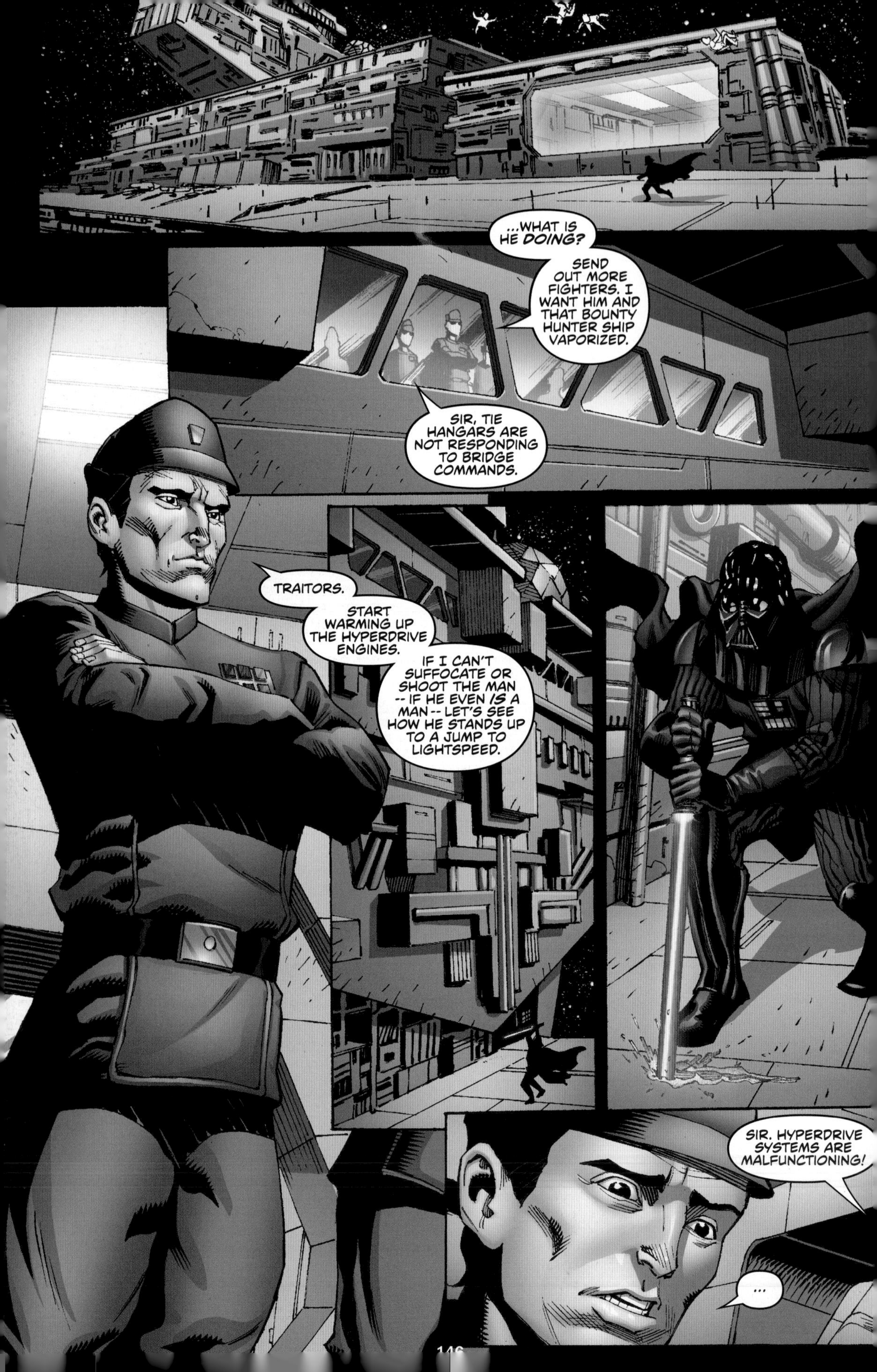
...WHAT IS HE DOING?
SEND OUT MORE FIGHTERS. I WANT HIM AND THAT BOUNTY HUNTER SHIP VAPORIZED.
SIR, TIE HANGARS ARE NOT RESPONDING TO BRIDGE COMMANDS.
TRAITORS.
START WARMING UP THE HYPERDRIVE ENGINES.
IF I CAN'T SUFFOCATE OR SHOOT THE MAN -- IF HE EVEN IS A MAN -- LET'S SEE HOW HE STANDS UP TO A JUMP TO LIGHTSPEED.
SIR. HYPERDRIVE SYSTEMS ARE MALFUNCTIONING!
...

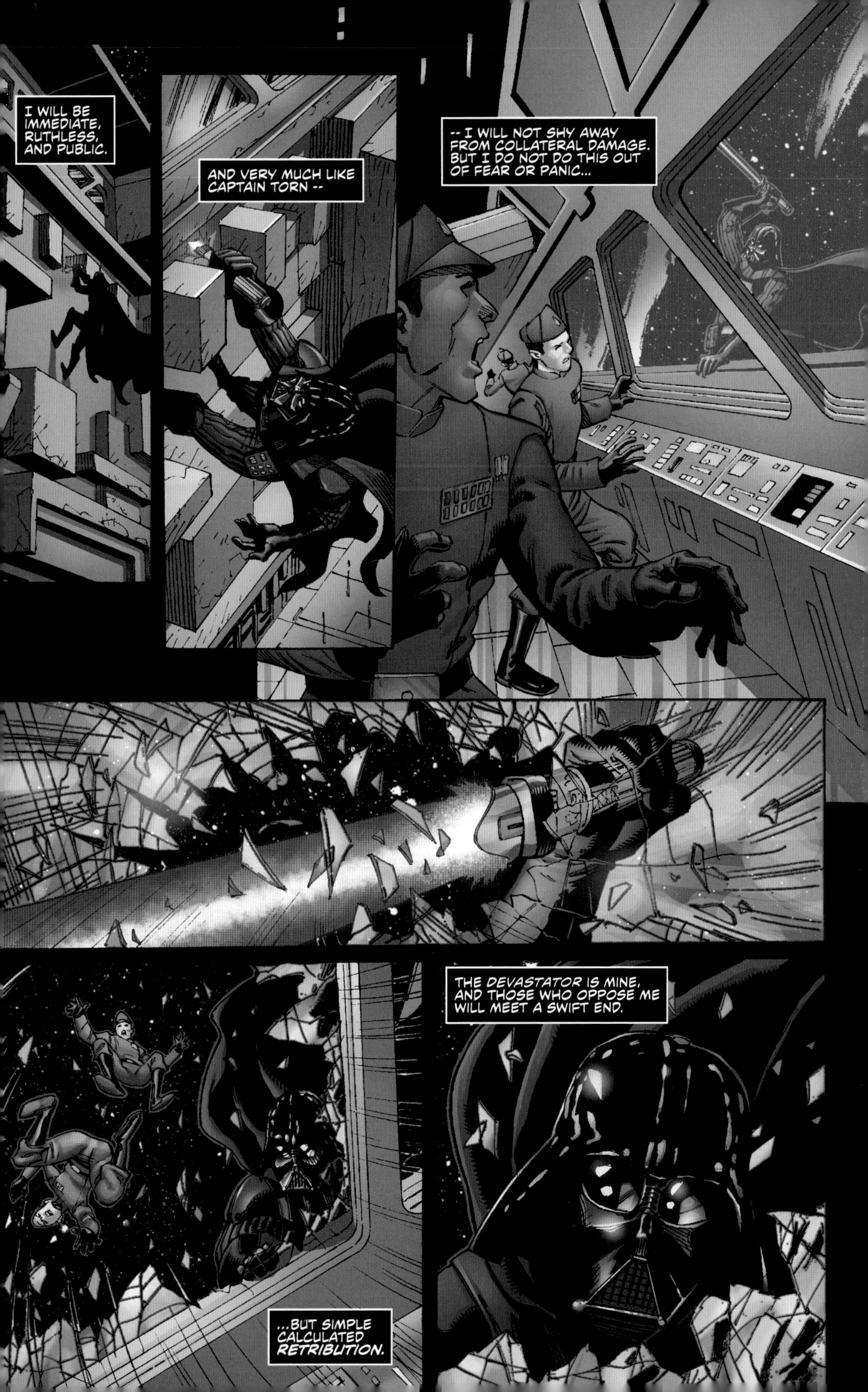

I WILL BE IMMEDIATE, RUTHLESS, AND PUBLIC.
AND VERY MUCH LIKE CAPTAIN TORN --
-- I WILL NOT SHY AWAY FROM COLLATERAL DAMAGE. BUT I DO NOT DO THIS OUT OF FEAR OR PANIC...
...BUT SIMPLE CALCULATED *RETRIBUTION.*
THE *DEVASTATOR* IS MINE, AND THOSE WHO OPPOSE ME WILL MEET A SWIFT END.

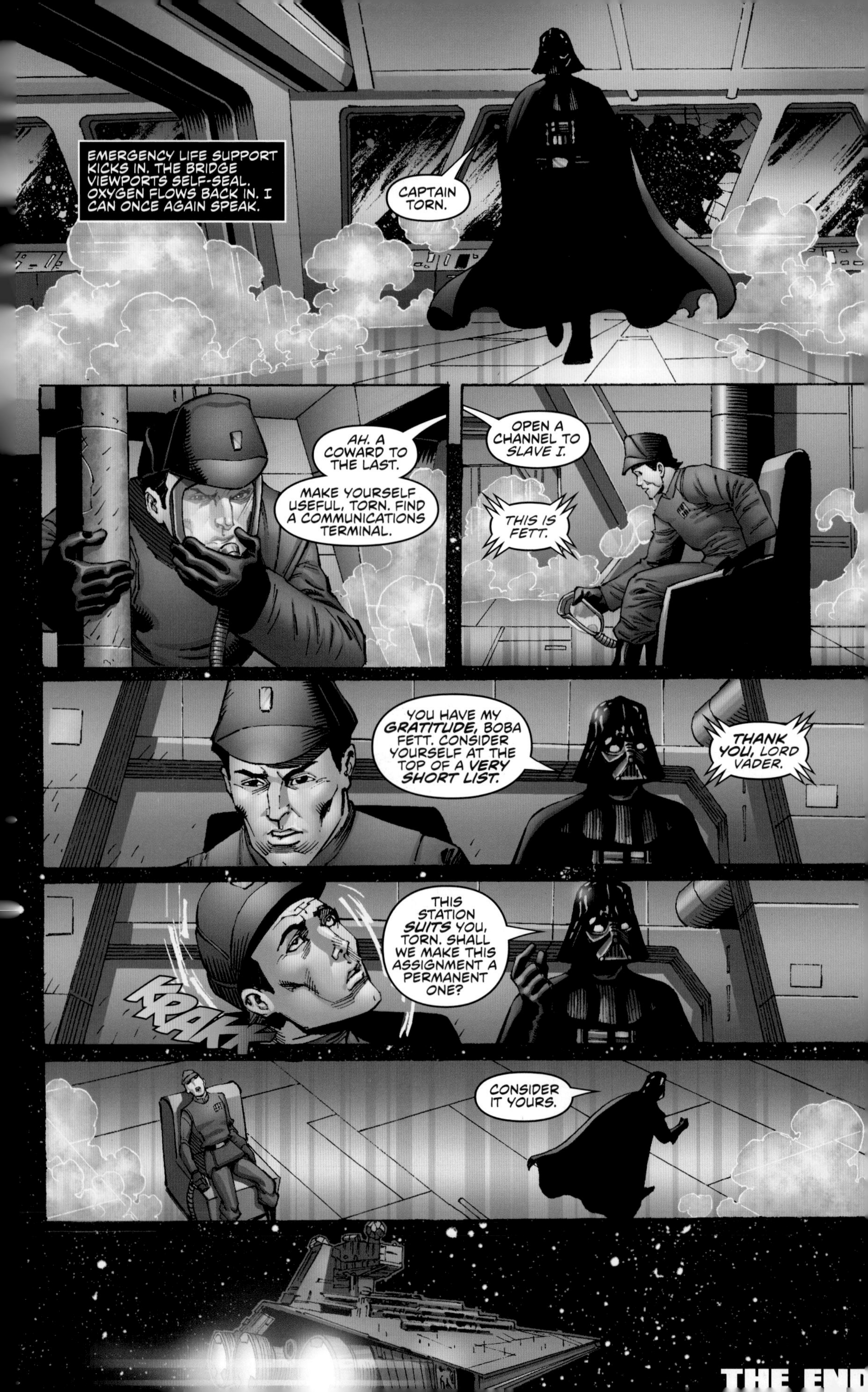
EMERGENCY LIFE SUPPORT KICKS IN. THE BRIDGE VIEWPORTS SELF-SEAL. OXYGEN FLOWS BACK IN. I CAN ONCE AGAIN SPEAK.
CAPTAIN TORN.
AH. A COWARD TO THE LAST.
MAKE YOURSELF USEFUL, TORN. FIND A COMMUNICATIONS TERMINAL.
OPEN A CHANNEL TO SLAVE I.
THIS IS FETT.
YOU HAVE MY GRATITUDE, BOBA FETT. CONSIDER YOURSELF AT THE TOP OF A VERY SHORT LIST.
THANK YOU, LORD VADER.
THIS STATION SUITS YOU, TORN. SHALL WE MAKE THIS ASSIGNMENT A PERMANENT ONE?
KRAKK
CONSIDER IT YOURS.
THE END

STAR WARS GRAPHIC NOVEL TIMELINE (IN YEARS)

Dawn of the Jedi—36,000 BSW4

Omnibus: Tales of the Jedi—5,000–3,986 BSW4

Knights of the Old Republic—3,964–3,963 BSW4

The Old Republic—3678, 3653, 3600 BSW4

Lost Tribe of the Sith—2974 BSW4

Knight Errant—1,032 BSW4

Jedi vs. Sith—1,000 BSW4

Jedi: The Dark Side—53 BSW4

Omnibus: Rise of the Sith—33 BSW4

Episode I: The Phantom Menace—32 BSW4

Omnibus: Emissaries and Assassins—32 BSW4

Omnibus: Quinlan Vos—Jedi in Darkness—31–30 BSW4

Omnibus: Menace Revealed—31–22 BSW4

Honor and Duty—22 BSW4

Blood Ties—22 BSW4

Episode II: Attack of the Clones—22 BSW4

Clone Wars—22–19 BSW4

Omnibus: Clone Wars—22–19 BSW4

Clone Wars Adventures—22–19 BSW4

Darth Maul: Death Sentence—20 BSW4

Episode III: Revenge of the Sith—19 BSW4

Purge—19 BSW4

Dark Times—19 BSW4

Omnibus: Droids—5.5 BSW4

Omnibus: Boba Fett—3 BSW4–10 ASW4

Agent of the Empire—3 BSW4

The Force Unleashed—2 BSW4

Omnibus: At War with the Empire—1 BSW4

Episode IV: A New Hope—SW4

Star Wars—0 ASW4

Classic Star Wars—0–3 ASW4

Omnibus: A Long Time Ago. . . .—0–4 ASW4

Empire—0 ASW4

Omnibus: The Other Sons of Tatooine—0 ASW4

Omnibus: Early Victories—0–3 ASW4

Jabba the Hutt: The Art of the Deal—1 ASW4

Episode V: The Empire Strikes Back—3 ASW4

Omnibus: Shadows of the Empire—3.5–4.5 ASW4

Episode VI: Return of the Jedi—4 ASW4

Omnibus: X-Wing Rogue Squadron—4–5 ASW4

The Thrawn Trilogy—9 ASW4

Dark Empire—10 ASW4

Crimson Empire—11 ASW4

Jedi Academy: Leviathan—12 ASW4

Union—19 ASW4

Chewbacca—25 ASW4

Invasion—25 ASW4

Legacy—130–138 ASW4

Dawn of the Jedi
36,000 years before
Star Wars: A New Hope

Old Republic Era
25,000–1000 years before
Star Wars: A New Hope

Rise of the Empire Era
1000–0 years before Star
Wars: A New Hope

Rebellion Era
0–5 years after
Star Wars: A New Hope

New Republic Era
5–25 years after
Star Wars: A New Hope

New Jedi Order Era
25+ years after
Star Wars: A New Hope

Legacy Era
130+ years after
Star Wars: A New Hope

Vector
Crosses four eras in timeline

Volume 1 contains:
Knights of the Old Republic Volume 5
Dark Times Volume 3
Volume 2 contains:
Rebellion Volume 4
Legacy Volume 6

Infinities
Does not apply to timeline

Sergio Aragones Stomps Star Wars
Star Wars Tales
Omnibus: Infinities
Tag and Bink
Star Wars Visionaries

BSW4 = before *Episode IV: A New Hope*. ASW4 = after *Episode IV: A New Hope*.

STAR WARS HARDCOVER VOLUMES

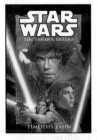

STAR WARS
THE THRAWN TRILOGY
TIMOTHY ZAHN

STAR WARS: THE THRAWN TRILOGY

Collects the comics adaptations of Timothy Zahn's best-selling novels *Heir to the Empire*, *Dark Force Rising*, and *The Last Command*. Years after the fall of the Empire, the last of the Emperor's warlords, Admiral Thrawn, is ready to destroy the New Republic—and the odds are stacked against Luke, Leia, and Han!

ISBN 978-1-59582-417-2 | $34.99

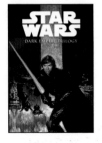

STAR WARS
DARK EMPIRE TRILOGY

STAR WARS: DARK EMPIRE TRILOGY

Six years after the fall of the Empire in *Return of the Jedi*, the battle for the galaxy's freedom rages on. The Empire has been mysteriously reborn . . . Princess Leia and Han Solo struggle to hold together the New Republic while Luke Skywalker fights an inner battle as he is drawn to the dark side . . .

ISBN 978-1-59582-612-1 | $29.99

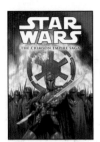

STAR WARS
THE CRIMSON EMPIRE SAGA

STAR WARS: THE CRIMSON EMPIRE SAGA

The blood-soaked tale of the last surviving member of Emperor Palpatine's Royal Guard is now complete! From revenge to redemption, the story of Kir Kanos takes him from the deserts of Yinchorr, to the halls of Imperial power, and to the inner circle of the New Republic.

ISBN 978-1-59582-947-4 | $34.99

STAR WARS

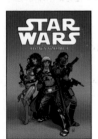

STAR WARS: LEGACY

The future of Star Wars and the future of the Skywalkers is told in John Ostrander and Jan Duursema's acclaimed *Star Wars: Legacy*. A Sith legion has conquered the Empire, the Jedi have been scattered, and the galaxy is divided. Into this comes Cade Skywalker, heir to the Skywalker legacy . . .

Book 1: ISBN 978-1-61655-178-0 | $34.99

Book 2: ISBN 978-1-61655-209-1 | $34.99

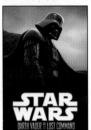

STAR WARS
DARTH VADER AND THE LOST COMMAND

STAR WARS: DARTH VADER AND THE LOST COMMAND

Still haunted by the death of Anakin Skywalker's beloved Padmé, Darth Vader is tasked with a mission to locate a lost Imperial expeditionary force—led by the son of Vader's rising nemesis, Moff Tarkin. Vader's journey is compounded by traitors among his crew and the presence of the mysterious Lady Saro.

ISBN 978-1-59582-778-4 | $24.99

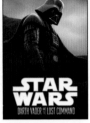

STAR WARS
DARTH VADER AND THE GHOST PRISON

STAR WARS: DARTH VADER AND THE GHOST PRISON

A traitorous uprising against the Galactic Empire leaves Emperor Palpatine close to death. Saving the Emperor—and the Empire—appears to be a lost cause . . . unless Darth Vader and a young lieutenant can uncover the secrets of the Jedi Council and locate the mysterious "Ghost Prison."

ISBN 978-1-61655-059-2 | $24.99

DARK HORSE BOOKS

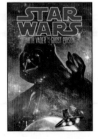

AVAILABLE AT YOUR LOCAL COMICS SHOP OR BOOKSTORE!

To find a comics shop in your area, call 1-888-266-4226

For more information or to order direct: • On the web: DarkHorse.com • E-mail: mailorder@darkhorse.com • Phone: 1-800-862-0052 Mon.–Fri. 9 AM to 5 PM Pacific Time

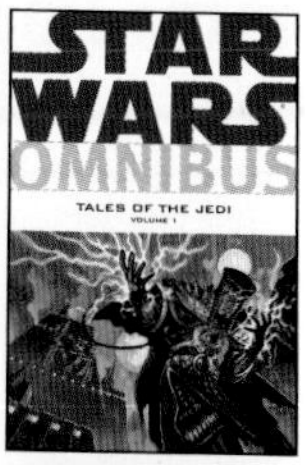
STAR WARS
OMNIBUS
TALES OF THE JEDI
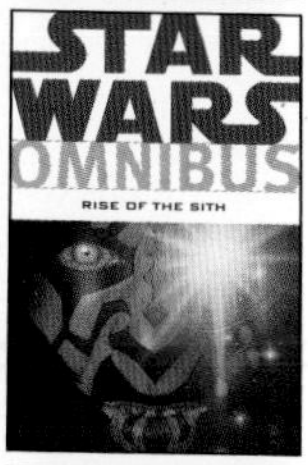
STAR WARS
OMNIBUS
RISE OF THE SITH
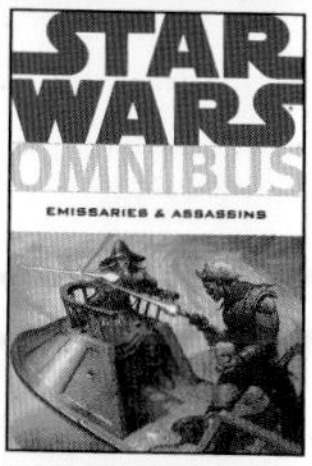
STAR WARS
OMNIBUS
EMISSARIES & ASSASSINS
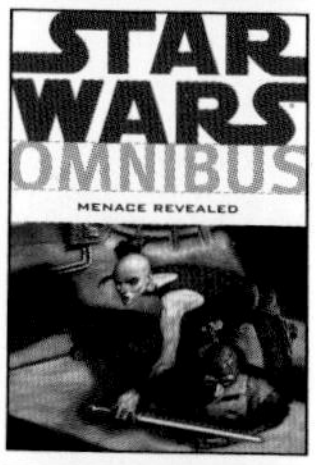
STAR WARS
OMNIBUS
MENACE REVEALED
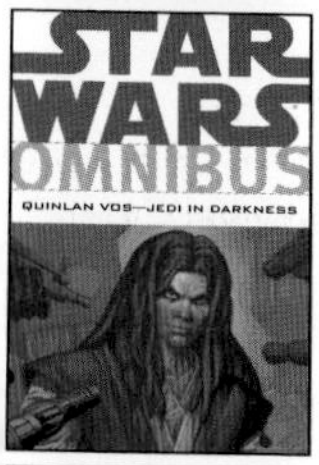
STAR WARS
OMNIBUS
QUINLAN VOS—JEDI IN DARKNESS
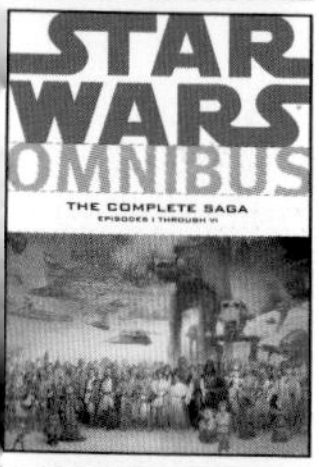
STAR WARS
OMNIBUS
THE COMPLETE SAGA
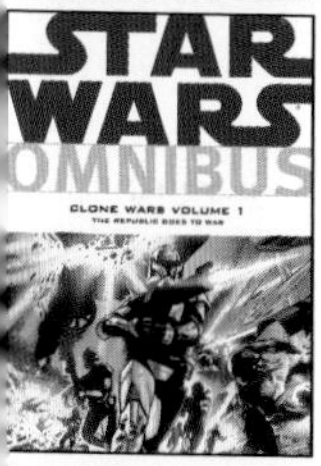
STAR WARS
OMNIBUS
CLONE WARS VOLUME 1
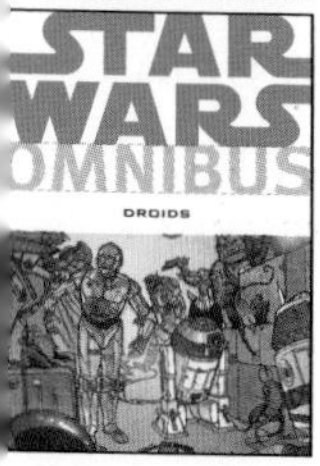
STAR WARS
OMNIBUS
DROIDS

STAR WARS OMNIBUS COLLECTIONS

STAR WARS: TALES OF THE JEDI

Including the *Tales of the Jedi* stories "The Golden Age of the Sith," "The Freedon Nadd Uprising," and "Knights of the Old Republic," these huge omnibus editions are the ultimate introduction to the ancient history of the *Star Wars* universe!

Volume 1: ISBN 978-1-59307-830-0 | $24.99 **Volume 2: ISBN 978-1-59307-911-6 | $24.99**

STAR WARS: KNIGHTS OF THE OLD REPUBLIC

Padawan Zayne Carrick is suddenly a fugitive framed for the murder of his fellow Jedi-in-training. Little does the galaxy know, Zayne's own Masters are behind the massacre and dead set on recovering him before he can reveal the truth.

Volume 1: ISBN 978-1-61655-206-0 | $24.99

STAR WARS: RISE OF THE SITH

These thrilling tales illustrate the events leading up to *Episode I: The Phantom Menace*, when the Jedi Knights preserved peace and justice . . . as well as prevented the return of the Sith.

ISBN 978-1-59582-228-4 | $24.99

STAR WARS: EMISSARIES AND ASSASSINS

Discover more stories featuring Anakin Skywalker, Amidala, Obi-Wan, and Qui-Gon set during the time of *Episode I: The Phantom Menace*!

ISBN 978-1-59582-229-1 | $24.99

STAR WARS: MENACE REVEALED

Included here are one-shot adventures, short story arcs, specialty issues, and early *Dark Horse Extra* comic strips! All of these tales take place after *Episode I: The Phantom Menace*, and lead up to *Episode II: Attack of the Clones*.

ISBN 978-1-59582-273-4 | $24.99

STAR WARS: QUINLAN VOS—JEDI IN DARKNESS

From his first appearance as a mind-wiped amnesiac to his triumphant passage to the rank of Jedi Master, few Jedi had more brushes with the powers of the dark side and the evil of the underworld than Quinlan Vos.

ISBN 978-1-59582-555-1 | $24.99

STAR WARS: THE COMPLETE SAGA—EPISODES I THROUGH VI

The comics adaptations of the complete *Star Wars* film saga—in one volume! From the first fateful encounter with Darth Maul to Luke Skywalker's victory over the Sith and Darth Vader's redemption, it's all here.

ISBN 978-1-59582-832-3 | $24.99

STAR WARS: CLONE WARS

The Jedi Knights who were once protectors of the peace must become generals, leading the clone armies of the Republic to war! These stories follow *Attack of the Clones* and feature Jedi heroes Obi-Wan Kenobi, Anakin Skywalker, Mace Windu, and Quinlan Vos.

Volume 1: The Republic Goes to War ISBN 978-1-59582-927-6 | $24.99
Volume 2: The Enemy on All Sides ISBN 978-1-59582-958-0 | $24.99
Volume 3: The Republic Falls ISBN 978-1-59582-980-1 | $24.99

STAR WARS: DROIDS

Before the fateful day Luke Skywalker met Artoo and Threepio, those troublesome droids had some amazing adventures all their own—and they stick together in a dangerous galaxy where anything can happen!

ISBN 978-1-59307-955-0 | $24.99

STAR WARS: DROIDS AND EWOKS

Based on the children's television cartoon series of the same names, *Droids and Ewoks* explores further adventures in the lives of the Ewoks on Endor and the droids R2-D2 and C-3PO.

ISBN 978-1-59582-953-5 | $24.99

DARK HORSE BOOKS

AVAILABLE AT YOUR LOCAL COMICS SHOP OR BOOKSTORE!

To find a comics shop in your area, call 1-888-266-4226
For more information or to order direct: • On the web: DarkHorse.com • E-mail: mailorder@darkhorse.com
• Phone: 1-800-862-0052 Mon.–Fri. 9 AM to 5 PM Pacific Time

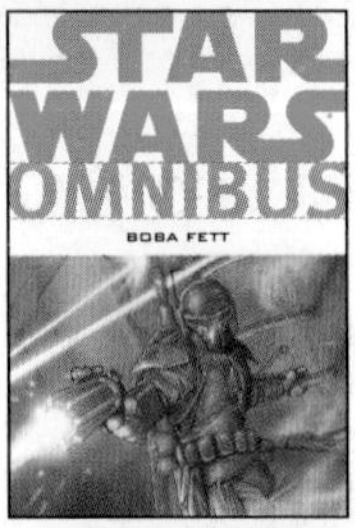
STAR WARS OMNIBUS
BOBA FETT

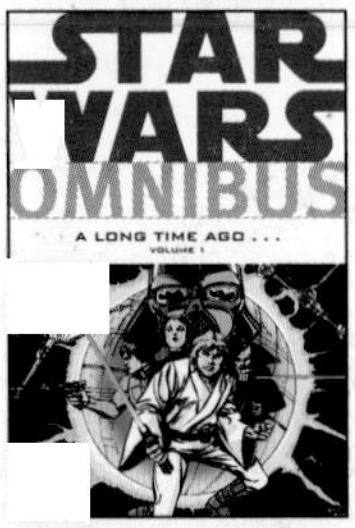
STAR
OMNIBUS
A LONG TIME AGO . . .

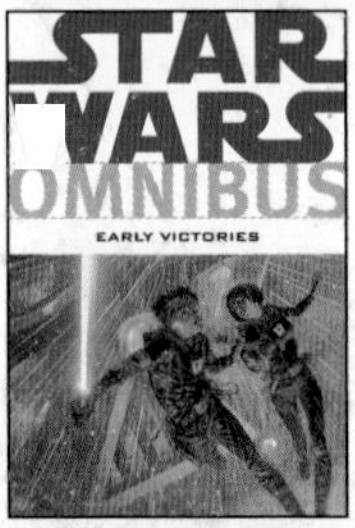
STAR
OMNIBUS
EARLY VICTORIES

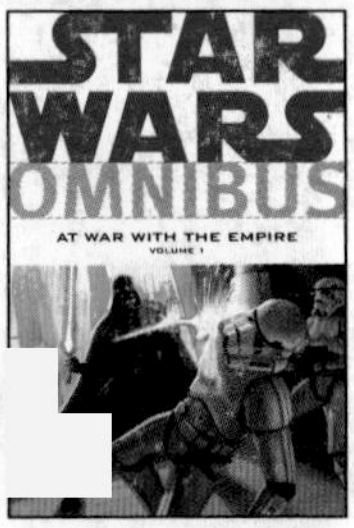
STAR WARS OMNIBUS
AT WAR WITH THE EMPIRE

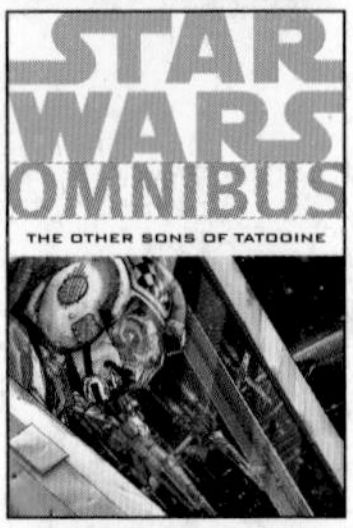
STAR WARS OMNIBUS
THE OTHER SONS OF TATOOINE

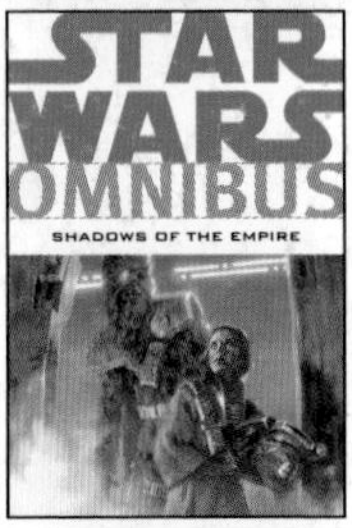
STAR WARS OMNIBUS
SHADOWS OF THE EMPIRE

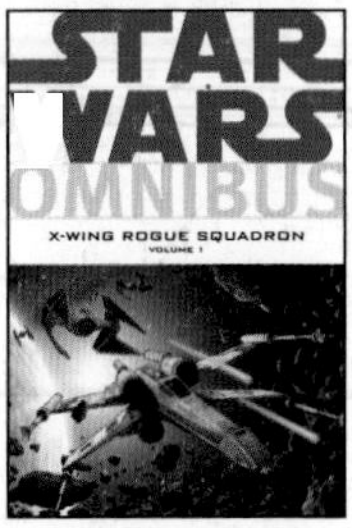
STAR
OMNIBUS
X-WING ROGUE SQUADRON

STAR WARS OMNIBUS COLLECTIONS

STAR WARS: BOBA FETT

Boba Fett, the most feared, most respected, and most loved bounty hunter in the galaxy, now has all of his comics stories collected into one massive volume!

ISBN 978-1-59582-418-9 | $24.99

STAR WARS: INFINITIES

Three different tales where *one thing* happens differently than it did in the original trilogy of *Star Wars* films. Luke Skywalker, Princess Leia, Han Solo, and Darth Vader are launched onto new trajectories!

ISBN 978-1-61655-078-3 | $24.99

STAR WARS: A LONG TIME AGO. . . .

Star Wars: A Long Time Ago. . . . omnibus volumes feature classic *Star Wars* stories not seen in over twenty years! Originally printed by Marvel Comics, these recolored stories are sure to please Star Wars fans both new and old.

Volume 1: ISBN 978-1-59582-486-8 | $24.99
Volume 2: ISBN 978-1-59582-554-4 | $24.99
Volume 3: ISBN 978-1-59582-639-8 | $24.99
Volume 4: ISBN 978-1-59582-640-4 | $24.99
Volume 5: ISBN 978-1-59582-801-9 | $24.99

STAR WARS: WILD SPACE

Rare and previously uncollected stories! Contains work from some of comics' most famous writers and artists (including Alan Moore, Chris Claremont, Archie Goodwin, Walt Simonson, and Alan Davis), plus stories featuring the greatest heroes and villains of *Star Wars*!

Volume 1: ISBN 978-1-61655-146-9 | $24.99
Volume 2: ISBN 978-1-61655-147-6 | $24.99

STAR WARS: EARLY VICTORIES

Following the destruction of the first Death Star, Luke Skywalker and Princess Leia find there are many more battles to be fought against the Empire and Darth Vader!

ISBN 978-1-59582-172-0 | $24.99

STAR WARS: AT WAR WITH THE EMPIRE

Stories of the early days of the Rebel Alliance and the beginnings of its war with the Empire—tales of the *Star Wars* galaxy set before, during, and after the events in *Star Wars: A New Hope!*

Volume 1: ISBN 978-1-59582-699-2 | $24.99
Volume 2: ISBN 978-1-59582-777-7 | $24.99

STAR WARS: THE OTHER SONS OF TATOOINE

Luke's story has been told time and again, but what about the journeys of his boyhood friends, Biggs Darklighter and Janek "Tank" Sunber? Both are led to be heroes in their own right: one of the Rebellion, the other of the Empire . . .

ISBN 978-1-59582-866-8 | $24.99

STAR WARS: SHADOWS OF THE EMPIRE

Featuring all your favorite characters from the *Star Wars* trilogy—Luke Skywalker, Princess Leia, and Han Solo—this volume includes stories written by acclaimed novelists Timothy Zahn and Steve Perry!

ISBN 978-1-59582-434-9 | $24.99

STAR WARS: X-WING ROGUE SQUADRON

The starfighters of the Rebel Alliance become the defenders of a new Republic in these stories featuring Wedge Antilles and his team of ace pilots known throughout the galaxy as Rogue Squadron.

Volume 1: ISBN 978-1-59307-572-9 | $24.99
Volume 2: ISBN 978-1-59307-619-1 | $24.99
Volume 3: ISBN 978-1-59307-776-1 | $24.99

AVAILABLE AT YOUR LOCAL COMICS SHOP OR BOOKSTORE!

To find a comics shop in your area, call 1-888-266-4226

For more information or to order direct: • On the web: DarkHorse.com • E-mail: mailorder@darkhorse.com • Phone: 1-800-862-0052 Mon.–Fri. 9 AM to 5 PM Pacific Time •